Integrity in Business and Management

This book highlights the interconnectedness of integrity with philosophical history, leadership, managerial decision making, and organizational effectiveness in a wide variety of contexts (e.g., time theft in organizations or integrity in family business). Well-known researchers in business ethics from all around the world reframe the literature on integrity in business and management and develop updated and more comprehensive models of integrity.

Integrity in Business and Management not only connects integrity to both ancient thought and the modern philosophy of pragmatism but also explains how contemporary societal trends may shape the way we think about integrity. The final chapter warns against oversocialized conceptualizations of integrity and argues for a clear differentiation between personal integrity and moral integrity.

Aimed at researchers and academics in the fields of business ethics and organizational leadership, *Integrity in Business and Management* explicates and critiques prior models of managerial integrity in a wide variety of disciplines, covering economics, moral philosophy, business ethics, organizational behavior, sociology, history, and psychology and offers a helpful set of readings in advanced undergraduate and postgraduate courses of business ethics, corporate governance, corporate social responsibility, and leadership to stimulate discussions about personal integrity, moral integrity, and organizational leadership.

Marc Orlitzky is Chair in Management, University of South Australia Business School, Australia.

Manjit Monga is a lecturer in the School of Management at the University of South Australia Business School, Australia.

Routledge Studies in Business Ethics

For a full list of titles in this series, please visit www.routledge.com

Originating from both normative and descriptive philosophical backgrounds, business ethics implicitly regulates areas of behaviour which influence decision making, judgment, behaviour and objectives of the leadership and employees of an organization. This series seeks to analyse current and leading edge issues in business ethics, and the titles within it examine and reflect on the philosophy of business, corporations and organizations pertaining to all aspects of business conduct. They are relevant to the conduct of both individuals and organizations as a whole.

Based in academic theory but relevant to current organizational policy, the series welcomes contributions addressing topics including: ethical strategy; sustainable policies and practices; finance and accountability; CSR; employee relations and workers' rights; law and regulation; economic and taxation systems.

Integrity in Business and Management

Edited by Marc Orlitzky
and Manjit Monga

Routledge
Taylor & Francis Group

LONDON AND NEW YORK

First published 2018 by Routledge

2 Park Square, Milton Park, Abingdon, Oxfordshire OX14 4RN

52 Vanderbilt Avenue, New York, NY 10017

Routledge is an imprint of the Taylor & Francis Group, an informa business

First issued in paperback 2019

Library of Congress Cataloging-in-Publication Data
A catalog record for this book has been requested

ISBN: 978-1-138-80877-5 (hbk)
ISBN: 978-0-367-87078-2 (pbk)

Typeset in Sabon
by Apex CoVantage, LLC

Dedication Photo Acknowledgment:
Creative Commons Attribution 2.0 Generic
Author: Paul van de Velde
Title: Diamonds are forever . . . these evaporate (Explore)
Photo taken on May 5, 2016
URL: https://www.flickr.com/photos/dordrecht-holland/27131791731
Link to license: https://creativecommons.org/licenses/by/2.0/legalcode

Dedicated to
Manjit's beloved mother, Kuljit, and father,
Late Sri Trilok Singh Monga,
for their moral courage and integrity

as well as

Ursula and Rainer Orlitzky
für die schönsten Jahre.

Contents

Figures

Preface and Acknowledgments

Integrity in business and management has become a popular topic for discussion in the scholarly literature and popular press. Although there is wide agreement on the vital role of integrity in business and management, it has proved to be an elusive construct. The first chapter of this volume, "The Multiple Facets of Integrity in Business and Management," discusses the complexities associated with the meaning of integrity in the organizational and leadership literature and offers an overview of the other chapters. The following chapters cover important research on integrity by scholars from all around the world, illuminating the different aspects and contexts of integrity and its potential to influence decision making in various organizational contexts. The final chapter is a critique of the concept from the perspective of the particular historical moment in which we find ourselves.

Marc: A few months after joining the University of South Australia Business School in 2013, a research team was most generously supported by an internal School of Management Grant (Project Protocol Number 0000031818) for this research project, examining integrity in business and management. As the lead researcher, I am deeply grateful for this grant. The final stage of the book was prepared, in part, while I was on Professional Experience Program study leave. I would like to express my heartfelt gratitude to the contributors who responded to our requests for revisions in such a timely and cooperative way. The contributor and coeditor whose assistance was most outstanding was Manjit Monga. Without her constructive ideas, this book would never have such an international flavor with so many international contributors. Finally, I would also like to acknowledge the excellent editorial assistance and guidance by Megan Smith, Brianna Ascher, and David Varley at the Taylor & Francis Publishing Group.

Manjit: I wish to acknowledge the University of South Australia Business School, especially the School of Management for its support of the project. I am especially thankful to all the organizations that agreed to participate and found time to contribute to my study, reported in Chapter 6. The chief editor of this volume and my coauthor, Professor Marc Orlitzky, has been exceptionally helpful and supportive throughout the development of this venture. I am also grateful to Professor Cheri Ostroff for her guidance and advice. Finally, I am very thankful to all my friends especially Dr Sukhbir Sandhu and colleagues who encouraged me along the way.

About the Contributors

Richard Bent is a senior lecturer in Business and Enterprise at Queen Margaret University in Edinburgh and a member of FASE (Family and Smaller Enterprises research group). He has published in a variety of journals over the past 20 years with a focus on smaller and family enterprises. In recent years he has engaged with a range of enterprises in both Knowledge Exchange projects and with the challenges faced by the traditional British High Street. A regular contributor on BBC Radio Scotland, he currently looks after the QMU PG Business Masters programs at home and overseas.

Joanna Crossman, School of Management, is a member of the Centre for Workplace Excellence at the University of South Australia. Her international career in Scandinavia, the United Arab Emirates, Malaysia, the United Kingdom, and Australia has included the general management of an international company, accreditation consultancy, educational management, and academic positions. She has authored more than 50 peer-reviewed publications in the form of journal papers and book chapters, largely concerned with business ethics and workplace spirituality, internationalization, interculturality, and experiential management education. She has also coauthored four McGraw-Hill textbooks on business communication and coedits the Emerald journal *Journal of International Education in Business.*

Werner H. Erhard is a critical thinker who has influenced the academic community worldwide with his revolutionary ideas first expressed in The est Training. He introduced the 20th-century notion of transformation and has had an enormous impact as a thought leader and humanitarian. In 1973 Erhard, committed to making a difference, founded the Werner Erhard Foundation. The foundation's original name was the Foundation for the Realization of Man, a name in keeping with the intention of the foundation. Erhard established this foundation as an expression of his own personal commitment to transforming the quality of life for all human beings, and as a vehicle for graduates of The est Training to participate in making a difference in their local communities

xiv *About the Contributors*

and throughout the world. Erhard, and the entire board of directors, served the foundation pro bono, with Erhard committing a significant amount of time generating funds for the Foundation. Erhard founded over a dozen separate charities and has been recognized for his commitment to humanity with the Mahatma Gandhi Humanitarian Award in 1988 and the Humanitarian of the Year Award in 2003.

Frederick Greene, a graduate of the State University of New York at Buffalo (BS, MBA, PhD), has more than three decades of involvement in all aspects of small business. He has been active in establishing and operating small businesses as well as researching, publishing, teaching, consulting, and advocating with regard to issues of concern in this field. In 1987, he was appointed to the position of Director of the Manhattan College Small Business Development Center (SBDC)—The Bronx Regional Center within the New York State Small Business Center Network—allowing him the opportunity to work with a wide range of businesses. Dr. Greene was also on the faculty of the Managerial Sciences Department in the School of Business at Manhattan College, where he was once chairman of the department and since 1979 has served as Director of the Small Business Institute.

David C. Jacobs is an associate professor of labor and sustainability at the Graves School of Business at Morgan State University in Baltimore, Maryland. He has also taught at American University, the University of Michigan–Flint, Kansas State University, the Residential College of the University of Michigan, and Case Western Reserve University. Jacobs has published articles in *Academy of Management Learning and Education*, the *Academy of Management Review, Ephemera, Labor Studies Journal, Negotiation Journal, Perspectives on Work,* and other refereed outlets. He is author or editor of six books, including *The Future of the Safety Net and the Disunited States of America*, the 2001 and 2014 research volumes of the Labor and Employment Relations Association. Jacobs is a past chair of the Critical Management Studies Division of the Academy of Management.

Michael C. Jensen, Jesse Isidor Straus Professor of Business Administration, Emeritus, joined the faculty of the Harvard Business School in 1985 founding what is now the Negotiations, Organizations and Markets Unit in the school. He joined the Monitor Company in 2000 as Managing Director of the Organizational Strategy Practice, became Senior Advisor in 2007, and as of 2009 is no longer associated with Monitor. He was LaClare Professor of Finance and Business Administration at the William E. Simon Graduate School of Business Administration, University of Rochester from 1984 to 1988, professor from 1979 to 1984, associate professor from 1971 to 1979, and assistant professor from 1967 to 1971.

He founded the Managerial Economics Research Center at the University of Rochester in 1977 and served as its director until 1988.

Manjit Monga is a lecturer at the University of South Australia Business School, in the School of Management. She teaches and researches in business ethics and human resource management areas. Prior to joining UniSA, she had a successful career in private-sector businesses overseas and in Australia. She brought the practical experience and knowledge of business to academia and to her research program. She has a master's degree and a PhD in Social Anthropology from Panjab University, Chandigarh, India. She has research interests in management ethics, research ethics, human resource diversity management, and social enterprises.

Marc Orlitzky (PhD in Business Administration, University of Iowa) is Chair of Management at the University of South Australia Business School. His previous positions included lecturer at UNSW, Senior Lecturer above the Bar at the University of Auckland, and tenured associate professor at Penn State University, Altoona. With an L-Index (Belikov & Belikov, 2015) of 6.59, he has published research in, among others, *Organizational Research Methods, Business Ethics Quarterly, Academy of Management Perspectives, Journal of Business Ethics, Academy of Management Learning & Education, Personnel Psychology,* and *Organization Studies.* His research has received several awards, including the 2004 Moskowitz award for outstanding quantitative study in the field of social investing and the 2001 Best Article Prize awarded by the International Association for Business & Society in association with *California Management Review.* Orlitzky et al.'s (2003) meta-analysis has become the most highly cited article ever published in the journal *Organization Studies.*

Sanjee Perera is a lecturer at the University of South Australia Business School. She received her PhD from the University of South Australia. Prior to commencing her academic career, she worked for several years in human resource management in both the service and manufacturing sectors. Her research interests include emotion in the workplace and workforce diversity. Current projects examine stereotype threat among mature-age workers and jobseekers, and emotion management of family business coworkers.

Carolyn Predmore, PhD, is a professor of marketing. She is an active member in the American Marketing Association. Her research interests cover entrepreneurship, innovation and creativity perceptions of ethical issues by business students, retailing and terrorism, salesmanship, Internet usage, and retailing on both a national and international basis. She has published in the *e-learning Digest, Management Decisions,* the *Journal of Business*

Ethics, and the *Journal of the Association of Marketing Educators*, as well as having written chapters on entrepreneurship and social media.

Janet Rovenpor is a professor of management at Manhattan College, Riverdale, New York. She teaches courses in Introduction to Management; Human Behavior in Organizations; Business, Government and Society; and Strategic Management. Her research combines her training in organizational behavior with her concern for successful strategic management outcomes for corporations. Her articles, published in such journals as *Business and Society Review*, the *Journal of Vocational Behavior*, the *Journal of Psychology*, and the *Journal of Business and Psychology*, focus on the impact that personality traits have on employee productivity and organizational performance. She has also published case studies on Respironics, Stoli Group USA, and New York Life Insurance Company in *Case Research Journal*.

Claire Seaman is a reader in enterprise and family business at Queen Margaret University in Edinburgh and editor in chief of the *Journal of Family Business Management*. She has published more than 30 journal articles on family businesses in the United Kingdom, New Zealand and Latin America and is a regular contributor to family business conferences worldwide. Her recent book, *The Modern Family Business*, was developed with colleagues and published by Palgrave McMillan. She has been integral to the development a Family Business Education Pathway for Scotland, including two masters programs at Queen Margaret University and is a regular supervisor and examiner at doctoral level.

Duane Windsor is the Lynette S. Autrey Professor of Management in the area of strategy and environment. He has been with the Jones Graduate School at Rice University since 1977. He received the Distinguished Service Award from the International Associate for Business and Society in 2014 and was elected a fellow of that organization in 2006. He served as the editor of *Business & Society* from 2007 to 2014 and as the consulting editor for 2015 and 2016. Professor Windsor received his BA in political science from Rice University and his AM and PhD in political economy and government from Harvard University. His research interests are in business ethics, corporate environmental and social performance, CSR, corporate governance, social enterprise, stakeholder theory, leadership, and public and nonprofit management. His teaching interests are in the area of business ethics, corporate governance, and social enterprise.

Steve Zaffron is CEO of Vanto Group, a consulting firm specialized in the design and implementation of large-scale initiatives to elevate organizational performance. He has worked with organizations in different industries worldwide including Walgreens, NASA, Reebok, BHP-Billiton, Dalmia Group (India), Petrobras (Brazil), and Polus Group (Japan). As an internationally respected leadership authority, Zaffron is noted for his provocative new perspectives on breakthrough performance, organizational change, transformational leadership, and integrating competitive advantages. He has been a guest lecturer at universities in the United States and Europe, including Harvard Business School, Simon School of Business at the University of Rochester, Marshall School of Business at the University of Southern California, and Erasmus University (Holland).

1 The Multiple Facets of Integrity in Business and Management

Marc Orlitzky and Manjit Monga

Integrity has been the subject of considerable debate in management and business ethics for a long time. In a complex business environment, accompanied by the loss of morality on various fronts, there is a need to reconsider the concept of *integrity* and its potential for a more realistic alignment between managerial practice and ethics (Solomon, 1992, 1999). Although there is strong consensus on the importance of integrity in personal and organizational situations, there is also much disagreement on the definition and the broader implications of integrity (Bauman, 2013). Undoubtedly, integrity is an inherently complex construct to define and measure. In fact, it has been defined in so many ways that the meaning of integrity and its implications have remained elusive (e.g., Audi & Murphy, 2006; Becker, 1998; Orlitzky & Jacobs, 1998; Palanski & Yammarino, 2009; Parry & Proctor-Thomson, 2002).

In this chapter, as a backdrop to the contributions made by the researchers in this volume, we first provide a brief sketch of the variety of ways integrity has been conceptualized and analyzed in the Management and Business Ethics literature. We then preview the individual chapters included in the book. As we argue in the following, each featured researcher in this volume emphasizes one aspect of integrity relatively more than other aspects, with the normatively loaded conceptualization, numbered 3 in the following, being the most common in this book.

The Meanings of Integrity

Palanski and Yammarino's (2007) influential review of the organizational literature on integrity identified five different facets of integrity: (1) behavioral consistency, (2) steadfastness in adversity, (3) demonstrating moral or ethical behavior, (4) authenticity, and (5) wholeness. In the following, these five aspects of integrity are presented in the same order as the chapters focus on one of these aspects of integrity relatively more than the other four.

1. Behavioral Consistency

One meaning of integrity that seems very prevalent in the Management literature is consistency between words and actions, also known as *behavioral consistency* (Bews & Rossouw, 2002; Jensen, 2009; Kirkpatrick & Locke, 1991; Paine, 2005; Simons, 2002, 1999; Simons, Friedman, Liu, & McLean-Parks, 2007; Tracey & Hinkin, 1994; Worden, 2003). It includes both the perceived fit between espoused and enacted values and promise-keeping.

A possible and oft-cited criticism of this conceptualization is that, if integrity is defined purely as consistency between words and actions or explicit promise-keeping, it may also refer to promises that are unethical or immoral in nature. For example, I give my word to a potential contractor that in return of a kickback, he or she will be given the contract. After I follow through on this promise, can I be called a person of integrity because I kept my word and gave away the contract in return for a kickback? Such consistency would, according to some scholars (e.g., Badaracco & Ellsworth, 1991; Koehn, 2005), miss the true meaning of integrity. Therefore, one may argue that the content of the words and actions (see Aspect 3) must also be taken into account. However, other philosophers (e.g., Audi & Murphy, 2006; Cox, LaCaze, & Levine, 2016; Palanski & Yammarino, 2009) emphasize that integrity is morally neutral.

2. Integrity as Steadfastness in Adversity

Steadfastness in adversity is another important meaning of integrity in the literature (Carter, 1996; Duska, 2005; McFall, 1987; Paine, 2005; Posner, 2001; Worden, 2003) and implies the presence of a choice or choices, which may influence integrity. Conceptually, this view of integrity overlaps with consistency between words and actions, but the two conceptualizations are distinct. Steadfastness in adversity reflects the need to resist unethical temptations or choices, even at a high personal cost. McFall (1987) goes as far as to claim that if there is no adversity or moral temptation involved, then integrity cannot meaningfully be demonstrated. Although this conceptualization can be regarded as an essential feature of integrity, it arguably does not, by itself, fully encompass the meaning of integrity. So, it is usually argued that the nature of the values and principles be defined along with the moral content of the word given, which is the conceptualization previewed next.

3. Integrity as Moral or Ethical Behavior

This is the normative view of integrity as moral or ethical behavior, related to making a judgment about good or bad, right or wrong. A number of scholars have associated integrity with key moral values, for example, justice and respect (Baccili, 2001; Bews & Rossouw, 2002; Den Hartog & Koopman, 2002; Rawls, 1971), empathy/compassion (Koehn, 2005; Lowe, Cordery, &

Morrison, 2004), and trustworthiness (Baccilli, 2001; Den Hartog & Koopman, 2002; Trevino, Hartman, & Brown, 2000). In the organizational behavior, human resource management, and psychology literature on integrity and integrity tests, the value of honesty (Den Hartog & Koopman, 2002; McFall, 1987; Newman, 2003; Peterson & Seligman, 2004; Posner, 2001; Trevino et al., 2000; Yukl & VanFleet, 1992) features most prominently. In addition, some authors have associated integrity with a general sense of morality and ethics (Baccilli, 2001; Batson, Thompson, Sueferling, Whitney, & Strongman, 1999; Becker, 1998; Carter, 1996; Lowe et al., 2004; Maak, 2008; McFall, 1987; Mayer, Davis, & Schoorman, 1995; Newman, 2003). Murphy (1999) considers fairness, trust, respect, and empathy to be the core virtues of integrity. More generally, striving to achieve integrity is at once a moral, philosophical, and practical endeavor and suggests a sense of moral soundness (Badaracco & Ellsworth, 1991). Consistent with such a broad conceptualization, Parry and Proctor-Thomson (2002) argue that integrity should be based on a, or any, morally justifiable set of values.

There is an important stream of management literature that has attempted to identify and specify the content of the moral principles and values underpinning integrity (Becker, 1998; Locke & Becker, 1998). According to this Objectivist perspective (Peikoff, 1991), a morally justifiable code of principles and values is one that promotes the long-term survival and well-being of individuals as rational beings (Becker, 1998). According to the philosophy of Objectivism, the ultimate standards of morality are survival and happiness. The pursuit of self-interest for survival in the Objectivist view implies a rejection of the Christian and Kantian orthodoxy of altruism (Rand, 1964). Unsurprisingly, Becker's (1998) and Locke and Becker's (1998) Objectivist definition of integrity generated heated debate among scholars (Barry & Stephens, 1998; Orlitzky & Jacobs, 1998), who highlighted the limitations of the Objectivist perspective.

4. Integrity as Authenticity

Authenticity is another meaning of integrity found in the Management literature, which means being true to oneself (Baccilli, 2001; Calhoun, 1995; Cox, LaCraze, & Levine, 2003; Howell & Avolio, 1995; Kaptein, 1999, 2003; Koehn, 2005; Lowe et al., 2004; McFall, 1987; Morrison, 2001; Paine, 2005; Peterson & Seligman, 2004; Posner, 2001; Rawls, 1971; Yukl & VanFleet, 1992). Being true to oneself means consistency between espoused values and enacted values. This conceptualization of integrity overlaps, at least to some extent, with the *behavioral consistency* and *steadfastness in adversity* definitions of integrity discussed before (Aspects 1 and 2 discussed earlier) because it means acting in accordance with a person's espoused beliefs and values, irrespective of the circumstances or consequences of the action.

This meaning of integrity implies that a person may appear to be acting in accordance with their beliefs and values, but in reality this may be difficult to ascertain (like most psychological, intangible variables, of course). This intractability makes it nearly impossible for others to determine if the person is acting in compliance with his or her deeply held values. Often, the motives of an organizational decision can only be (imperfectly) inferred from organizational actions (for more details, see also Chapter 6).

This dimension of integrity has various terms associated with it. For example, Palanski and Yammarino (2007) call this aspect *personal integrity*. Personal integrity means the alignment of one's words, actions, and internalized values—which is different from public integrity, the alignment of one's words and actions only. Peterson and Seligman (2004) call it private and public aspects of integrity. This highlights the intrinsic nature of integrity, where only the person himself or herself can determine if he or she acted with integrity (Monga, 2016). Arguably, for integrity to occur, there needs to be a unification of personal integrity with public integrity.

5. Integrity as Wholeness

The fifth and final meaning of integrity is the broadest but probably also in closest alignment with its etymology. The Latin meaning of *integer* is closely associated with wholeness (see also Chapter 9), which can be applied to a variety of situations. It can be applied to an object, machinery, the natural environment—and to humans. When applied to an object like a piece of art, it can mean intactness, completeness, or purity. Applied to wilderness, it indicates the most undisturbed wild natural areas left on Earth. *Webster's New World Dictionary* defines *integrity* as the "quality or state of being complete: unbroken condition; wholeness" and the "quality or state of being of sound moral principle; uprightness, honesty and sincerity." So, this meaning captures the spirit of its Latin root *integer* most accurately.

When applied to a "person of integrity," the image that comes to mind is that of a person who acts in accordance with high moral standards and does so consistently even if challenged by unfavorable/adverse circumstances, which may result in some personal loss. Similarly, the *Oxford Dictionary* defines integrity as "quality of being honest and having strong moral principles . . . the state of being whole and undivided." Several scholars, such as Badaracco and Ellsworth (1991), Koehn (2005), Lowe et al. (2004), Trevino et al. (2000), Worden (2003), Kaptein (2003, 1999), George (2003), and McFall (1987), include wholeness as a key aspect of integrity. Integrity as wholeness also suggests that there are multiple aspects or dimensions to it that must be integrated to result in such a state of wholeness.

If we apply this meaning to human beings, it is nearly synonymous with character. According to philosopher Robert Solomon (1992, 1999), integrity represents the synthesis of virtues working together to form a coherent character, an identifiable and trustworthy personality, with moral courage—the will and willingness to do what one knows one ought to do—as its key trait. Thus, integrity refers to a superordinate virtue, or supervirtue, characterizing someone who lives up to his or her own standards (Korsgaard, 1996). In an organizational context, the notion of wholeness points toward a person's overall consistency of behavior, thoughts, and emotions across time and situations, characterizing the overall person and not only certain aspects of a person.

Audi and Murphy (2006) describe integrity as an adjunctive virtue, like courage and conscientiousness, rather than a substantive moral virtue, like honesty and fairness, which are morally good in themselves. According to these business ethicists, adjunctive virtues do not necessarily imply a commitment to moral standards; however, their presence may strengthen a person's moral character. In the synthetic sense of integrity as wholeness, such an adjunctive virtue is important for adherence to high moral standards because it facilitates moral reasoning and ethical conduct.

The various meanings of integrity in the management literature fail to fully capture the meaning of integrity or wholeness. This conceptual shortcoming makes it essential to identify various dimensions or aspects of integrity that, when aligned and integrated, form a complete whole—the state of integrity. Maak (2008) has addressed this at individual and organizational levels by taking a different approach. He tries to capture the multidimensionality of the construct by assigning seven essential conditions, which form the undivided whole. These seven necessary conditions for integrity are commitment, conduct, content, context, consistency, coherence, and continuity.

Preview of the Chapters

This brief sketch of the variety of ways in which integrity has been conceptualized and studied is indicative of the need for more nuanced and clearer frameworks for a better understanding of the concept. Given the ambiguities and inconsistencies of the conceptual and operational definitions of integrity in business and management, the chapters in this volume advance the study of integrity by illuminating both the antecedents and consequences of this elusive construct.

In Chapter 2, Erhard, Jensen, and Zaffron present an eminently well-argued, positive model of integrity, which clearly differentiates integrity from morality and ethics. They argue that integrity, a necessary condition for the workability and optimum performance of organizations, exists in a positive realm and, therefore, can be the subject of social scientists' descriptive, observational study of behavior. Their definition of integrity as *honoring your word* is clearly differentiated from the normative realm of morality, ethics, and legality. The authors show that defining integrity as honoring one's word provides an unambiguous and actionable access to the opportunity for superior performance and competitive advantage at different levels of analysis and empowers the three virtue phenomena of morality, ethics, and legality. This chapter is most consistent with the conceptualization as behavioral integrity, the first facet of integrity introduced above.

In Chapter 3, Crossman and Perera develop an integrity-based approach for managing and alleviating time theft, which can be committed not only by employees but also by employers. Time theft, defined as the abuse of expectations about how time or other resources are used (Ketchen, Craighead, & Buckley, 2008; Martin, Brock, Buckley, & Ketchen, 2010), is reportedly on the rise and a significant ethical issue that drains organizational profits and national economies. Managing time theft is problematic in its complexity, intensified by the rise of knowledge work and flexible human resource policies. Perera and colleagues argue that an integrity-based approach enables a holistic, proactive, flexible, and sustainable framework to guide management decision making, relevant to both employee and organizational time theft. Such an integrity-based approach, the authors argue, carries less risk of damaging repercussions that would emerge if a compliance-oriented, employee-focused approach were adopted. Because Perera et al. emphasize the context of challenging or difficult conditions for time theft (see p. 43 of this chapter), we classified this chapter as most aligned with the aspect of integrity as steadfastness in adversity.

In Chapter 4, titled "Financial Motives for Integrity and Ethical Idiosyncratic Credit in Business: A Multilevel Conceptual Model," Predmore et al. introduce a multilevel conceptual model that describes how leadership integrity, combined with ethical idiosyncratic credit, may originate at the highest levels of management and cascade down the firm, eventually contributing to greater overall profitability. The leader who consistently acts with integrity sends a powerful message to others and creates great momentum within the organization by engendering subordinate trust, promoting ethical behavior among employees, and fostering the emergence of an ethical culture which in turn results in shared governance, the attraction of talented employees, a stellar reputation, a long-term strategic orientation, and favorable stakeholder perceptions. Through many real-world examples of ethical and unethical business conduct, the authors illustrate how each stage in the model works and how empirical studies support the viability of their model. Because Predmore et al. focus on the relationship of integrity to ethical idiosyncratic credit, we would classify as mainly relating to integrity as moral behavior.

In Chapter 5, "The Role of Family Values in the Integrity of Family Business," Seaman and Bent bring to the fore the importance of family values and the role they play in achieving integrity in family business. The literature in this area is still in its infancy, and their chapter makes an important contribution by proposing a model that synthesizes family values and the development of business integrity. They draw on the work of Petrick and Quinn's (2000), using process, judgment, development, and system as the four dimensions of their integrity construct. Because they extend this seminal model by focusing on internalized ethical values, we classify this chapter as relating most directly to integrity as moral behavior.

In the sixth chapter, "'Doing the Right Thing' in the Banking Sector: Integrity from an Upper Echelons Perspective," Monga presents the findings of her qualitative interview study in the Australian banking industry, illuminating the meaning of integrity from an executive's perspective. Monga argues that it is vital that practitioners' understandings of the concept are taken into consideration because they are tasked with the implementation of integrity in the workplace. The findings suggest that integrity is mainly seen (by the interviewed Australian bank executives) to be synonymous with ethical actions ("doing the right thing"). The study develops two propositions for further research: (1) practitioners' understanding of integrity is multifaceted (set of beliefs systems and actions consistent with them), and (2) commitment to a set of sound ethical and moral principles is a prerequisite to the achievement of integrity. Again, like the two preceding chapters, Chapter 6 is most consistent with the conceptualization of integrity as moral behavior.

In Chapter 7, Windsor carefully develops an integrated model of managerial integrity and compliance. Windsor argues that integrity and compliance are mutually compatible and presents a compelling case for the alignment of internal and external governance mechanisms in order to increase the likelihood of achieving organizational integrity. To illustrate his model empirically, Windsor contrasts four mini-cases of corruption (integrity failure) in Germany and Japan, on one hand, with the integrity-based and compliance-oriented approach at General Electric, on the other. Although Windsor's comprehensive model emphasizes moral principles, his theoretical starting point is "being true to oneself" (see p. 138 in this chapter). So, the theorizing in this chapter is, at least in part, reflective of the authenticity view of integrity.

In Chapter 8, "Pragmatism and Integrity: A Second Look," Jacobs extends his earlier arguments (Jacobs, 2004) for a pragmatist philosophical foundation of integrity. He argues that the organizational context plays a critical role in decision making where multiple stakeholders shape the decisions and decision-making processes. He suggests his pragmatist approach to integrity effectively addresses the limitations in the current models and conceptualizations of integrity in the management literature. Jacobs's perspective, blending John Dewey with Reinhold Niebuhr, subjects organizations and organizational routines to question; organizations are understood as merely provisional instruments of human collaboration. Of the various aspects of integrity, Jacobs arguably (see pp. 158 in his chapter) relies on wholeness more than the other conceptualizations.

Orlitzky's final chapter presents a critique of the integrity concept in a postvirtues era. First, he explains the etymological roots of *integer* and *integritas* and illustrates how the modern concept of integrity, especially in the organizational literature, is disconnected from its Latin roots. Second, he critiques ubiquitous virtue signaling, which seems to have replaced genuine integrity-based decision making in business, politics, and society. Third, he offers several examples of what genuine integrity could mean today—rather than merely the appearance of integrity—and a few fruitful directions for future research, which, based on his partly historical, partly psychoanalytic critique, ought to investigate in much greater depth the conceptual aspects of wholeness and authenticity.

In sum, each of the chapters included in this book reflects at least one of the facets of integrity discussed earlier. Behavioral consistency is reflected in the next chapter (i.e., Chapter 2), while Chapter 3 on time theft is most closely aligned with the second facet, steadfastness in adversity. The following three chapters (Chapters 4–6) are mainly about the normative conceptualization of integrity as moral behavior—the third aspect. Whereas Windsor's Chapter 7 uses authenticity (Facet 4 of diversity) as its starting point, Jacobs's pragmatist foundation of integrity (Chapter 8) seems to consider wholeness (Integrity Facet 5) its most central aspect. The last chapter emphasizes Facets 4 and 5 of integrity (authenticity and wholeness) to an equal extent. It ought to be noted that no chapter focuses on one facet of integrity exclusively. For example, Chapter 2 puts heavy emphasis on wholeness as well. The conceptual alignments noted earlier are merely our editorial suggestions as to the *main* emphasis of each chapter.

References

Audi, R. & Murphy, P. E. (2006). The many faces of integrity. *Business Ethics Quarterly, 16*(1), 3–21.

Baccilli, P. A. (2001). Organization and manager obligations in a framework of psychological contract development and violation. Unpublished dissertation. Claremont Graduate University, Claremont, CA.

Badaracco Jr, J. L. & Ellsworth, R. R. (1991). Leadership, integrity and conflict. *Journal of Organizational Change Management, 4*(4), 46–55.

Barry, B. & Stephens, C. U. (1998). Objections to an objectivist approach to integrity. *Academy of Management Review, 23*(1), 162–169.

Batson, C. D., Thompson, E. R., Sueferling, G., Whitney, H., & Strongman, J. A. (1999). Moral hypocrisy: Appearing moral to oneself without being so. *Journal of Personality and Social Psychology, 77,* 525–537.

Bauman, D. C. (2013). Leadership and the three faces of integrity. *The Leadership Quarterly, 24*(3), 414–426.

Becker, T. E. (1998). Integrity in organizations: Beyond honesty and conscientiousness. *Academy of Management Review, 23,* 154–161.

Bews, N. F. & Rossouw, G. J. (2002). A role for business ethics in facilitating trsutworthiness. *Journal of Busienss Ethics, 39,* 377–389.

Calhoun, C. (1995). Standing for something. *Journal of Philosophy, 92*(5), 235–260.

Carter, S. L. (1996). *Integrity.* New York: Harper Perennial.

Cox, D., LaCaze, M., & Levine, M. (2016). Integrity. In E. N. Zalta (Ed.), *The Stanford Encyclopedia of Philosophy.* Retrieved from https://plato.stanford.edu/archives/win2016/entries/integrity/

Cox, D., LaCraze, M., & Levine, M. (2003). *Integrity and the fragile self.* Burlington, VT: Ashgate.

Den Hartog, D. N. & Koopman, P. L. (2002). Leadership in organizations. In D. S. Ones, N. Anderson, H. K. Sinangil, & V. Chockalingam (Eds.), *Handbook of industrial, work and organizational psychology* (Vol 2, pp. 166–187). London: Sage.

Duska, R. F. (2005). A look at integrity in financial services. *Journal of Financial Services Professionals, 59*, 26–28.

George, B. (2003). *Authentic leadership.* San Francisco, CA: Jossey-Bass.

Howell, J. M. & Avolio, B. J. (1995). Charismatic leadership: Submission or liberation? *Business Ethics Quarterly, 60*, 62–71.

Jacobs, D. C. (2004). A pragmatic approach to integrity in business ethics. *Journal of Management Inquiry, 13*(3), 215–223.

Jensen, M. C. (2009, January 14). Integrity: Without it nothing works. *Rotman Magazine*, 16–20.

Kaptein, M. (1999). Integrity management. *European Management Journal, 17*(6), 625–635.

Kaptein, M. (2003). The diamond of managerial integrity. *Europeon Management Journal, 21*(1), 99–108.

Ketchen, J., Craighead, C., & Buckley, R. (2008). Time bandits: How they are created, why they are tolerated, and what can be done about them. *Business Horizons, 51*(2), 141–149.

Kirkpatrick, S. A. & Locke, E. A. (1991). Leadership: Do traits matter? *The Executive, 5*, 48–60.

Koehn, D. (2005). Integrity as a business asset. *Journal of Business Ethics, 58*(1–3), 125–136.

Korsgaard, C. M. (1996). *The sources of normativity.* Cambridge: Cambridge Press.

Locke, E. A. & Becker, T. E. (1998). Rebuttal to a subjectivist critique of an objectivist approach to integrity in organizations. *Academy of Management Review, 23*(1), 170–175.

Lowe, K. B., Cordery, J., & Morrison, D. (2004). *A model for the attribution of leader intergrity: Peeking inside the black box of authentic leadership.* Paper presented at the 2004 Gallup Leadership Institute Conference, Lincoln, NE.

Maak, T. (2008). Undivided corporate responsibility: Towards a theory of corporate integrity. *Journal of Business Ethics, 82*, 353–368.

McFall, L. (1987). Integrity. *Ethics, 98*, 5–20.

Martin, L., Brock, M., Buckley, R., & Ketchen, D. (2010). Time banditry: Examining the purloining of time in organizations. *Human Resource Management Review, 20*(1), 26–34.

Mayer, R. C., Davis, J. H., & Schoorman, F. D. (1995). An integrative model of organizational trust. *Academy of Management Review, 20*, 709–734.

Monga, M. (2016). Integrity and its antecedent: A unified conceptual framework of integrity. *Journal of Developing Areas, 50*(5), 415–421.

Morrison, A. (2001). Integrity and global leadership. *Journal of Business Ethics, 31*, 65–76.

Murphy, P. E. (1999). Character and virtue ethics in international marketing: An agenda for managers, researchers and educators. *Journal of Business Ethics, 18*(1), 107–124.

Newman, B. (2003). Integrity and presidential approval, 1980–2000. *Public Opinion Quarterly, 67*, 335–367.

Orlitzky, M. & Jacobs, D. (1998). A candid and modest proposal: The brave new world of objectivism. *Academy of Management Review, 23*(4), 656–658.

Paine, L. S. (2005). Integrity. In P. H. Werhane & R. E. Freeman (Eds.), *The blackwell encyclopedia of management: Business ethics*, (2nd ed., pp. 247–249). Malden, MA: Blackwell Publishing.

Palanski, M. E. & Yammarino, F. J. (2007). Integrity and leadership: Clearing the conceptual confusion. *European Management Journal, 25*(3), 171–184.

Palanski, M. E. & Yammarino, F. J. (2009). Integrity and leadership: A multilevel conceptualization. *The Leadership Quarterly, 20*(3), 405–420.

Parry, K. W. & Proctor-Thomson, S. B. (2002). Perceived integrity of transformational leaders in organizational settings. *Journal of Business Ethics, 35*, 75–96.

Peikoff, L. (1991). *Objectivism: The philosophy of Ayn Rand.* New York: Meridian.

Peterson, C. & Seligman, M. E. P. (2004). *Character strengths and virtues.* New York: Oxford University Press.

Petrick, J. A. & Quinn, J. F. (2000). The integrity capacity construct and moral progress in business. *Journal of Business Ethics, 23*(1), 3–18.

Posner, B. Z. (2001). What does it mean to act with integrity? *Teaching Business Ethics, 5*, 461–473.

Rand, A. (1964). *The virtue of selfishness: A new concept of egoism.* New York: New American Library.

Rawls, J. (1971). *A theory of justice.* Cambridge: Harvard University Press.

Simons, T. L. (1999). Behavioral integrity as a critical ingredient for transformational leadership. *Journal of Organizational Change Management, 12*, 89–104.

Simons, T. L. (2002). Behavioral integrity: The percieved alignment between managers' words and deeds as a research focus. *Organization Science, 13*, 18–35.

Simons, T. L., Friedman, R., Liu, L. A., & McLean-Parks, J. (2007). Racial differences in sensitivity to behavioral integrity: Attitudinal consequences, in-group effects, and "trickle down" among black and non-black employees. *The Journal of Applied Psychology, 92*, 650–665.

Solomon, R. C. (1992). Ethics and excellence: Cooperation and integrity in business. New York: Oxford University Press.

Solomon, R. C. (1999). A better way to think about business: How personal integrity leads to corporate success. New York: Oxford University Press.

Tracey, J. B. & Hinkin, T. R. (1994). Transformational leaders in hospitality industry. *Cornell Hotel and Restaurant Administration Quarterly, 35*, 18–24.

Trevino, L. K., Hartman, L. P., & Brown, M. (2000). Moral person and moral manager: How executives develop a reputation for ethical leadership. *California Management Review, 42*, 128–142.

Worden, S. (2003). The role of integrity as a mediator in strategic leadership: A recipe for reputational capital. *Journal of Business Ethics, 46*, 31–44.

Yukl, G. A. & VanFleet, D. D. (1992). Theory and research on leadership in organizations. In M. D. Dunette & L. M. Hugh (Eds.), *Handbook of industrial and organizational psychology* (92nd ed., Vol 3, pp. 147–197). Palo Alto, CA: Consulting Psychologists Press.

2   Integrity

A Positive Model that Incorporates the Normative Phenomena of Morality, Ethics, and Legality (Abbreviated Version)

Werner H. Erhard, Michael C. Jensen, and Steve Zaffron

1. A New Model of Integrity

Integrity: Prologue

What follows is our new model of integrity. We began our effort to clarify the nature of integrity by researching its common usage as it appears in dictionaries and by examining the philosophical discussion on integrity. In both cases, as we show later, we found confusion and confounding among integrity, morality, and ethics. We chose first to see if it was possible to eliminate the confusion and confounding among those three terms, while accounting for the essence of the common usage definitions and the important elements of what philosophy says about integrity. At the same time, we avoided inventing any new definitions.

Our aim in settling on our definitions of each of the three terms was to honor the general common usage and philosophical meaning of each of the terms, while at the same time eliminating the confusion and confounding amongst them.

In defining integrity in our model, we honor common usage by using the first two definitions that appear in *Webster's Dictionary*.[1] We eliminate the third and final definition that includes "morality" and therefore generates the confusion and confounding between integrity and the virtue terms of *morality* and *ethics* (*ethics* being found in the definition of *morality*). However, in our new model we have honored the commonly held philosophical idea reflected in common usage that morality and ethics are somehow related to integrity by showing exactly how the virtue phenomena of morality and ethics are related to integrity as a positive phenomenon.

What we mean by the term *virtue* in the phrases "virtue concepts" and "virtue phenomena" are concepts and phenomena that deal with the normative standards of right and wrong, desirable and undesirable, and good and bad.

A fundamental basis for this new model is the assignment of appropriate realms for each of the four phenomena (integrity, morality, ethics, and legality). For us, the appropriate realms are those that make them effective tools for understanding and affecting human behavior. We assign each of the four phenomena to one of two realms, namely, a normative realm of virtues and a positive realm devoid of normative values. In our model, morality, ethics, and legality exist in the normative virtue realm, whereas integrity exists in the positive realm.[2]

Integrity as a Positive Model

For those who may be unfamiliar with the term *positive* in the way it is used here, *positive* does not mean the opposite of *negative*; that is, by "positive theory" we don't mean a theory of what is good or right as contrasted with what is bad or wrong. By *positive theory*, we mean a model that describes the way the world "behaves"—that is, the way the world actually is and how it operates independent of any value judgments about its desirability or undesirability, and a theory that is empirically testable—falsifiable in the Popperian sense (Popper, 1959).

Positive in the way it is used here contrasts with *normative*, where normative means establishing, relating to, or deriving from a human standard or norm that indicates what is considered to be good and right, or bad and wrong. Or, more specifically, normative means what is considered desirable or undesirable in conduct or behavior—that is, a value judgment about what should be or should not be.[3] In short, *positive* as it is used here is about "what is," while *normative* is about what human beings think "ought to be."

Note that, when fully developed, this new theory ultimately transforms the normative *concepts* of integrity, morality, ethics, and legality into positive *phenomena*. *Concept* is defined in *Webster's New World Dictionary* (2008)[4] as "an idea or thought, esp. a generalized idea of a thing or class of things; abstract notion." *Concept* sharply contrasts with *phenomenon*, which is defined as "any event, circumstance, or experience that is apparent to the senses and that can be scientifically described or appraised."

Consequently, when integrity, morality, ethics, and legality are taken to be normative virtues, they fit the definition of *concept*, but when in this new theory they are shown to be positive entities; they fit the definition of *phenomenon*. Consistent with this difference, when we are speaking about integrity, morality, ethics, and legality in their *normative* sense, we use the term *concepts* (as in *normative concepts*). In contrast, when we are speaking about integrity, morality, ethics, and legality in their *positive* sense, as they are revealed by this new theory, we use the term *phenomena* (as in *positive phenomena*).

Integrity: Definition

In *Webster's New World Dictionary integrity* is defined as "1. the quality or state of being complete; unbroken condition; wholeness; entirety; 2. the quality or state of being unimpaired; perfect condition; soundness; and 3. the quality or state of being of sound moral principle; uprightness, honesty, and sincerity."

As with the definitions of morality and ethics, including "sound moral principle" in the definition of integrity (Definition 3 in *Webster's* definition mentioned earlier) confounds and confuses the distinction between each of these three. In our new model, the definition of integrity specifically does not include Webster's Definition 3, "the quality or state of being of sound moral principle; uprightness, honesty, and sincerity." While the virtue concepts mentioned in definition 3 are not included in our definition of *integrity*, the way integrity is treated in our new model does take account of morality, ethics, and legality by making these standards part of one's word, unless one has publicly announced one's refusal to abide by one or more of those standards and agrees to accept any consequences for such refusal.

As we have said, in our new model, the three phenomena of morality, ethics, and legality are normative virtue phenomena, and integrity is not. Integrity, as we distinguish it, is a purely positive phenomenon, independent of normative value judgments. Integrity is thus not about good or bad, or right or wrong, or even about what should be or what should not be.

In this new model of integrity, "integrity" exists in the positive realm, and within that realm its *domain* is one of the *objective state* or *condition*, and within that domain we define *integrity* as *a state or condition of being whole, complete, unbroken, unimpaired, sound, perfect condition.*

Hereafter, we sometimes use the term *whole and complete* to represent this entire definition.

2. The Integrity of Objects and Systems, and the Universal Consequences of Diminished Integrity

Integrity of an Object

In this new model, we distinguish integrity for objects and systems as being a matter of the components that make up the object or system and the relationship between those components, and their design, the implementation of the design, and the use to which they are put. For an object or system to have integrity, all the foregoing must fit our definition of integrity (be whole, complete, unbroken, unimpaired, sound, and in perfect condition).

Consider a bicycle wheel as an example of an object and its integrity. As we remove spokes from the bicycle wheel, the wheel is no longer whole and complete. Because the wheel is no longer whole and complete, the integrity of the wheel is diminished.

Workability

As a consequence of the diminution of the integrity of the wheel (a diminution of whole and complete), there is an obvious corresponding diminution in the workability of the wheel. The *Oxford Dictionary* defines *workable* as "capable of producing the desired effect or result."[5]

Workability—Definition

In this new model of integrity, we define workability as the state or condition that determines the available opportunity for performance (the "opportunity set").

As we remove spokes from the wheel, integrity is more and more diminished, and as integrity is more and more diminished, the wheel becomes less and less workable. Indeed, when we have removed enough spokes, the wheel has no integrity, and therefore, the wheel collapses into complete failure and will not work at all.

In short, we assert the following simple, general rule: As integrity declines, workability declines, and when workability declines, the opportunity for performance (the opportunity set) declines.

Performance

We mean the word *performance*[6] in its broadest sense and leave the choice of definition and measures of performance up to individuals or organizational entities—for example, for organizations: profits or value creation; or for societies: concerns about environment, peace, or quality of life; or for individuals: being whole and complete as a person, the quality of one's life, happiness, or the welfare of one's children.

In effect, integrity as we distinguish and define it is an important factor of production (using the language of economists) comparable to knowledge and technology. Our model reveals the causal link between integrity and the available opportunity for performance (the opportunity set) for individuals, groups, and organizations. And our model provides actionable access to that causal link to individuals, families, executives, economists, philosophers, policy makers, leaders, and legal and governmental authorities. Revealing the causal link between integrity and performance makes clear what is currently obscured; namely, as integrity declines, the available opportunity for performance declines—however one wishes to define *performance*.[7] As will be seen in the following, this is an empirically testable proposition.

The Relationship Between Integrity and Performance

We can now extend and thereby complete our definition of workability to include the definition of *performance* (the final word used in the definition of *workability*). We define *workability* as *the state or condition that constitutes the available opportunity for something or somebody or a group or an organization to function, operate, or behave to produce an intended outcome, that is, to be effective; or the state or condition that determines the opportunity set from which someone or a group or an organization can choose outcomes, or design or construct for outcomes.*

In our bicycle-wheel example, we saw that as a consequence of the diminution of integrity there is a diminution in the workability of the wheel. Now we see that as a consequence of the diminution of the workability of the wheel, there is a corresponding diminution in the opportunity for performance. As spokes are removed, the integrity of the wheel is diminished. And as the integrity of the wheel is diminished, the workability of the wheel is diminished. And as the workability of the wheel is diminished, the opportunity for performance is diminished.

Thus, there is a cascade beginning with integrity, flowing to workability, and from workability to performance. As a result of this cascade, any diminution of whole and complete (a diminution of integrity) is a diminution of workability, and any diminution of workability is a diminution in the opportunity for performance. Integrity is thus a requisite condition for maximum performance.

There is a clear and unambiguous relationship between integrity and performance. It is not that performance is caused by integrity; rather, integrity is a necessary condition for performance. More rigorously, as integrity declines, so, too, does the opportunity set for performance available to the actor or decision maker. Hence, we speak about the *available opportunity set* for performance. Integrity is thus a necessary (although not sufficient) condition for performance. Some level of integrity is required for any level of performance. For example, as we said, when enough spokes are removed from the bicycle wheel, the wheel collapses, and there is no opportunity for performance.

In short, we assert the following simple, general rule: ceteris paribus (all other things held constant), as integrity declines, the opportunity for performance declines.

As is the case with the physical laws of nature (such as gravity), integrity as we have distinguished and defined it operates as it does regardless of whether one likes it or not (the question regarding how one might know something is whole and complete or not is entirely separable from its being so or not, and separable from the impact on performance of its being so or not.) Something is objectively whole, complete, unbroken, sound, perfect condition, or it is not. If it is, it has maximum workability. If it is not, to the degree that it is not, workability is diminished. And to the degree that workability is diminished, the opportunity for performance is diminished. This yields what we have termed

THE ONTOLOGICAL LAW OF INTEGRITY: To the degree that integrity is diminished, the opportunity for performance (the opportunity set) is diminished.

And this includes the opportunity for being whole and complete as a person, thus enriching the quality of one's life.

In order to reach the standard of being a law, a proposition must describe the workings or behavior of something, the stated workings or behavior of which are observed with unvarying uniformity under the same conditions. We believe that our Ontological Law of Integrity meets this standard while recognizing that the required formal empirical evidence has yet to be generated.

We include in the domain of objects, objects that are wholly human, for example, a person's body. If the condition of a person's body is less than whole, complete, unbroken, unimpaired, sound, and in perfect condition, then that person's body is diminished in physical integrity. As a body, this individual will have a diminished available opportunity for performance. However, the person, while diminished in physical integrity and therefore diminished in the available opportunity for physical performance, may at the same time be in full integrity as a person, as will be seen in the unique way we distinguish integrity for a person.[8]

Systems

All the foregoing is also true for systems. The opportunity for performance of a system to any standard of performance for which the system is designed diminishes as the integrity of any component, or relationship between components, necessary to the designed standard of performance is diminished, that is, is less than whole and complete. We see a repeat of the cascade from integrity to performance. When the integrity of any necessary component or necessary relationship between components of a system diminishes (i.e., becomes less whole and complete, including being absent entirely), the workability of the system diminishes, and as the workability of the system diminishes, the opportunity for performance to the designed standard of performance of that system diminishes. Thus, again we see that, ceteris paribus, as the integrity of a system declines, the available opportunity for performance of that system declines—an empirically testable proposition.

Other ways that the integrity of a system (or object) can be compromised and thereby result in diminished performance are when the design itself (integrity-of-design) or the implementation (integrity-of-implementation) of the design lacks integrity. When the design of a system or the implementation of the design lacks any component, or relationship between components, required to perform at the available designed-for opportunity for performance, the design or its implementation is less than whole and complete, and that violates the definition of integrity.

Finally, the integrity of a system (or object) can be compromised and thereby result in diminished performance when the operation (use) of the system by the user lacks integrity (integrity-of-use). When a system is used to produce performance where the design does not allow for such performance, the system is being used other than as it is meant to be used, and such use is unsound, and that leaves the use of the system out of integrity.[9] We note that the likelihood of an out-of-integrity use of a system rises in proportion to the degree that the user of the system is out of integrity as a person.

Our model says nothing about the standard of performance to which a system is designed; that definition is left totally to the discretion of the designer or to the design standard specified by or is agreed to by the user (be it a person, a group, or an organization).

We include in the domain of systems (including what we have said about the integrity of systems) (1) aspects of systems that are used by people (e.g., operating instructions or manufacturing protocols), (2) systems that have an impact on people (e.g., corporate human resource strategies), and (3) systems that utilize people (e.g., business processes and manufacturing processes). As with human objects, if such systems that include people in some way are less than whole, complete, unbroken, unimpaired, sound, perfect condition, then that human-including system is diminished in integrity. As a system, the system will have a diminished available opportunity for performance. However, the person (or persons) using the system, or impacted by the system, or utilized by the system, while confronted with a system diminished in system integrity and therefore diminished in the available opportunity for system performance, may at the same time be in full integrity as persons—as will be clear in the way we distinguish integrity for persons, groups, and organizational entities. Conversely, if the entire system is otherwise in integrity but one or more humans who are a part of the system are personally out of integrity, the system is likely to be out of integrity as well.

In summary, the available opportunity set for performance of a system is conditional on the integrity of the components and on the relationship among components necessary to the designed standard of performance, the integrity-of-design, and the integrity-of-use.

3. Integrity for a Person

Integrity for Persons, Groups, and Organizations

We distinguish integrity for an individual as being solely a matter of that person's word, and for a group or organizational entity as being comprised solely of what is said by or on behalf of the group or organization (the group or organization's word). (In the following, we define explicitly and completely what constitutes "one's word.") For a person, group, or organizational entity to have integrity, the word of the person, group, or organizational entity must be whole, complete, unbroken, unimpaired, sound, and in perfect condition. In our new model this is achieved by *honoring one's word*.

Integrity for a Person Is a Matter of That Person's Word

In this new model, integrity for a person is a matter of that person's word, nothing more and nothing less. Be it my word to myself (e.g., making a promise to myself, or a comment to myself about myself), or my word to others, in fact it is my word through which I define and express myself, both for myself and for others.

Even in the case where my "actions speak louder than words," it is what is *said* by my actions (the *speaking* of the actions rather than the actions per se) that constitute and expresses me, for myself and for others. It is as my word that others encounter me. And, while less obvious, it is also as my word (to others as well as to myself) that I encounter myself.[10] Indeed, in this new model, who I *am* is my word, at least in the matter of integrity. Because of its importance, we discuss this proposition in some detail.

One's Word Defined

In this new model of integrity, we define a person's word as consisting of each of the following:

Word-1. **What You Said:** Whatever you have said you will do or will not do, and in the case of do, by when you said you would do it.

Note A—Requests of You Become Your Word Unless You Have Timely Responded to Them: When you have received a request, you may accept, decline, make a counter-offer, or promise to respond at some specific later time. If you do not timely respond to a request with a decline, counter-offer, or promise to respond at some specific later time (which promise you timely honor), you have in effect accepted (given your word to) that request. If, when you receive a request, you do not timely respond to that request with one of the four legitimate responses, you have, in effect, accepted (given your word to) that request. That is, that request is part of your word (What You Said: Word-1).

Note B—In Contrast, Your Requests of Others Do Not for You Become Their Word When They Have Not Responded in a Timely Fashion: The efficacy (workability) of the asymmetry between Note A and this Note B is explained in note of "Word-3 Note."

Word-2. **What You Know:** Whatever you know to do or know not to do, and in the case of do, doing it as you know it is meant to be done and doing it on time, unless you have explicitly said to the contrary.

Word-3. **What Is Expected:** Whatever you are expected to do or not do (even when not explicitly expressed), and in the case of do, doing it on time, unless you have explicitly said to the contrary.

Note—In Contrast, Your Expectations of Others Are Not for You the Word Of Others: What you expect of others and have not explicitly expressed to them is not part of their word as defined in this new model. Only those expectations you have of others that you have made clear to them by a request is part of their word (unless they decline or counterpropose your request).

Word-4. **What You Say Is So:** Whenever you have given your word to others as to the existence of some thing or some state of the world, your word includes being willing to be held accountable that the others would find your evidence for what you have asserted also makes what you have asserted valid for themselves.[11]

Word-5. **What You Stand For:** What you stand for is fundamental to who you are for yourself and who you are for others. What you stand for is a declaration constituted by (1) who you hold yourself to be for yourself as that for which you can be counted on from yourself (whether specifically articulated by you or not) and (2) who you hold yourself out to be for others as that for which you can be counted on by others (or have allowed others to believe as that for which you can be counted on). The importance of this aspect of one's word in the matter of integrity is pointed to by Cox et al. in the *Stanford Encyclopedia of Philosophy*, who devote an entire section to "Integrity as Standing for Something."

Word-6. **Moral, Ethical, and Legal Standards:** The *social moral standards*, the *group ethical standards*, and the *governmental legal standards* of right and wrong, good and bad behavior, in the society, groups, and state in which one enjoys the benefits of membership are also part of one's word (what one is expected to do) unless (a) one has explicitly and publicly expressed an intention to not keep one or more of these standards and (b) one is willing to bear the costs of refusing to conform to these standards (the rules of the game one is in).

Note that what we have defined here is what constitutes a *person's word*—not what constitutes integrity for a person, which is explicitly defined next.

Clarifications of "One's Word" as Defined Earlier

Word-1. Most people will not have a problem with Word-1 (their word being constituted by that to which they have given their word).

Many people will have a problem in Word-1 with Note B: Your Requests of Others Do Not for You Become Their Word When They Have Not Responded in a Timely Fashion. Assuming that the nonresponse of another to your request is an acceptance on their part invites a breakdown in workability and a consequential decline in the opportunity for performance. Where another has not timely responded to your request, you avoid the chance of such a breakdown if you hold yourself accountable for obtaining a response.

Note that integrity is a matter of being whole and complete as to one's word, integrity is not an issue of fairness.

Word-2. Some people may have a problem with Word-2 (their word also being constituted by what they *know to do and doing it as it was meant to be done*) because there might be situations in which they don't know what to do or may not know how it is meant to be done. If one does not know what to do, and one *does not know* that one does not know what to do, that does not fit the definition of one's word as stated in Word-2 (*doing what you know to do*). However, if one does not know what to do and one *knows* that one does not know, that does fit the definition of one's Word-2, and explicitly saying that one does not know what to do would be a part of one's word; otherwise, the other would be left with the belief that one does know what to do. Likewise with knowing how it is meant to be done.

Word-3. Many people will have a problem with their word being constituted by Word-3 (*whatever is expected of them unless they have said to the contrary*). Of course, if someone has an expectation of me and has then expressed that expectation in the form of a request, I can accept, decline, or counteroffer that request—no problem with that. It is being obligated by expectations of me that have not been expressed explicitly, and certainly those about which one is unaware (unexpressed requests), with which many people will have a problem. When these are also considered as being part of one's word, it occurs for many as wrongful that one should be burdened by the unexpressed expectations (unexpressed requests) that others have of one. There are six points to be considered:

a. Suppose someone has an expectation (unexpressed request) of another. Even if one is unaware of the expectation, if that expectation is not met, like it or not, the outcome is much the same as having given one's word and not kept that word; specifically, workability declines, and consequently the opportunity for performance declines.

b. For better or for worse, what is expected of one is expected of one; in life, there is no escaping expectations (unexpressed requests). And if there is an expectation (even if you are unaware of that expectation), and you do not either meet that expectation or uncover it and explicitly declare that you will not meet it, there will be a breakdown, and workability will decline. As with an object or a system, when a relationship is less than whole and complete, workability declines, and consequently the opportunity for performance declines.

c. The notion of it being wrong or right (or bad or good, or unfair or fair) that you are affected by the unannounced expectations (unexpressed requests) of others is a normative value judgment, and in this new model of integrity, integrity is devoid of such normative value judgments. Whether you like it or not is irrelevant from the standpoint of integrity, workability, and performance. Given the obvious impact of unmet expectations on the workability of relationships, when you recognize that the expectations of others matter and you take all expectations of those with whom you desire to have a workable relationship as part of your word unless you have explicitly declared you will not meet them, your integrity will increase, the workability of your life will increase, and your opportunity for performance (however defined) will be greater. It all follows willy-nilly (i.e., willingly or unwillingly).

d. In light of the preceding three points, it follows that for a person's word to be whole and complete and to thereby create a life with high workability and high performance, one has to be "cause in the matter" of what is expected of one. By taking the position (a declaration, not an assertion[12]) that I am a cause in the matter of what people expect of me, I am then led to be highly sensitive and motivated to ferret out those expectations and to take action to manage them. And if I am straight with those who have expectations of me that I will not fulfill, my integrity will increase, the workability of my life will increase, and my performance (however defined) will be greater.

e. While we are still defining a person's word and have not yet gotten to defining integrity for a person, as will be seen later when we do, when declining an expectation (unexpressed request) of you, you do not have to deal with any mess that arises as a result of your decline, given that expectations of you are your word only if you have failed to decline them. Note that there may well be a mess as a result of your decline. You may well choose to do something to deal with the mess that results from the decline, but this is not a matter of keeping your word whole and complete and is, therefore, not a matter of your integrity to do so.

f. In summary, one's word as we have defined it in this new model is not a matter of being obligated or not (or even of being willing or not willing) to fulfill the expectations of others; if there is an expectation (unexpressed request), there is an expectation, and if you do not fulfill the expectation and have not said that you will not fulfill the expectation, the consequence on workability and performance is the same as that to which you have explicitly given your word. And this is true even though you do have a justification for not fulfilling the expectation. For example, like it or not, a person's performance is often judged against expectations (unexpressed requests), even if that person has never agreed to, or was not even aware of, those expectations. Thus, to create workability with those with whom you desire to have a relationship, you must clean up any mess created in their lives that result from their expectations of you that you do not meet and that you have not explicitly declined. This is what it means to take yourself to be a cause in the matter of expectations of you.

Word-3 Note. There is an asymmetry here in Word-3 (your expectations, unexpressed requests, of others are not the word of others). As we said above, your word includes the unexpressed expectations of others, unless you formally decline them; yet, your unexpressed expectations are not the word of others. Thus, you cannot hold others accountable for fulfilling your unexpressed expectations. Indeed, holding others accountable for fulfilling your unexpressed expectations will result in a diminution of workability and performance, a consequence of your being out of integrity. This asymmetry—in effect, an instance of "what's good for the goose is not good for the gander"—is required to be whole and complete with oneself and with others.

Word-4. With respect to Word-4 (what you say is so), some people will have a problem that one's word as to the existence of some thing or some state of the world includes being accountable that the other would find valid for themselves the evidence that one had for asserting something to be the case. Of course, there are times when one says that this or that is so, or not so, but one would not be willing to be held to account for having evidence that the other would find valid. In such cases, one's word would include acknowledging that, and perhaps saying what level of evidence one does have, for example, when one assumes that something is the case.

Word-5. With respect to Word-5 (what you stand for), it is important to be aware that what you stand for is essentially a matter of who you say you can be counted on to be for yourself (whether specifically articulated by you or not) and who you say that others can count on you to be for them (whether specifically declared or not). The explicit content of what you stand for is not a matter of your integrity. However, the impact on who you are for yourself and the impact on who you are for others is determined by the nature of what you stand for, and the integrity with which you handle it. And, to a large extent, the magnitude of what you stand for determines your opportunity set for performance in the world, with others, and with yourself.

Word-6. With respect to Word-6 (moral, ethical, and legal standards), in the unabbreviated version of this paper (URL: https://papers.ssrn. com/sol3/papers2.cfm?abstract_id=920625), we explicate in detail the arguments that lead to the proposition that moral, ethical, and legal standards are a part of one's word. It suffices here to recognize that Word-6 recontextualizes the moral, ethical, and legal standards of the society, group, and governmental entities in which one enjoys membership from something inflicted on me—someone else's will or in the language of this new model "someone else's word"—to my word, thus, leaving me with the power to honor my word either by keeping it or by saying I will not and accepting the consequences.

Integrity Is Honoring One's Word

In this new model of integrity, we define integrity for a person as *honoring one's word* (as one's word is defined in the preceding sections).

Notice that we did not say that integrity is a matter of *keeping* one's word; we said that integrity is *honoring* one's word.

In this new model of integrity, we define *honoring your word* as

1. *Keeping* your word (and on time).
    And, whenever you will *not be keeping* your word:
2. Just as soon as you become aware that you will not be keeping your word (including not keeping your word on time), saying to everyone who is impacted

    a. that you will not be keeping your word, and
    b. that you will keep that word in the future, and by when, or that you won't be keeping that word at all, and
    c. what you will do to deal with the impact on others of the failure to keep your word (or to keep it on time).

Notice that "honoring your word" includes two conditions, where the second condition comes into play whenever the first condition is not met. Integrity is an "*and*" proposition. In other words, to be a person of integrity all you have to do is "honor your word," which means you keep your word (Condition 1), *and when you will not*, then you say you will not and clean up any consequences (Conditions 2.a, 2.b, and 2.c).

However, we have found it useful for discussions regarding the impact of integrity to sometimes use "honoring your word" in another way. While we want to emphasize that, strictly speaking, integrity for human entities is honoring their word as specified earlier, when speaking about the consequences of integrity we will sometimes speak as though integrity is an "either/or" proposition where you either "keep your word" (Condition 1) or you "honor your word" (Conditions 2.a, 2.b, and 2.c). We have not yet found a situation, where in context, the way we are using "honor your word" is ambiguous.

The Impossibility of Always Keeping One's Word

A person who always *keeps* his or her word is almost certainly living a life that is too small. Thus, unless you are playing a small game in life, you will not always *keep* your word. However, it is always possible to *honor* your word. Integrity is *honoring* your word.

While always keeping your word may not be possible, honoring your word as we have defined *honoring* in our new model of integrity is always possible. Therefore, it is always possible to have integrity, that is, to be whole and complete as a person. Having integrity is a simple, although not always easy, matter of honoring your word.

The state of being whole, complete, unbroken, unimpaired, sound, and in perfect condition is our definition of integrity, but that definition says nothing about the pathway, or what one can or must do to create, maintain or restore integrity. Because honoring your word is the pathway to integrity it gives us access to integrity; it is actionable. In other words, you can't "do" whole and complete, you can "do" honor your word, and honoring your word leaves you whole and complete. This is what we mean when we say a proposition is "actionable."

It is worth repeating that integrity, as distinguished in this new model, is independent of normative value judgments. While one can have a normative value judgment regarding whether or not one likes integrity as distinguished in this new model (as one can have a normative value judgment about whether or not one likes gravity), the effect of integrity on performance is a positive (empirical) proposition. And to emphasize the point, the purely positive nature of integrity is independent of whether you believe honoring your word is a good or a bad thing. That is, the consequences of honoring or not honoring your word are independent of whether you believe it is a good or bad thing. We mean by this that, ceteris paribus, the closer a person, group, or entity is to full integrity, the larger will be the opportunity set for performance available to the entity. Moreover, because we have said nothing about how performance is defined or measured, our model of integrity is free of value judgments regarding what performance is. Integrity has no virtue value as we are defining it. Indeed, some might choose to give their word to what we might judge to be dishonorable activities or goals—"honor amongst thieves," for example.

The integrity mountain has no top, so you better learn to love climbing. Doing so makes it OK for each of us to recognize that we are not always a person of "integrity."

Our proposition is that whatever it is you are committed to, you maximize the opportunity for success if you honor your word. We have also found that honoring your word is privately optimal in the sense that it requires no cooperation from anyone else. Even if everyone else is out of integrity, it is in your personal best interest to be a man or woman of integrity. Do not naively assume that everyone you are dealing with in life is a person of integrity; deal with people as they actually act. If you behave with integrity in your interactions with them, they will come to trust you, and that is valuable to you. As we said earlier, deal with these others exactly as they act (i.e., as lacking integrity and therefore untrustworthy).

In the full document, we emphasize the fact that in this new model of integrity, your word includes the ethical, moral, and legal standards of the groups or entities in which you enjoy the benefits of membership (unless you have already publicly expressed that you will not keep one or more of these standards, and you willingly bear the consequences of not doing so). And we discuss how treating integrity as a positive phenomenon increases the likelihood that individuals will honor their word regarding the standards of the virtue phenomena. Thus, individuals' efforts to behave with integrity (as we distinguish integrity in this new model) support morality, ethics, and legality in their lives.

Maintaining One's Integrity When Not Keeping One's Word—Paradox Resolved

Unless we give our word to virtually nothing, it is impossible in practice to always be able to keep our word and certainly to keep our word on time. If integrity is understood to be *keeping* one's word (as it often is), this creates a paradox for a person of integrity when confronted with instances where it is impossible or inappropriate for that person to keep his or her word. Faced with this paradox, even people committed to integrity often wind up engaging in out-of-integrity behavior, such as avoiding the issue or engaging in long-winded explanations in an attempt to somehow counterbalance not keeping their word. And such efforts sometimes extend to what turns out to be highly counterproductive out-of-integrity behavior, for example, lying, covering up, or laying the blame on others.

There is a high personal cost to oneself from such out-of-integrity behavior— that is, the cost of being less than whole and complete as a person (a disintegration of self)—combined with an inevitable decline in quality of life, not to mention the loss of trust in oneself by others. However, that the out-of-integrity behavior is the source of this cost is inevitably hidden. In Section 8 of the full document, we define and discuss at length what we term the "veil of invisibility"[13] that conceals the impact of virtually all out-of-integrity behavior and the costs it imposes on individuals, groups, organizations, and societies. We summarize that discussion in Appendix A.

By defining integrity for persons, groups and entities as honoring one's word, the paradox associated with taking integrity as keeping one's word (as is so often recommended by those who do not perceive the damage caused by taking integrity to be *keeping* one's word) is resolved, and a pathway is established for handling not keeping one's word with integrity.

In the full document, we discuss the situation in which it was impossible for Johnson & Johnson (J&J) to keep its word (as we define an organization's word) that its products were safe. Because cyanide had been put in some Tylenol capsules and then replaced on retailer's shelves, it was impossible for J&J to keep its word that its Tylenol capsules were safe. In fact, a number of Tylenol consumers died. By simply honoring its word when it could not keep its word, J&J was able to maintain its integrity and thereby maintain its customers' trust in J&J and Tylenol. As a consequence, it resurrected Tylenol as a leading pain killer in a remarkably short time and did so under circumstances in which experts predicted it could not be done.

There will also be cases where an entity will *choose* not to keep its word. For example, one of the functions of a governmental authority in a well-developed society is to maintain a monopoly over the legitimate use of violence to protect the rights of citizens, in particular, to protect them from violent acts by their fellow citizens—including bodily harm or theft of or damage to their property. The commitment to use the government's monopoly on violence to maintain peace by preventing the private use of violence by citizens on each other can be understood as the state's word. Yet, in some cases, it pays both the state and its citizens for the state to use its monopoly on violence on citizens in cases where violence of others is not being prevented. Consider cases like mad cow and avian flu diseases, where it is considered appropriate for the governmental authority to use its powers to destroy herds or flocks in order to stamp out local infections so as to prevent the spread of disease and the loss of human life. In some, but not all, cases the rules of the game will provide for compensation for the loss of property by such actions (as, e.g., in cases of eminent domain where a public taking is ruled to be in the overall public interest).

There will also be cases in which we simply make a choice to not keep our word. For example, in a situation where when it comes time to keep our word, we are faced with two conflicting commitments and must choose one over the other. In such cases, whether as an individual, group, or organizational entity, maintaining integrity always requires one to clean up the mess one has caused for those depending on one's word by honoring one's word.

The preceding examples help us see that a great deal of the mischief that surrounds integrity is a product of the paradox created by limiting the definition of integrity to keeping one's word in a reality in which it is not possible or even appropriate to always keep one's word. By defining integrity for individuals, groups, and organizations as honoring one's word we resolve this paradox that undermines the power of integrity. Honoring our word provides the opportunity to maintain our integrity when it is not possible or appropriate to keep our word, or we simply choose not to keep our word.[14]

In his early insightful work, Simons (1999, p. 90) quite rightly emphasizes "behavioral integrity" as "the perceived degree of congruence between the values expressed by words and those expressed through action" and points to the importance of what he terms "word–action" misfit. Simons's paper "proposes that the divergence between words and deeds has profound costs as it renders managers untrustworthy and undermines their credibility and their ability to use their words to influence the actions of their subordinates" (p. 89).[15] We agree and find his statement a clear illustration of what we said earlier, namely, that as the integrity of one's word declines, the available opportunity for performance declines.

Simons points at the critical distinction that integrity for a person is a matter of that person's word. However, as an example of the almost universal treatment of integrity, Simons defines integrity as keeping one's word, but our model does not. In order for "the perceived degree of congruence between the values expressed by words and those expressed through action"[16] to be an effective model of integrity, the model must provide an opportunity to maintain one's integrity in situations in which one cannot keep one's word or makes a choice to not keep one's word (a condition that Simons also implies is necessary but does not state in his discussion). As we said previously, there are cases where because of the complexities of the situation or external factors, it is not always optimal or appropriate for managers (indeed all individuals) to keep their word.

Our definition of *integrity* as "honoring one's word" provides a complete model that includes a way to maintain integrity when one is for any reason not going to keep one's word. When one honors one's word exactly as we define it in the preceding sections (including dealing with the consequences to others of not keeping one's word), there are none of the "profound costs" that Simons rightly associates with not being able to keep one's word.

In fact, failing to keep one's word, but fully honoring that word can generate substantial benefits in that such behavior provides a vivid signal to others that one takes one's word seriously. In their *Journal of Marketing* study of favorable and unfavorable incidents in service encounters in the airline, restaurant, and hotel businesses, Bitner, Booms, and Tetreault (1990, pp. 80–81) were surprised to find (using our language) the power of honoring one's word when one does not keep one's word. Their study revealed that 23.3% of the

> "memorable satisfactory encounters" involve difficulties attributable to failures in core service delivery. . . . From a management perspective, this finding is striking. It suggests that even service delivery system *failures* can be remembered as highly satisfactory encounters if they are handled properly. . . . One might expect that dissatisfaction could be mitigated in failure situations if employees are trained to respond, but the fact that such incidents can be remembered as very satisfactory is somewhat surprising.
> (Bitner et al., 1990, pp. 80–81)

We are not surprised by the favorable response of customers to such "properly handled" service failures; in fact, from the perspective of our new model such outcomes are predictable. While apparently counterintuitive, customers are frequently surprised and delighted when individuals or organizations honor their word when they have failed to keep their word. Indeed, such occasions are often viewed by customers as extraordinary performance. In fact, when the failure is newsworthy, the actions the organization takes to honor its word are also newsworthy. Thus, the results of the Bitner, Booms, and Tetreault study illustrate our postulated relation between integrity and performance—in this case, performance as viewed by the organization's customers. And the results imply (counter to the arguments of Simons and others) that one will create trust by others more quickly when one fails to *keep* one's word, but *honors* one's word.

Integrity as the Integration of Self

In the *Stanford Encyclopedia of Philosophy*, Cox, La Caze, and Levine (2005)[17] point out that "integrity is primarily a formal relation one has to oneself." This is an important theme that runs through the philosophical discourse on integrity—it relates to integrity directly as "being whole and complete as a person." We extract the various following phrases that relate to being personally whole and complete from a much longer quotation in the *Stanford Encyclopedia of Philosophy*:

- "'integrity' refers to the wholeness, intactness or purity of a thing—meanings that are sometimes . . . applied to people."
- ". . . maintains its integrity as long as it remains uncorrupted. . . ."
- ". . . the most important of them being: (i) integrity as the integration of self; (ii) integrity as maintenance of identity; (iii) integrity as standing for something. . . ."
- "Integrity as self-integration. . . ."

The ideas pointed to by the preceding quotes are represented in this chapter by our phrase "being personally whole and complete" or "being whole and complete as a person."

We now deal directly with how integrity creates being whole and complete as a person and how being whole and complete as a person relates to the quality of one's life.

The Role of One's Body

While, in everyday speaking, we might say that people identify with their body, on closer examination it is not their body per se with which they identify; that is, it is not their body per se that they are for themselves. Rather it is what they say to themselves and to others about their body, their interpretation of their body, with which they identify.

For example, two different people lose both legs. One of the two says to herself, "I am less of a person," and as a result may contemplate suicide, or perhaps experience depression. The other of the two says to herself, "I have lost my legs, but I am no less of a person," and as a result goes on to live a productive and fulfilled life, and does so despite having an impaired body. It is what I say, that is, my word, with which I identify rather than my body per se.

Indeed, to emphasize the point, it is never one's body per se that one is for oneself; rather, it is what one says about one's body—one's judgments, evaluations, for example, the pride or shame about one's body with which one identifies. This further clarifies why, in a previous section, we made the distinction between the integrity of a person and the integrity of that person's body. As we said, at least for purposes of integrity, we treat a person's body as an object or system and distinguish a person's body from the person. The integrity of a person's body has to do with the wholeness and completeness of that person's body. The integrity of a person has to do with the wholeness and completeness of that person's word.

The Role of One's Feelings

Similarly, some of us think we are our feelings; that is, we identify with our feelings. However, with a deeper examination of ourselves it becomes clear that it is not our feelings per se (what is happening in our brain and endocrine system, or even any resultant sensations or feelings about which we become aware) that we are for ourselves. Rather, it is what I say I am feeling and what I say about what I am feeling (i.e., my interpretation of those sensations and feelings) that I am for myself.

If you experience an emotion, let's say annoyance, that you interpret as inappropriate to the circumstances in which you find yourself, with incredulity you might say, "Why am I feeling annoyed?" In your questioning of the appropriateness of the feeling, you have identified your self with what you say about the feeling (your interpretation of the feeling), not with the feeling itself. On the other hand, if you experience annoyance that you interpret as appropriate to the circumstances, with definiteness you might say, "I am annoyed!" In your conclusion of the appropriateness of the feeling, again, you have identified your self with what you say about the feeling (your interpretation), not with the feeling itself. Moreover, unless one is in some way mentally deficient, one acts consistent with one's interpretation rather than acting consistent with the emotion itself.[18]

The Role of One's Thinking

Finally, some might argue that we identify with our thinking. If we pay attention to our thought process, it is clear that we have different kinds of thinking.

In one kind of thinking, a good many of our thoughts are thoughts that we just have. That is, many thoughts just seem to come into mind willy-nilly. In fact, we sometimes reject the thought that we just had as being inaccurate or inappropriate to the situation, rather than identifying with it. Again, as with the emotions we experience, it is our interpretation of the thoughts we have—that is, what we say to ourselves about those thoughts—with which we identify.

Another kind of thinking is when we generate thoughts intentionally, when we are thinking rather than having thoughts. This includes when we think creatively; commonly we call this "having a new idea about something." In this creative thinking, we are speaking to ourselves about something—in words or symbols or images. We also go on to speak to ourselves about our new idea—that is, what we said when we were thinking creatively. In this speaking to ourselves about our new idea, we reject certain statements we made in the new idea, modify others, and accept yet others. Whether it be what we say to ourselves in formulating the original idea or what we say to ourselves about the original idea, it is what we say to ourselves with which we identify.

Of course, we have all experienced situations in which we later discover that what we said in our interpretation was, in fact, erroneous or was inappropriate to the situation. Nevertheless, accurate or inaccurate, it is with what we say in our interpretations at the time that we identify. And this includes when we discover an error in an earlier statement of interpretation that leads to a new interpretation.

One's Word to Oneself: The Foundation of Integrity

Being a person of integrity begins with my word to myself that I am a person of integrity. If I attempt to start with my word to others to be a person of integrity without having given my word to myself to be a person of integrity, I am almost certain to fail to be a person of integrity. Once I have given my word to myself that I am a person of integrity, I am more likely to notice opportunities to act with integrity regarding my word to others. (In addition, one is likely to act with more caution and care in giving one's word to others.) If in this process one does not practice dealing with one's word to one's self with integrity, one will fail to be a person of integrity. Ultimately, when one's word to one's self is whole, complete, unbroken, unimpaired, sound, and in perfect condition, it serves as a foundation on which one is likely to deal with one's word to others with integrity.

In the end, it is honoring what I say to myself when I say I am a person of integrity that is the beginning and end of being a person of integrity.

When giving our word to others, one would think that it would be obvious to us that we have in fact given our word (although later we argue that for most people, even when giving their word to others, they are often unaware that they have given their word). At the same time, when we give our word to ourselves, we seldom recognize that we have in fact given our word. For an example of this failure, think of occasions when the issue of self-discipline comes up, and the ease with which we often dismiss it—of course, always "just this one time." In such self-discipline cases, we fail to recognize that we are not honoring our word to ourselves and that in doing so, we have undermined ourselves as a person of integrity.

As we have said, integrity for a person is a matter of that person's word, nothing more and nothing less; and one's word to one's self is a critical part of one's word. By not being serious when we give our word to ourselves, we forfeit the opportunity to maintain our integrity by honoring our word to ourselves. We take the conversations we have with ourselves as merely "thinking." And when in those conversations, we give our word, giving our word occurs to us as just more thinking, rather than having just committed ourselves (given our word) to ourselves. For example, thinking to myself that I will exercise tomorrow. But, when tomorrow comes, I have either simply forgotten my word to myself, or if remembered, I easily dismiss my word as nothing more than a thought (a good idea) I had yesterday. What it costs not to treat your word to yourself with integrity is that you become less powerful as a person, and with less power, you will find yourself using force to deal with the world (guile, anger, bossiness, subterfuge, righteousness, defensiveness, manipulation, and the like—or at the other end of the spectrum but still a matter of force, playing the victim, helplessness, and the like).

An important aspect of my word to myself is my word to others. For example, when I give my word to someone to meet them at a given time tomorrow, in effect I have also given my word to myself to be there tomorrow at the appointed time and place. Likewise, with any time I give my word to others, I have also given my word to myself to be good for my word.

If I hold myself up as a person of integrity and do not honor my word to myself, it is highly unlikely that I will be able to be in integrity with others. Most of us hold ourselves to be a "man of integrity" or a "woman of integrity," but if one does not treat one's word to oneself as a matter of integrity, being a person of integrity is simply not possible. Unfortunately, most of us human beings believe that we are people of integrity, but as Chris Argyris (1991, 1993) concludes after 40 years of studying human beings, we humans consistently act inconsistently with our view of ourselves. More specifically, and said in the language of our model, we consistently hold ourselves up as people of integrity but do not honor our word to ourselves, and moreover are blind to this contradiction.

Referring back to what was said at the beginning of a previous section about the philosophical discourse of integrity's relation to being whole and complete as a person—"integrity as the integration of self," "quality of character," "uncorrupted," "exhibiting integrity throughout life," "maintenance of identity"—one's word to oneself can be said to be central in being personally whole and complete.

When I am not serious about my word to myself, it will show up consistently as various problems and difficulties in my life, the actual source of which I will obscure with various explanations and justifications. Moreover, I will show up for others variously as inconsistent, unfocused, scattered, unreliable, undependable, unpredictable, and generally unsatisfied as a person. In conclusion, honoring your word to yourself provides a solid foundation for self-discipline.

When an occasion for self-discipline shows up for you as an occasion for honoring your word to yourself, and you see that as a way to maintain yourself whole and complete as a person, that empowers you to deal with the matter with integrity.

Summary

Whether it be one's body, or one's emotions, or one's thoughts, it is our interpretation (what we say to ourselves, our word to ourselves) that ultimately defines who we are for ourselves. Who one is in the matter of integrity is one's word—nothing more, nothing less.

One's Relationships Are Constituted by One's Word

Before, we looked at a person's integrity from the perspective of what it takes for that person to be whole and complete, and now we look at integrity from the perspective of what it takes for the relationship created by the person's word to be whole and complete.

The power of taking one's self to be constituted by one's word becomes even clearer when examined in light of the fact that giving one's word to another creates a relationship (or a new aspect of an existing relationship). When I give my word, I have a new relationship not only to the other but, less obviously, with myself as well. Therefore, it is important to hold one's word in a context that includes both one's word as itself and the relationships that it creates.

Simply put, when I give my word to another, that act creates various conditions of "counting on" or "reliance on," in the relationship between me and the other. Given that one's word creates the relationship, it follows that when one's word is whole and complete, the aspect of the relationship it creates is whole and complete. In a critical sense, who I am for another *is* my word,[19] that is, my expression of my self. For a relationship to have integrity (to be whole and complete), one's word must be whole and complete. As Shakespeare said, "this above all: to thine own self be true, *it must follow, as the night the d*ay, Thou cans't not be false to any man."[20] When one is true to one's word (which is being true to one's self), one cannot be but true to any man.

Of course, there are at least two sides to a relationship. If one side has integrity and the other does not (the word of the other is not whole and complete), there is a diminution of integrity in the relationship resulting in a diminution of the available opportunity for performance in (or resulting from) the relationship—however performance is defined. Nevertheless, when the other person in a relationship is out-of-integrity and therefore diminishes the workability of that relationship, your being in-integrity allows you to continue to be effective in the relationship and to contribute positively to the workability of that relationship. And therefore, in spite of the other being out-of-integrity, you personally benefit. Your being in-integrity leaves you whole and complete both *outside* of the relationship and *inside* the relationship. Thus, as we said earlier, integrity is privately optimal; it does not require the cooperation of the other. You benefit even though the other is out-of-integrity.

Conclusion: An Actionable Pathway

In conclusion, in our new model, the way in which integrity is distinguished and defined for individuals, groups, and organizations reveals the impact of integrity on workability and trustworthiness and, consequently, on performance. Even more important, our new model provides an actionable pathway (i.e., direct access[21]) to integrity and, therefore, to workability and trustworthiness, and, consequently, to elevating performance itself.

4. Appendix

There are eleven factors contributing to what we term the "veil of invisibility" that conceals the impact of out-of-integrity behavior on individuals, groups, organizations, and societies.

Eleven Factors of the "Veil of Invisibility" That Conceal
the Effects of Out-of-Integrity Behavior

1. Not seeing that who you are as a person is your word

That is, thinking that who you are as a person is anything other than your word. For example, thinking that who you are is your body, or what is going on with you internally (your mental/emotional state, your thoughts/ thought processes and your bodily sensations), or anything else you identify with such as your title or position in life, or your possessions, among others, leaves you unable to see that when your word is less than whole and complete, you are diminished as a person.

   A person is constituted in language. As such, when a person's word is less than whole and complete they are diminished as a person.

2. Living as if My Word Is Only What I Said (Word-1) and What I Assert Is True (Word-4)

Even if we are clear that in the matter of integrity our word exists in six distinct ways, most of us actually function as if our word consists only of *what I said* or *what I assert is true*. This guarantees that we cannot be men or women of integrity. For us, Words-2, -3, -5, and -6 are invisible as our word:

- Word-2: What You Know to do or not to do
- Word-3: What Is Expected of you by those with whom you wish to have a workable relationship (unless you have explicitly declined those unexpressed requests)
- Word-5: What You Stand For

- Word-6: Moral, Ethical and Legal Standards of each society, group, and governmental entity of which I am a member.

When we live (function in life) as though our word is limited to Word-1: What I Said and Word-4: What I Say Is So, we are virtually certain to be out of integrity with regard to our word as constituted in Words-2, -3, -5, and -6. In such cases, all the instances of our word (be it the word of an individual or organization) that are not spoken or otherwise communicated explicitly are simply invisible as our word to such individuals or organizations. In our lives, all the instances of our Words-2, -3, -5, and -6 simply do not show up (occur) for us as our having given our word.

3.   "Integrity is a virtue."

For most people and organizations, integrity exists as a *virtue* rather than as a *necessary condition for performance* (see also Monga, 2017; Orlitzky & Monga, 2017). When held as a virtue rather than as a factor of production, integrity is easily sacrificed when it appears that a person or organization must do so to succeed. For many people, virtue is valued only to the degree that it engenders the admiration of others, and as such it is easily sacrificed especially when it would not be noticed or can be rationalized (see also Orlitzky, 2017). Sacrificing integrity as a virtue seems no different from sacrificing courteousness or new sinks in the men's room.

4.   Self-deception about being out-of-integrity

People are mostly unaware that they have not kept their word. All they see is the reason, rationalization, or excuse for not keeping their word. In fact, people systematically deceive (lie to) themselves about who they have been and what they have done. As Chris Argyris (1991, p. 103) concludes, "put simply, people consistently act inconsistently, unaware of the contradiction between their espoused theory and their theory-in-use, between the way they think they are acting and the way they really act."

And if you think this is not you, you are fooling yourself about fooling yourself.

Because people cannot see their out-of-integrity behavior, it is impossible for them to see the cause of the unworkability in their lives and organizations—the direct result of their own attempts to violate the Law of Integrity.

5.   Integrity is keeping one's word

The belief that integrity is keeping one's word—period—leaves no way to maintain integrity when this is not possible, or when it is inappropriate, or when one simply chooses not to keep one's word. This leads to concealing not keeping one's word, which adds to the veil of invisibility about the impact of violations of the Law of Integrity.

6. Fear of acknowledging you are not going to keep your word

When maintaining your integrity (i.e., acknowledging that you are not going to keep your word and cleaning up the mess that results) appears to you as a threat to be avoided (like it was when you were a child) rather than simply a challenge to be dealt with, you will find it difficult to maintain your integrity. When not keeping their word, most people choose the apparent short-term gain of hiding that they will not keep their word. Thus, out of fear we are blinded to (and, therefore, mistakenly forfeit) the power and respect that accrue from acknowledging that one will not keep one's word or that one has not kept one's word.

7. Integrity is not seen as a factor of production

This leads people to make up false causes and unfounded rationalizations as the source(s) of failure, which, in turn, conceals the violations of the Law of Integrity as the source of the reduction of the opportunity for performance that results in failure.

8. *Not* doing a cost/benefit analysis on *giving* one's word

When giving their word, most people do not consider fully what it will take to *keep* that word. That is, people do not do a cost/benefit analysis on giving their word. In effect, when giving their word, most people are merely sincere (well meaning) or placating someone, and don't even think about what it will take to keep their word. Simply put, this failure to do a cost/benefit analysis on giving one's word is irresponsible. Irresponsible giving of one's word is a major source of the mess left in the lives of people and organizations. People generally do not see the giving of their word as "I *am* going to *make* this happen," but if you are not doing this, you will be out-of-integrity. Generally, people give their word *intending* to keep it. That is, they are merely sincere. If anything makes it difficult to deliver, then they provide *reasons* instead of results.

9. *Doing* a cost/benefit analysis on *honoring* one's word

People almost universally apply cost/benefit analysis to *honoring* their word. Treating integrity as a matter of cost/benefit analysis guarantees you will not be a trustworthy person, or with a small exception, a person of integrity.

If I apply cost/benefit analysis to honoring my word, I am either out of integrity to start with because I have not stated the cost/benefit contingency that is in fact part of my word (I lied), or to have integrity when I give my word, I must say something like the following:

> I will honor my word when it comes time for me to honor my word if the costs of doing so are less than the benefits.

Such a statement, while leaving me with integrity will not engender trust. In fact, it says that my word is meaningless.

10. Integrity is a mountain with no top

People systematically believe that they are in integrity, or if by chance they are at the moment aware of being out of integrity, they believe that they will soon get back into integrity.

In fact, integrity is a mountain with no top. However, the combination of (1) generally not seeing our own out-of-integrity behavior, (2) believing that we are persons of integrity, and (3) even when we get a glimpse of our own out-of-integrity behavior, assuaging ourselves with the notion that we will soon restore ourselves to being a person of integrity keeps us from seeing that in fact integrity is a mountain with no top. To be a person of integrity requires that we recognize this and "learn to enjoy climbing."

11. Not having your word in existence when it comes time to keep your word

People say "talk is cheap" because most people do not honor their word when it comes time to keep their word. A major source of people not honoring their word is that when it comes time for them to do so, their word does not exist for them in a way that gives them a reliable opportunity to honor their word.

Most people have never given any thought to keeping their word in existence so that when it comes time for them to keep their word, there is a reliable opportunity for them to honor their word. This is a major source of out-of-integrity behavior for individuals, groups, and organizations.

In order to honor your word, you will need an extraordinarily powerful answer to the question, "Where Is My Word When It Comes Time for Me to Keep My Word?" If you don't have a way for your word to be powerfully present for you in the moment or moments that it is time for you to take action to honor your word, then you can forget about being a person of integrity, much less a leader.

Notes

1. Webster's, Webster's New World Dictionary on PowerCD version 2.1, based on Webster's New World Dictionary®, Third College Edition 1994.

2. Drawing on *Webster's New World Dictionary,* we use the following definitions of *morality, ethics,* and *legality:* In this new model of integrity, "morality" exists in the normative realm, and within that realm morality is in the *social virtue domain,* and within that domain we define morality as a term as *in a given society, in a given era of that society, morality is the generally accepted standards of what is desirable and undesirable; of right and wrong conduct, and what is considered by that society as good behavior and what is considered bad behavior of a person, group, or entity.* In this new model of integrity, "ethics" exists in the normative realm, and within that realm ethics is in the *group virtue domain* (where a group is defined as a subclass of a given entity), and within that domain we define ethics as a term as *in a given group (the benefits of inclusion in which group a person, subgroup, or entity enjoys), ethics is the agreed on standards of what is desirable and undesirable; of right and wrong conduct; of what is considered by that group as good and bad behavior of a person, subgroup, or entity that is a member of the group, and may include defined bases for discipline, including exclusion.* In this new model of integrity, "legality" exists in the normative realm, and within that realm legality is in the *governmental virtue domain,* and within that domain we define legality as a term as *the system of laws and regulations of right and wrong behavior that are enforceable by the state (federal, state, or local governmental body in the United States) through the exercise of its policing powers and judicial process, with the threat and use of penalties, including its monopoly on the right to use physical violence.*
3. See Keynes (1891, pp. 34–35, and p. 46) *The Scope and Method of Political Economy*; and Friedman, 1996, "The Methodology of Positive Economics," in M. Friedman (ed.), *Essays in Positive Economics* (pp. 145–178). Chicago: University of Chicago Press.
4. This is the dictionary we use throughout the full document and this abridged version, in which dictionary the definitions are generally consistent with other dictionaries.
5. Oxford American Dictionaries, 2005, *Dictionary and Thesaurus,* Version 1.0.1: Apple Computer, Inc.
6. The relevant entries in the *Encarta Dictionary* (Encarta, 2004, Microsoft® Encarta® Reference Library 2004: Microsoft Corporation) define performance as "the manner in which something or somebody functions, operates, or behaves; the effectiveness of the way somebody does his or her job."
7. It should be noted that operating with integrity increases the available opportunity set for performance without regard to the objective of one's performance. This leads to the uncomfortable conclusion that behaving with integrity will allow one to more effectively accomplish ends that others may consider inappropriate or undesirable. However, given the relation between integrity and the virtue elements of morality, ethics, and legality, this holds only if one is acting morally, ethically, and legally. This last requires a broader discussion. For example, does the context of the morals, ethics, and legality of a larger group trump the context of the morals, ethics, and legality of a significantly smaller or less powerful group?
8. Of course, there are certain physical components required for a human body to be whole and complete. If these are lacking, there is no opportunity for full integrity for that human body.
9. For example, if a man of 300 pounds attempts to save his life with a life preserver flotation device designed to be used by a child of 50 pounds, he will drown unless he can swim. In addition, if he were to use a life preserver flotation device designed to be used by a man of 300 pounds, but he ties it around his ankles, the user's operation of the system is unsound, he will die.
10. I encounter myself either authentically or inauthentically. If you believe Chris Argyris (as we do), we human beings almost universally encounter ourselves

in many respects inauthentically, that is "people consistently act inconsistently, unaware of the contradiction . . . between the way they think they are acting and the way they really act" (Argyris, 1991, p. 103). When we encounter ourselves inauthentically we are not whole and complete and thus are out of integrity.

11. See Searle, 1969, *Speech Acts: An Essay in the Philosophy of Language*, Cambridge, UK: Cambridge University Press, especially for his discussion of assertions.

12. See Searle, 1969, *Speech Acts: An Essay in the Philosophy of Language*, Cambridge, UK: Cambridge University Press, especially for his discussion of assertions.

13. To use a variant of the term "veil of ignorance" originally used by Rawls, 1971, *A Theory of Justice*, Cambridge: Harvard University Press, Chapter 3.

14. There is a useful parallel/application of this principle in the law. Lucian Bebchuk pointed out to us in a private communication that "the idea that integrity does not require keeping one's word no matter what relates to Oliver Wendell Holmes' notion that a contract is not a promise to execute it no matter what, but rather to execute it or bear the financial consequences stipulated by the law."

15. See also Simons, 2002, "Behavioral Integrity: The Perceived Alignment between Manager's Words and Deeds as a Research Focus," *Organization Science* 13, no. 1: 18–35.

16. Simons, 1999, "Behavioral Integrity as a Critical Ingredient for Transformational Leadership," *Journal of Organizational Change Management* 12, no. 2: 90 (89–104).

17. Cox, La Caze and Levine, "Integrity," in Edward N. Zalta (ed.), *The Stanford Encyclopedia of Philosophy* (Fall 2005 Edition). Accessed April 9, 2006, http://plato.stanford.edu/archives/fall2005/entries/integrity/

18. For the human animal, the action (or inaction) response to emotion is mediated by interpretation which occurs in language. For an animal without language, the animal's action (or inaction) response to emotion is not mediated by interpretation. (That animal's brain may sort through stored neuronal patterns in "selecting" the particular action or inaction it triggers in reaction to the emotion. An observer might ascribe interpretation to such selecting, but the selecting of the stored neuronal pattern is triggered by the emotion, not by any interpretation.) For an animal without language, there is nothing present like the interpretation experienced by the human animal.

19. My word is constituted not only literally in words, but in the "speaking" of my actions (including facial countenance, body language, and the like), that is, what these actions say to others. To be clear, "my word" includes what my word literally says in words and what my actions say. Therefore, my word includes what I say literally in words and what my actions say. Of course, as is the case with what I say in words, what is said by my actions will often be interpreted by the other. And, therefore who I ultimately am for the other is a product of my word including what is said by my actions, as the other interprets my word. Being aware of this opens up the opportunity to do something to ensure that the other has not misinterpreted my word, including what is said by my actions.

20. Shakespeare, *Hamlet*, Act II. (Italics added for emphasis.)

21. What Chris Argyris defines as "actionable research." See Argyris, 1993, *Knowledge for Action: A Guide to Overcoming Barriers to Organizational Change*, San Francisco, CA: Jossey-Bass.

References

Argyris, C. (1991, May–June). Teaching smart people how to learn. *Harvard Business Review, 69*(3), 99–109.

Argyris, C. (1993). Knowledge for action: A guide to overcoming barriers to organizational change. San Francisco, CA: Jossey-Bass, Inc.

Bitner, M. J., Booms, B. H., & Tetreault, M. S. (1990). The service encounter: Diagnosing favorable and unfavorable incidents. *Journal of Marketing, 54*, 71–84.

Cox, D., La Caze, M., & Levine, M. (2005). Integrity. In E. N. Zalta (Ed.), *The Stanford Encyclopedia of Philosophy* (Fall 2005 ed.). Retrieved from http://plato.stanford.edu/archives/fall2005/entries/integrity/. Accessed on April 9, 2006.

Friedman, M. (1996). The methodology of positive economics. In M. Friedman (Ed.), *Essays in positive economics* (pp. 145–178). Chicago: University of Chicago Press.

Keynes, J. N. (1891). *The scope and method of political economy*. London, UK: Macmillan.

McCabe, D. L., Butterfield, K. D., & Trevino, L. K. (2006). Academic dishonesty in graduate business programs: Prevalence, causes, and proposed action. *The Academy of Management Learning and Education, 5*(3), 294–305.

Monga, M. (2017). 'Doing the right thing' in the banking sector: Integrity from an upper echelons perspective. In M. Orlitzky & M. Monga (Eds.), *Integrity in business and management* (pp. 105–135). New York: Routledge/Taylor & Francis.

Orlitzky, M. (2017). Virtue signaling: Oversocialized "integrity" in a politically correct world. In M. Orlitzky & M. Monga (Eds.), *Integrity in business and management* (pp. 172–187). New York: Routledge/Taylor & Francis.

Orlitzky, M., & Monga, M. (2017). The multiple facets of integrity in business and management. In M. Orlitzky & M. Monga (Eds.), *Integrity in business and management* (pp. 1–10). New York: Routledge/Taylor & Francis.

Oxford American Dictionaries. (2005). *Dictionary and thesaurus* (Version 1.0.1). Cupertino, CA: Apple.

Popper, K. (1959). *The logic of scientific discovery*. New York: Basic Books.

Searle, J. (1969). *Speech acts: An essay in the philosophy of language*. Cambridge, UK: Cambridge University Press.

Simons, T. (1999). Behavioral integrity as a critical ingredient for transformational leadership. *Journal of Organizational Change Management, 12*(2), 89–104.

Simons, T. (2002). Behavioral integrity: The perceived alignment between managers' words and deeds as a research focus. *Organization Science, 13*(1), 18–35.

3   Time Theft[1]

An Integrity-Based Approach to Its Management

Joanna Crossman and Sanjee Perera

Introduction

"Organizations are complex systems" (Lorsch & McTague, 2016, p. 98; Perrow, 1986) that managers at all levels need to negotiate. In this chapter, we suggest that an integrity-based approach can be effective in challenging organizational contexts and illustrate this perspective by taking time theft as an example of a significant and complex organizational issue. We argue that an integrity-based approach captures the complexity of the phenomenon and allows managers to consider the interaction between the employee and the organizational context, necessary to understand and address time theft.

Described as "common" (Henle, Reeve, & Pitts, 2010, p. 53), "omnipresent" (Ketchen, Craighead, & Buckley, 2008, p. 141), and increasing (Henle et al., 2010; Lim, 2002; Snider, 2002), the literature on time theft documents a host of damaging consequences for organizational functioning. These consequences impact both micro and macro levels of organizations in terms of, for example, mission, goals, interests, morale, interpersonal relationships, and productivity (Ketchen et al., 2008, p. 141; Liu & Berry, 2013, p. 77; McKenzie, 2004). Managing time theft involves complex assessments, and navigating an array of perspectives and practices that may confuse rather than assist organizational decision making and, as we later argue, mismanagement may compound the problem. The rise of knowledge work and flexible work practices has also intensified ambiguity about boundaries between personal and work time, further confounding efforts to take an effective and strategic approach to managing the issue.

One rationale for exploring time theft lies in its cost to organizations and ultimately, economies. Unfortunately, assessments of time theft seem to be somewhat subjective and lack hard evidence that can be measured or predicted, especially in knowledge organizations and less structured employment (Brock, Martin, & Buckley, 2013, p. 309). Quantifying the financial impact of time theft is invariably based on calculations around the estimated percentage of the workforce participating in the behavior and how much time is misused. In a self-reporting study of 135 participants, Henle et al. (2010), for example, found that 84% of participants had engaged in time theft during a 2-month period. Atkinson (2006) estimated that time theft equates 5 weeks of lost time per employee each year, inflating the hourly pay rate by 50% to 100%. Jackson (2008) suggested that 25% of the working day is spent in social chatting or surfing the internet alone. At the national and economic level in the United States, estimated costs of time theft rose considerably from about $177 billion during the 1990s (McGee & Fillon, 1995) to $759 billion more recently (Martin, Brock, Buckley, & Ketchen, 2010, p. 26).

Despite estimates of the costs of time theft, the behavior is reportedly virtually ignored in many organizations (Ketchen et al., 2008, p. 143; Kulas, McInerney, Rachel, & Jadwinski., 2007; Liu & Berry, 2013, p. 73; McKenzie, 2004). Nonaction, in the hope that the problem will disappear, however, is not advised (Robinson & O'Leary-Kelly, 1998, p. 670) because even though human resource managers factor in nearly 1 hour a day to compensate for time theft, if left unchecked, the behavior may well intensify and, with it, the negative impact on profits (Brock et al., 2013, p. 310; Martin et al., 2010, p. 27).

This chapter puts forth an integrity-based approach as an effective tool in the management of time theft as a complex and significant organizational issue. Two key rationales for adopting an integrity approach to address time theft are linked to its conceptual flexibility, useful in, first, adopting a holistic approach and, second, its capacity to transcend contextual variations and move beyond the current and somewhat limited "bad apple" and rule-based response to the problem.

Understanding Integrity

Honesty and Integrity

Both honesty and integrity are commonly discussed in the business ethics literature (Audi & Murphy, 2006) and understood in various ways. For example, Crossman and Doshi (2014) have considered honesty in terms of transparency and the courage required to be truthful in acknowledging a lack of knowledge. Xu and Ma (2015) have referred to honesty as truth telling. The concept is also discussed through its antonym and correspondingly, associated with fakery, concealing unethical behavior, using others for gain (Smith, 2006), deceitful behavior, lying (Xu & Ma, 2015), or avoiding full disclosure (Crossman & Doshi, 2014).

From an individual perspective, honesty has been associated with personal character in the literature since ancient Greek times (Crossman & Noma, 2013) and is considered by many business ethicists to be a virtue, both moral and epistemic (Carr, 2014; Crossman & Doshi, 2014; Smith, 2006). When viewed as a moral good, honesty can be understood through the roots of Aristotelian practical wisdom and has been explored, at least in analogous ways, by Socrates and Plato (Carr, 2014).

Curiously, honesty and integrity are often used interchangeably (Audi & Murphy, 2006; Becker, 1998; Gosling & Huang, 2009) even though they are far from being conceptually synonymous. The literature suggests that integrity is a broader concept than honesty in that it is also associated, for example, with conscientiousness and trustworthiness (Becker, 1998; Palanski & Yammarino, 2007). Honesty is closely related to truthfulness, but given that integrity encompasses other constituents, honesty is considered "a necessary but not sufficient condition for integrity" (Becker, 1998, p. 158). In other words, a person of integrity is more than simply honest (Audi & Murphy, 2006).

Conceptualizing Integrity

Increasing interest in integrity has been noted by various authors, but little agreement exists about its meaning in business literature (Audi & Murphy, 2006; Gosling & Huang, 2009; Koehn, 2005; Palanski & Yammarino, 2009), shrouded as it is in ambiguity (Monga, 2016). Rooted in the Latin term, *integer*, meaning to be integral and whole, the concept of integrity is associated with multiple meanings. Interpretations include a commitment to being true to self and a set of principles, consistency in behavior across time and between words and action (Palanski & Yammarino, 2007), although Badaracco and Elllsworth (1991) warn against facile assumptions, asserting "cookie cutter consistency will not do" (Badaracco & Ellsworth, 1991, p. 46). Facile or not, this form of what is known as behavioral integrity is claiming some attention in empirical research studies, given the influence perceptions of word–deed alignment patterns among managers have on employees (Yang, Tsai, & Liao, 2014, p. 154). In addition to meanings associated with wholeness and consistency, it is also generally accepted that high moral standards, good character (Audi & Murphy, 2006), and virtue (Palanski & Yammarino, 2007) are essential aspects of integrity.

Becker's (1998) assertion that integrity involves a commitment to principles gives rise to discussion about whether one could have integrity regardless of, or independent from, the ethical nature of those principles. This kind of discussion basically explores the Objectivist and relativist assumptions that might be brought to understanding integrity, and Becker's (1998, p. 157) argument that "integrity involves acting in accordance not with *any* value system but with a *morally justifiable* one" reveals his own position in that regard.

Many business ethics scholars agree that integrity can be considered a virtue pertaining to character (Audi & Murphy, 2006; Palanski & Yammarino, 2007, 2009), but paradoxically as both a substantive and an adjunctive virtue. The former views integrity as intrinsically morally good, while the latter suggests it not necessarily good or bad (Palanski & Yammarino, 2007). Conceptualizing integrity as having a capacity for "consistency in adversity" (Palanski & Yammarino, 2007, p. 173) tends to suggest that integrity is an adjunctive virtue in that a racist person may thus be perceived as having integrity when he or she consistently demonstrates racism in words and deeds but may not be regarded as morally good.

In the work of Gosling and Huang (2009), Palanski and Yammarino (2007, p. 173), and Verhezen (2008), an underlying sense exists that integrity, as a virtue, is most potent and relevant when considered in challenging or difficult contexts, but being tested is not explicitly argued as a defining prerequisite of the construct. Integrity in contexts of being tested by adversity does, however, have relevance to time theft, for example, when employees feel they are not trusted or have been treated unfairly or when managers face ethical dilemmas in managing time theft as we discuss later in this chapter.

Integrity at the Individual or Organizational Level

Objectivists (e.g., Becker, 1998) tend to focus on integrity as operating at the level of the individual. However, most scholars acknowledge that individuals cannot realistically be separated from their social contexts, given that integrity requires continual and conscious social judgment and is consensually reinforced and validated (Gosling & Huang, 2009; Jacobs, 2004; Palanski & Yammarino, 2007; Verhezen, 2008). A degree of symmetry exists in the treatment of integrity by scholars at both individual and organizational levels. For example, references to consistency in words and action, as a personal aspect of integrity, are mirrored in conceptions of organizational integrity, a phenomenon that, Palanski and Yammarino (2009, p. 417) suggest, rests on the assumption of isomorphism, whereby a higher level construct such as organizational integrity shares the function and structure of individual integrity, as a lower level construct. The notion of organizational integrity assumes that an organization's functions as a whole, as an acting entity, for example, by displaying consistency in words and actions including enacted and stated values, even though organizations cannot speak or act as individuals do (Palanski & Yammarino, 2009).

Other work has explored integrity at the organizational level and the interplay of organizational climate and integrity. Maak (2008) framed corporate integrity as the alignment of seven conditions of commitment to moral principles. These conditions are identified as moral conduct, content, context (i.e., relating to all stakeholders), consistency of words and deeds, coherence between moral principles and moral action, and continuity over time (Maak, 2008). That integrity is considered vital to business ethicists and organizations alike is evidenced, as Gosling and Huang (2009) have observed, by the frequency of its appearance in organizational mission and value statements. How much those mission statements are manifested in or consistent with practices throughout organizations is less clear, but certainly, as Verhezen (2010) suggests, for an attitude of integrity to be effective it will need to be consistently addressed and demonstrated at all levels of the organization.

Previous work on organizational integrity suggests that, by adopting an integrity-based approach, organizations stand to gain more than simply being able to manage time theft more effectively. Organizational integrity has been associated with increased market value, enhanced reputation, investor confidence, (Arjoon, 2006; Koehn, 2005; Verhezen, 2008), and a sustainable competitive advantage (Maak, 2008; Verhezen, 2010). An integrity-based approach also has the potential to lessen the time involved in legal cases, associated with employee misconduct (Verhezen, 2008), and indeed, the same assumption might be made with respect to employer time theft. However, while these benefits of integrity tend to suggest that integrity has a market value, Koehn (2005) calls for a focus on the intrinsic value of integrity as a common good.

Conceptualizing Time Theft in Organizations

As Brock et al. (2013, p. 309) and Henle et al. (2010) have observed, little empirical work on time theft appears to exist in comparison with other forms of organizational theft (e.g., tangible and financial), perhaps because it is perceived as a comparatively minor issue and has a covert element to it, making confident assessments difficult. Deeply embedded in the human psyche and serving to limit or circumscribe experience, the concept of time has preoccupied humans since early Greek and Roman times (Lombardi, 2013, p. 691). Employers have always been mindful of the relationship between remuneration and the quality and quantity of labor (Snider, 2001, 2002). Time, as a measurable commodity governing organizational functioning, can be traced to the introduction of clocks during the Industrial Revolution in the 18th century and is the historical point, according to Marx, when the capitalist assumed the role of buyer, the laborer the seller, and working time became the same thing as production time (Marx, 1893/1971). This relationship forms the basis of how time theft has been conceptualized in the literature over time.

Early in the 20th century, Taylorist theories of productivity also influenced how time theft was viewed (Snider, 2001, 2002; Stevens & Lavin, 2007, p. 43). In his text *The Principles of Scientific Management*, Taylor referred to the practice of "soldiering" (laziness or shirking) as an evil causing universal suffering to employers (Taylor, 1911/2005). In so doing, he emphasized the moral element in time theft. Although considerable research on tardiness and absenteeism was undertaken prior to the 1980s (Gruys & Sackett, 2003, p. 30), the term *time theft* was arguably only adopted for the first time in Hollinger and Clarke's (1983) *Theft by Employees*, but *time banditry* tends to be used synonymously (see Martin et al., 2010, p. 31) in the literature.

Definitions and Behaviors

Definitions of time theft tend to focus on the practice of receiving compensation for work that has deliberately not been undertaken, the violation of organizational norms, and the damage the behavior does to the well-being of its members (Gruys & Sackett, 2003, p. 30; Liu & Berry, 2013, p. 77; Robinson & Bennett, 1995, p. 556). Other sources specifically refer to time theft as an abuse of expectations about how time or other resources are used (see Ketchen et al., 2008, p. 141; Martin et al., 2010). Few definitions encompass the perspective of an employee who is not appropriately compensated for work undertaken beyond negotiated hours or agreed outcomes, in other words, employer-initiated time theft. For example, Brock et al. (2013, p. 309), in defining *time banditry*, refer to the engagement of "an employee" in unsanctioned or unethical personal activities during work time but neglect to acknowledge that some organizations engage in time theft by encroaching on the unpaid, personal time of employees. This is an ethical point we will return to at a later stage in this chapter.

Time theft is addressed in literature concerned with employee theft, workplace deviance, and counterproductive workplace behavior (see Ketchen et al., 2008, p. 141; Ünal, 2013; Weatherbee, 2010) but is distinguished from other forms of counterproductive work behavior (Brock et al., 2013, p. 309). Within the context of workplace deviancy, time theft focuses on behavior that violates organizational norms whereas from a business ethics perspective, the behavior tends to be considered as the social construction of right or wrong moral behavior (Robinson & Bennett, 1995, p. 155).

Hollinger and Clark's (1982) seminal work distinguished between *property deviance* involving the theft of tangibles or embezzlement and *production deviance*, relevant to time theft in that it encompasses breaches of expectations about how work is accomplished qualitatively and quantitatively and relates to, for example, attendance, absence, tardiness, and long breaks (Gruys & Sackett, 2003, p. 31). In Robinson and Bennett's (1995) typology, the authors retained the term *production deviance* pertaining to minor misdemeanors concerned with the use of company time but curiously identified lying about hours worked (arguably a time-theft issue) as a form of property deviance. Concurring that time theft is a form of production deviance, Brock et al. (2013, p. 310) nevertheless suggest that time theft does not always involve a conscious intent to do malicious harm, unlike other forms of deviancy. We expand on this later in the chapter under relevant theoretical perspectives of time theft.

A variety of time theft behaviors has been documented in scholarly work. They include arriving late, leaving early, or deliberately working at a slower pace (Bowling, Burns, & Beehr, 2010; Brock et al., 2013, p. 310; Gruys & Sackett, 2003; Henle et al., 2010, p. 53; Liu & Berry, 2013; Robinson & Bennett, 1995). Many authors refer to the taking of longer or additional breaks for cigarette smoking perhaps or simply loitering to avoid returning to work

(Atkinson, 2006; Gruys & Sackett, 2003; Henle et al., 2010, p. 53; Jackson, 2008; Kulas et al., 2007; Martin et al., 2010, p. 27; McKenzie, 2004; Robinson & Bennett, 1995; Snider, 2001; Weatherbee, 2010). References to the pursuit of personal hobbies, entertainment, or communication, such as making phone calls and writing letters, are also noted (Atkinson, 2006; Ketchen et al., 2008, p. 141 Snider, 2001). Time theft is also associated with absenteeism by taking unwarranted sick leave or poor attendance generally (Atkinson, 2006; Gruys & Sackett, 2003). Finally, the falsification of records such as time sheets or "clocking in" for coworkers before they actually arrive at work are also cited as examples of time theft behavior (Martin et al., 2010, p. 27). This latter practice is now largely an anachronism, however, given new technologies, such as the introduction of biometric time attendance systems that recognize fingerprints or eye retinas or that scan bar codes (Atkinson, 2006). These behaviors suggest some intentionality on the part of the employee.

Technological advancement has generated interest in rather different forms of time theft behavior (Snider, 2001, p. 105), where employee intentionality is ambiguous. These behaviors are beginning to be specifically addressed through studies in cyber-deviancy despite some concerns about terminological inconsistencies and poor theoretical development (Brock et al., 2013, p. 310; Weatherbee, 2010). Assessments of online time-theft behaviors suggest that about an hour of the working day is spent on activities surfing the Internet, writing personal e-mails, instant messaging, and engaging with social media, such as Facebook, online shopping, or visiting pornographic websites (Atkinson, 2006; Brock et al., 2013, p. 310; Jackson, 2008; Kulas et al., 2007; Lim, 2002; Martin et al., 2010, p. 27; McKenzie, 2004; Snider, 2001, p. 112; Weatherbee, 2010).

Greater workplace flexibility, largely enabled by technology, has, in turn, served to deepen the theoretical and conceptual complexity of time theft behaviors. As Henle et al. (2010, p. 53) observed, some references to time theft behaviors during work hours may be less relevant in flexible workplaces. Whether flexible workplaces such as academia are hotbeds of time theft (see Ketchen et al., 2008, p. 142) or a means to meet expected outcomes by working evenings and weekends more traditionally reserved for relaxation is a matter for debate. These discussions are particularly challenging in that employers appear to have quite different perspectives on what constitutes productive or counterproductive workplace behavior. To illustrate, a social event with colleagues may be regarded as team building, morale raising, and enhancing working relationships by one individual and yet be viewed as time theft by another (Brock et al., 2013, p. 310; McKenzie, 2004).

The Antecedents of Time Theft

Understanding the antecedents of time theft is important for managers, given its impact on organizational functioning (Robinson, Wang, & Kiewitz,

2014, p. 124) and its relevance to determining its management. With some caution, work on the antecedents of employee theft more generally may be relevant, despite the fact that not all employee theft or indeed counterproductive work behaviors pertain to time theft (Brock et al., 2013, p. 310). Because Gruys and Sackett (2003) conclude that counterproductive work behaviors such as forms of employee theft and time theft are positively related to one another and that typologies have tended to view time theft as a form of employee theft (see Hollinger & Clark, 1982; Robinson & Bennett, 1995), some synergies in antecedents might be assumed.

Although researchers draw distinctions between individual, social, organizational, or environmental antecedents, doing so is a somewhat artificial practice given the dynamic relationship between these factors. To illustrate, an employee's propensity to peer pressure (individual factor) and his or her response to any social norms encouraging theft (organizational factor) will simultaneously play a part in influencing theft behavior (Greenberg, 2010; Lipman & McGraw, 1988). Similarly, associations between boredom and time theft (Brock et al., 2013, p. 310) may relate to poor management at the organizational level or an individual's inability to be proactive.

With respect to social and organizational conditions, it is widely argued that time theft flourishes where counterproductive behavior stands uncorrected, in ambiguous or lax environments lacking direction, rules, and policies (Arel, Besudoin, & Cianci, 2012, p. 353; Atkinson, 2006; Greenberg, 2010; Ketchen et al., 2008; Martin et al., 2010; Murphy, 1993; Weber, Kurke, & Pentico, 2003). Organizational norms influence employees and, in turn, any positive or negative peer group pressure concerned with time theft behavior. Robinson and O'Leary-Kelly's seminal paper "Monkey See, Monkey Do," published in the *Academy of Management Journal* in 1998, illustrated how social context and peer pressure play a part in antisocial worker behaviors including time theft.

A host of individual factors have also been linked to time theft and other counterproductive workplace behaviors. For example, how conscientious someone is, their job attitudes (Bowling et al., 2010; Brock et al., 2013, p. 318), personal commitment (Bailey, 2006), and membership in a certain generational cohort (Atkinson, 2006, p. 52; Henle et al., 2010; Snider, 2002), as well as personality differences such as being closed-minded and neurotic, although there appears to be no significant relationship between extraversion and time theft behavior (Brock et al., 2013; Kidder, 2005). Some literature also suggests that, by employees' own accounts and coworker accounts, when individuals are of low moral character they are more likely to engage in harmful, unethical, counterproductive, and delinquent behavior, compared to those with high moral character Cohen, Panter, Turan, Morse, & Kim, 2014, p. 1; Greenberg, 2010), and these conclusions are of relevance to time theft.

Some Theoretical Perspectives

Several theories are relevant to understanding the contribution that individual and organizational factors play in time theft behavior and how it can be managed, including reasoned behavior, planned behavior, and agency theory. The theory of reasoned behavior (TRB; Ajzen & Fishbein, 1980; Fishbein & Ajzen, 1975) and the theory of planned behavior (TPB; Ajzen, 1991), which extended TRB, have been used to understand and predict intentions and undesirable behavior in organizations, especially when perceived moral obligations are taken into account (Bailey, 2006, p. 803; Beck & Ajzen, 1991; Sparks & Shepard, 2002).

Both of these theories suggest that intention is an important determinant of behavior (Ajzen, 2011) and influenced by a number of factors. Attitudes (Fishbein & Ajzen, 1975; Henle et al., 2010, p. 55), self-efficacy (Fishbein, Hennessy, Yzer, & Douglas, 2003), and subjective norms, such as social pressures to behave in certain ways and perceptions of controls, all play a part, so where individual attitudes and subjective norms are positive, the greater the intention to behave in positive ways (Beck & Ajzen, 1991). However, it is important to remember that individuals do not always act on their intentions (Fishbein et al., 2003, p. 3). Also, those scholars that investigated intentionality in the context of counterproductive theft behaviors need to be distinguished from authors who refer to intentionality in the sense of willfulness, as an intensifying moral marker in their discourse. See, for example, the way in which Henle et al. (2010, p. 53) suggest that time theft is unethical because employees are compensated despite "intentionally" stealing time and is a reference to willfulness in the context of counterproductive behavior in the work of Kelloway, Francis, Prosser, and Cameron (2010, p. 18). Thus, the uncontested assumption that intention plays a defining role in making evaluations about time theft in all cases is misleading.

Agency theory incorporated an acknowledgment of social and situational influences in predicting counterproductive workplace behaviors, where the term *agent* refers to an individual who will always act opportunistically, thereby exhibiting self-interested behavior, arguably wishing to do the least work possible, and the *principal* as the employer, who wishes to extract maximum performance from the agent (Kidder, 2005, p. 391). However, although opportunity is logically a prerequisite of theft, agency theory is not so much concerned with whether someone has the opportunity to commit theft but whether he or she is inclined to take advantage of those circumstances (Greenberg & Barling, 1996). Assuming that individuals will instinctively serve their own interests when tempted, especially in anonymous contexts, tends to suggest that refraining from dishonest behavior will involve some self-control (Shalvi, Eldar, & Bereby-Meyer, 2012). Understanding the distinctions between a "will" hypothesis that assumes honesty requires resistance in the face of temptation and the "grace" hypothesis that honesty depends upon removing temptation altogether (Xu & Ma, 2015) helps to frame some of these ideas. Essentially, the work inspired by agency theory is based on the perspective that monitoring and control of employees are essential to limiting employee abuse of organizational resources, including time, and aim to ensure compliance with organizational policies and procedures by instilling fear of punishment among employees (Verhezen, 2010). This can be problematic.

We contend that planned/reasoned behavior theory is limited in its usefulness because with respect to intentionality, time theft may not always be intentional. As outlined previously, as a form of production deviance, Brock et al. (2013, p. 310) time theft does not necessarily involve a conscious intent to do malicious harm and as such is distinct from other forms of workplace deviance. Also, agency theory can be problematic in that, first, monitoring can backfire and, second, knowledge work and flexible work arrangements mediated by technology are difficult to track and complex to assess using these strategies and finally there is no evidence to suggest that opportunity to commit time theft necessarily leads to time theft. Both these theories emphasize time theft as deviance, but they do not allow us to examine employer time theft.

Problematic Issues Associated with Strategies for Managing Time Theft

Managing time theft can be a complex process, perhaps because it seems less visible and harder to control than, for example, the theft of tangible goods (Liu & Berry, 2013; McKenzie, 2004) and does not always include an intention to "steal" what is considered employer's property. Organizations have a number of strategies at their disposal to address employee time theft. According to Gross-Schaefer, Trigilio, Negus, and Ro (2000), organizations commonly adopt three broad and somewhat reactive strategies: (a) keeping potential miscreants out of the organizations, (b) preventing unwanted behaviors among existing staff, and (c) dealing with those who thieve. In this section, we also discuss strategies for managing time theft in a similar chronological manner, that is, first, by referring to strategies that filter out those who may present a risk during the recruitment process, for example, by implementing honesty tests; second, by exploring how time theft is sometimes managed by monitoring existing staff; and, third, by discussing strategies for responding to instances of time theft when discovered. We conclude the section by suggesting that none of these strategies is likely to be entirely effective, especially when flexible work is involved in the context of knowledge work. One main reason for the conclusion rests on the argument that the strategies of honesty tests, using peers, surveillance, rules, policies, and dismissal, for example, can themselves prove unethical, thus compounding, rather than resolving, a perceived time-theft problem.

Honesty tests, as a form of prescreening, have been implemented as a practice to predict counterproductive behaviors, such as theft and time theft

(Fine, 2013; Gruys & Sackett, 2003, p. 31). These tests are sometimes also referred to as integrity tests, a term criticized by Gosling and Huang (2009) because it is a popularized and imprecise descriptor of integrity. Additionally, individual traits, identified in prescreening, are only general guides, as behavior is also influenced by situational factors in the work context (Arjoon, 2006). Even where an individual scores highly on an honesty test, he or she would not necessarily be immune to a culture of mistrust and the abuse of organizational resources where the pressures to "fit in" with other colleagues may be compelling and give rise to time theft as a learned response (Bandura, Barbaranelli, Caprara, & Pastorelli, 1996; Dineen, Tomlinson, & Lewicki, 2006; Robinson & O'Leary-Kelly, 1998). Also, prescreening strategies do not appear to be very effective in dealing with employee theft in general (Gross-Schaefer et al., 2000), and it would seem unlikely that the complex context of time theft would reap a more promising outcome. Finally, prescreening in the form of honesty tests are problematic because they can be perceived as an intrusive form of monitoring that betrays trust relationships and may encourage self-interested and harmful behavior (Kidder, 2005, p. 392). For these reasons, it may be preferable to rely on other strategies, such as probing ethical values through background checks (Fenn, 1995) and during interviews (Niehoff & Paul, 2000).

Once employed, the influence of peers may operate negatively on employees, perhaps through legitimizing unethical behavior (McClurg & Butler, 2006; Poulston, 2008, p. 56). Correspondingly, peer influence may be harnessed as a force for managing time theft and other counterproductive behaviors through peer reporting systems (Curphy, Gibson, Macomber, Calhoun, & Wilbanks, 1998), which serve to convey the message that ethical responsibility is not simply a management issue. At the same time, peer reporting may be viewed as a "dark" measure, sanctioning "snitch lines" and "spies" who report on colleagues (Snider, 2001, p. 114).

Despite Robinson and Bennett's (1995, p. 155) insistence that the management of workplace deviance is not concerned with ethics or morality, Jones' (1991) work on moral intensity is revealing when considering the influence of social and contextual factors. These include, the magnitude of consequences, social consensus concerned with how much agreement exists over the extent to which an act is ethical or moral, probability of effect, temporal immediacy, concentration of effect, and, finally, social, cultural or physical proximity in that people tend to be more concerned about those who are closer to them (Jones, 1991; Leitsch, 2004). Consistent in some ways with this work of Jones (1991) on moral intensity, Curphy et al. (1998, p. 37) found that the intention to report on peers involves weighing up contextual information such as emotional closeness (referred to as *proximity* in Jones's 1991 work), the perceived severity of the offence and the presence of others as witnesses to unethical behavior—which presumably would enable Jones's (1991) *social consensus*, as an element in assessing moral intensity, to come into play.

The assumption that time theft springs, at least in part, from a lack of information (Snider, 2001, p. 111) or ignorance tends to suggest certain management responses. Addressing ignorance, as Socrates would have us believe, is one way to circumvent vice (Carr, 2014, p. 5). Professional development would seem to be a less intimidating strategy than honesty tests and peer reporting from the perspective of an employee and more appropriate, when the behavior appears to spring from a lack of information or ignorance (Snider, 2001, p. 111). Ongoing or orientation programs may focus on relevant policies and ethical training (Applebaum, Cottin, & Molson, 2006; Lipman & McGraw, 1988; Niehoff & Paul, 2000). Professional development also has a role in communicating how time theft harms organizations and the people in them, financially, psychologically, and physically (Henle et al., 2010; Promislo & Giacalone, 2013). Communicating information about ethical expectations may also occur at the individual level in meetings (Atkinson, 2006) where complex and ethical perspectives can be probed more deeply and with sensitivity.

Surveillance is used as a means of monitoring, controlling, and managing time theft (Moore, 2000, p. 705; Stevens & Lavin, 2007, p. 42). It may involve the installation of cameras in the workplace, using global positioning systems so movements out of the company location can be monitored, or filtering software that restricts Internet activity to non-work-related business websites (Moore, 2000; Stevens & Lavin, 2007). These forms of surveillance, however, can be perceived as a form of punishment (Stevens & Lavin, 2007, p. 42) and, as a result, may prove as much a part of the problem as a cure. The reason for this lies in studies associating surveillance with mental breakdowns, stress, depression, anxiety, experiencing lack of autonomy or empowerment, demotivation, resentment, and a deterioration of relationships owing to raised levels of competition, as well as physical symptoms, fear of taking bathroom breaks or being fired, absenteeism, and sleep disturbances (Moore, 2000; Snider, 2001; Stevens & Lavin, 2007, p. 48). Moore (2000) has also argued that encroaching on employee privacy and a lack of transparency when using surveillance systems present serious implications for ethical practice in organizations.

Implementing monitoring and punishment strategies also tends to involve instilling a fear of repercussions among employees that can lead to the issue going underground, thereby creating a culture of silence that has been identified in employee theft (Verhezen, 2010). Another risk is that monitoring strategies will motivate some employees to follow the rules, but others may respond by wanting to "beat the system" (Verhezen, 2008). On the other hand, a lack of monitoring or taking no disciplinary action and allowing for "acceptable" levels of employee theft (Gross-Schaefer et al., 2000) may also contribute to a culture where time theft is deemed acceptable and can be implicitly interpreted as sanctioned. Thus, the effectiveness of policies and procedures is limited at either end of the spectrum of strategies because both harsh rules and a complete lack of monitoring can equally lead to employee abuse of organizational resources (Dineen et al., 2006).

Other examples suggest that management responses to time theft can lead to unintended and undesirable consequences. For example, flexible working arrangements may be implemented to improve employee productivity, motivation, and job satisfaction (Baltes, Briggs, Huff, Wright, & Neuman, 1999) and to respond to time theft, resulting from work–life conflict (see Henle et al., 2010; Langner, 2010; Siegel, Post, Brockner, Fishman, & Garden, 2005; Snider, 2002). However, workplace flexibility has also been associated with higher levels of withdrawal, time theft, and other counterproductive behavior (see Baltes et al. 1999; Casper, Weltman, & Kwesiga, 2007; Ketchen et al., 2008, p. 142; Swanberg, Pitt-Catsouphes, & Drescher-Burke, 2005), especially where employees perceive that flexible arrangements are afforded to staff members inconsistently or unfairly (Casper et al., 2007).

If professional development and rewarding honesty (Murphy, 1993) are identified at one end of the spectrum, as positive approaches to time theft, then punitive measures lie at the other. Scholars who adopt a discourse characterized by references to fraud or dishonesty tend to recommend technical or legal solutions (Snider, 2001, p. 111) and punishments (Applebaum et al., 2006) in the form of pay reductions (Ketchen et al., 2008, p. 147) or even dismissal, but these responses may create feelings of job insecurity and misguidedly exacerbate time theft (Snider, 2001, p. 112) rather than manage it.

Time theft, at least in part, appears to stem from the underlying problem of a lack of trust between employers and employees. As Arjoon (2006) argues, monitoring and punishment, as advocated by agency theory, do not convey or build trust. Feelings of being disenfranchised are also associated with employee theft (Dineen et al., 2006) and possibly time theft, suggesting that poor trust in relationships between management and employees on some level has the potential to compound time theft.

The prevailing organizational response to time theft is to perceive the issue as one that concerns a "few bad apples" (reasoned behavior) or lax rules (agency theory; Arjoon, 2006). Strategies tethered to these theoretical assumptions, however, are flawed for a number of reasons, not least because they rest on the belief that time theft is always an intentional behavior. Research on employee theft, particularly petty theft and time theft, indicates that most employees do not realize that they are doing anything wrong or understand the impact their behavior has on the organizations (Dineen et al., 2006). While acknowledging a response to time theft based on *ignorantia juris non excusat* (ignorance of the law is no excuse; see Imbrisevic, 2010), indiscriminately treating employees engaging in time theft as thieves in the workplace context has its own complications, especially when communication around the issue of time on task is ambiguous. The complexity and variance of contextual factors would also suggest that time theft cannot be regulated effectively by one tool or a rule-based approach as a single strategy that may indeed also lead managers to become complacent, assuming that the rules will address any potential abuses (Arjoon, 2006). This calls for a holistic approach to the issue.

Time Theft From a Business Ethics and Values Perspective

Like Cohen et al. (2014, p. 2), we consider the terms *ethical* and *moral* roughly to be synonyms in this chapter, acknowledging that these concepts are challenging to define in distinctive ways. If one term is used rather than another, the rationale is to remain consistent with the work of an author under discussion, or in contexts where some value judgment is emphasized, the term *moral* is adopted in preference to *ethical*.

Deciding whether some employees are more moral or ethical than others and, thereby, less likely to engage in time theft is a difficult question to address because even when an individual is morally aware or has been trained in moral judgment, these factors alone do not necessarily lead to moral action since social and organizational influences also play a part (Baker, 2014, p. 571). Moral and ethical standards of behavior are influenced by perceptions of prevailing norms, opinions, and expectations around what is deemed legitimate in the workplace as a social context, based on observing the consequences of past actions and coworker behavior (Bandura et al., 1996, p. 364; Robinson & O'Leary-Kelly, 1998; Salancik & Pfeffer, 1978).

One study on moral differentiation (O'Fallon & Butterfield, 2011) has explored the situational and individual factors at play that affect whether an individual will be influenced by coworker unethical behavior. While affirming the principle of *monkey see, monkey do* referred to earlier in this chapter, O'Fallon and Butterfield (2011) believe it to have been overemphasized in the business ethics literature and conclude that a strong moral identity, low need for affiliation, and extraversion weaken the relationship between an individual and coworkers' unethical behavior. Other work suggests that a strong moral identity tends to inhibit dishonesty, whereas low moral identity requires greater willpower and is less likely to result in the resistance of dishonest behavior (Xu & Ma, 2015). Moral disengagement has also been associated with environments infused with counterproductive work behavior (Robinson et al., 2014, p. 134), but where a strong organizational identification exists, some evidence suggests that an employee may be less likely to become morally disengaged or to engage in unethical behaviors like time theft (see Liu & Berry, 2013, p. 77).

Various theories inform how time-theft behaviors can be explored from moral and ethical perspectives. The work of Bandura et al. (1996), for example, is useful in understanding how individuals who engage in unethical behavior may feel less culpable, less subject to self-censure, and less confident about the rightness of their actions. Because individuals need to feel affirmed either personally or socially, they will seek to justify dishonest behaviors (Shalvi et al., 2012, p. 1265). This process of moral justification is made possible through cognitive reconstrual that involves the displacement of personal responsibility for unethical behavior by comparing it with actions perceived as more reprehensible so that personal counterproductive behavior appears less blameworthy (Bandura et al., 1996, p. 365). A similar strategy can be adopted to achieve an opposite effect. That is, time theft can be compared to certain dysfunctional behaviors in order to intensify discourse arguing that it is a serious breach of ethical values in organizations. An example of this can be found in Atkinson's (2006, p. 49) work, where he compares time theft to the arguably morally less ambiguous theft of money from cash boxes or registers.

Another study in behavioral ethics and moral psychology has identified how two concepts, *moral consistency* and *moral compensation*, both affect moral behavior for different reasons (Joosten, van Dijke, Van Hiel, & Cremer, 2014, p. 71). Moral consistency research suggests that a salient self-concept as a moral person promotes moral behavior enabling productive reputation building and maintenance, yet at the same time, moral compensation suggests that a salient self-concept as an immoral person may also promote moral behavior because moral compensation may give rise to reactive, "damage control" responses in social situations (Joosten et al., 2014, p. 71). To illustrate, the moral compensator will be more likely to work overtime if he or she has been engaging in time-wasting behavior earlier in the day (Joosten et al., 2014, p. 72). Also, those who believe themselves to be moral may feel they can lay claim to a surplus of morality, allowing them to feel licensed to engage in less moral behavior without damaging their self-concept or self-presentation as a moral employee (Joosten et al., 2014, p. 72; Merritt, Effron, & Monin, 2010; Monin & Miller, 2001).

Thus, whether an employee perceives a particular act of time theft to be ethical and whether he or she engages in this behavior are dependent on an assessment of contextual conditions at the time (Marshall & Dewe, 1997). Like the concept of employee theft, moral intensity has been considered from the perspective of individual factors, such as level of education, gender, age, and personality, as well as any prevailing organizational ethical codes and climates that influence peer groups (Frey, 2000; Jones, 1991; McClurg & Butler, 2006; Poulston, 2008, p. 56).

Moral Discourse and Criminality in Time Theft

Ironically, if it is unusual for the topic of time theft to be explored through the lens of moral and business ethics literature (Henle et al., 2010; Liu & Berry, 2013), taking the moral high ground in discourse about time theft is not, especially in developing arguments that time theft constitutes criminal behavior. Indeed, Stevens and Lavin (2007) compared the moral discourse of contemporary scholars on time theft to that of Taylor (1911/2005) a century ago.

Economic evidence is brought to bear in developing arguments about the immorality of time theft and its seriousness. As Gössling (2003, p. 121) has observed, however, while it is not uncommon in the context of business ethics for morality to be associated with economic rationality, attaching a market price to moral behavior or being moral (and, by extension, perspectives on the immoral and the criminal) is misplaced. Businesses have always closely monitored productivity as a determinant of profit, but scholarly discourse associating poor productivity with criminality, normally reserved for acts injurious to citizens is a relatively recent and neoliberal call for new laws and a matter of concern among some scholars, conscious that so far, time theft is not deemed criminal in industrialized nations (see Snider, 2001, p. 108; Stevens & Lavin, 2007). The underlying assumption is that time theft constitutes criminal behavior because it limits profit making and violates propriety relations—a perspective succored by prevailing economic and political forces (Stevens & Lavin, 2007, p. 40).

On an individual basis and in similar ways to petty theft in the workplace, time theft may well be viewed in legal terms as *de minimis non curat praetor* (the law does not concern itself with trivial matters). Also, it is possible that time theft as a construct is too poorly developed to be criminalized. As Snider (2001, p. 109) concluded, for time-theft behavior to become criminalized, it will need to be isolated, identified, and distinguished from other behaviors. The public will need to be clear about why the activity is unacceptable, harmful, and widespread. Snider (2001) also maintained that communities would need to know much more about the psychological and demographic profiles of both organizations as the victims and as perpetrators. The literature suggests we are not there yet.

Another difficulty in criminalizing time theft is that "blameworthiness is to a significant degree in the eye of the beholder" (Bowers, 2010, p. 1669) or, in other words, socially and personally constructed and, inherently, morally relativist. If, from an ethical perspective, time theft is constructed in different ways from organization to organization, context to context, then laws that apply to the general population would be hard to implement because no consensus is achievable. As Arel et al. (2012) remarked, what is viewed as trifling in one context may not be elsewhere.

Employer Time Theft

Time theft is not limited to employees; it also extends to organizations. Working overtime without being paid is common and may particularly affect women and professionals in organizations where little flexibility exists (Conway & Sturges, 2014). Most of the literature cited in this chapter assumes that time theft is an unethical behavior in which individuals engage, but very little attention is given to unethical organizations that steal time from employees. According to Snider (2002), employers regularly engage in time theft by not remunerating employees for time worked over normal working hours. Faraz, Shamsi, and Bashir (2014, pp. 396–397) refer to unremunerated "off-the-clock work" taking place outside of scheduled hours and the practice of employers exacting retribution where employees speak out against such practices.

It is not unusual for employees to be provided with mobile phones and laptops and possible that doing so has created an expectation of 24/7 availability that intensifies the vulnerability of employees to become the victims of time theft by organizations, which rarely question the supremacy of productivity and the authority of business as a mantra (Atkinson, 2006; Snider, 2001). Constructing time theft from the perspective of both an employee and an organization can become difficult. As Snider (2001, p. 118) suggests, differentiating the exploited from the exploiter is challenging because when workers appropriate time, it is considered a criminal offense against capital, but when management steals the time of employees by expecting them to do extra work for no pay, the discourse around productivity and efficiency is sustained (Stevens & Lavin, 2007, p. 53).

So, while the corporate community expresses indignation at the damaging effects of time theft, they may well be simultaneously extracting more time to be spent on work tasks by fewer staff who have less and less job security (Stevens & Lavin, 2007, p. 44). Where double standards seem entrenched in organizations, a moral hypocrisy flourishes. No amount of spurious reporting of the financial consequences of employee time theft or suggestions that hundreds of billions of dollars are lost because of long lunches (Stevens & Lavin, 2007, p. 46) can quite obscure the possibility that organizational moral hypocrisy does also exist and may be directly related to employee time theft, driven by rationales of injustice, micromanagement, and entitlement in cases of poor conditions, as discussed earlier in this chapter.

Organizations as time-theft perpetrators at the extreme end of the spectrum raises questions about the human rights of employees. Stevens and Lavin (2007) illustrate this well in their study in the context of call centers, where the monitoring, documentation, and generation of exhaustive statistical information constitutes dehumanizing processes that shame and belittle workers. Thus, if organizations that create understaffed and pressured conditions give rise to employees feeling entitled to take additional breaks, for example (Atkinson, 2006), where does the moral responsibility ultimately lie? Stevens and Lavin (2007, p. 46), recast deviance and counterproductive work behaviors as the noble resistance of employees in the face of disempowerment and the erosion of their hard-won social justices, but employee and organizational time theft are probably dynamic and interrelated behaviors suggesting shared responsibility for addressing time theft and associated issues relevant to the behavior.

An Integrity-Based Approach to Managing Time Theft

Kant argued that moral laws are universal and therefore, arguably, no justification exists for dishonesty (Quinn, Reed, Browne, & Wesley, 1997, p. 1420), perhaps with the exception of life-threatening situations (Woiceshyn, 2008, p. 123). These assumptions, when applied to time theft, would explain a zero tolerance for the behavior without consideration of mitigating environmental or social factors. By comparison, moral relativism rejects the notion of absolute, moral principles and embraces subjectivity influenced by individual factors or cultural norms (Becker, 1998). These perspectives could provide a useful lens to evaluate time theft and its management more holistically at the organizational level.

Employee misconduct, like time theft, has been referred to as a form of dishonesty (Kidder, 2005, p. 389) that has the capability to damage social cohesion (Carr, 2014; Shalvi et al., 2012, p. 1269). One reason for this may be that dishonesty damages trust (Carr, 2014), but as we have argued earlier in the chapter, when trust is damaged, dishonesty may also follow, so the relationship between distrust and dishonesty is cyclical and relevant to the relationship between employee and employer in time theft contexts.

Hypocrisy, a concept referred to earlier in this chapter, in relation to unethical organizational practice, pertains to insincerity and falseness as a form of dishonesty (Quinn et al., 1997, p. 1419) and resonates with a lack of integrity, where integrity is interpreted as consistency between actions and words (Crossman & Doshi, 2014). When organizational codes of conduct in the matter of time theft become one way, focusing on employee time theft exclusively and ignoring employer time theft, the result is an organization that simply pays lip service to those codes, reducing them to "hypothetical window dressing" (Quinn et al., 1997, p. 1419). Thus, the virtue of honesty is breached, and its antithesis, hypocrisy, can lead to a kind of myopia, where time theft within the organizations as a whole entity, is likely to be addressed only in a limited way.

Arjoon (2006) and Verhezen (2008, 2010), focusing on an integrity-based approach, suggest the need to move beyond strict compliance with policies and procedures in time theft management. The implementation of rules and penalties for intentional breaches reflects an organizational strategy to combat dishonesty by enforcing honest behavior through compliance. While focusing on honesty may be appropriate in some contexts, a paradigm of integrity is likely to have a wider impact and prove more effective. As Verhezen (2008, p. 142) observed, "compliance with laws and regulations can never do what integrity can do" because integrity-based strategies enable the empowerment of individual employees, whereas the literature suggests that monitoring employee behavior to achieve compliance may only motivate employees to follow the letter of the law, at best. An integrity-based approach creates an organizational culture where the potential for both the letter and the spirit of the law to be addressed (Verhezen, 2008, p. 137).

Some evidence suggests that groups (arguably organizations) tend to be more strategic and less honest when economic benefits are clearly at stake (Cohen, Gunia, Kim-Jun, & Murnighan, 2009). When either individuals or organizations entertain time theft, they are essentially faced with a dilemma. Within business contexts, that dilemma is one where honesty may need to be reconciled with security (Quinn et al., 1997, p. 1422). In other words, the individual or the management of an organization may believe that behaving honestly is not entirely consistent, respectively, with maintaining well-being or profit levels, for example. In many respects, this perspective focuses on individual needs and concerns or organization's needs and concerns rather than taking a holistic approach that incorporates the needs and concerns of all stakeholders.

Given the complex nature of time in today's work environments, it is not possible to develop policies and procedures that take into consideration all possible contextual variations. However, an integrity-based approach founded on principles, rather than rules, allows for guidelines that can apply to varied organizational contexts and employee circumstances (Arjoon, 2006). An integrity-based approach would not necessarily obviate the need for policies and procedures, as one strategy, to combat time theft, but it does have the potential to be far more effective and flexible in addressing a complex issue. Thus, an integrity-based approach transcends mere compliance, creating organizations where genuine dialogues and deeper understandings about ethical issues (Verhezen, 2010), like time theft, can occur. An integrity approach, when championed and demonstrated by organizational leaders, according to Palanski and Yammarino (2007, 2009), has the capacity to influence followers and engender a culture of trust that as we have argued, is pertinent in time theft contexts.

An integrity-based approach throughout an organization implicitly encourages the organization as a whole, to review its own actions in terms of what time and tasks it demands of its employees and any evidence of exploitative practices creating an imbalance in the time/effort and rewards equation. Such an appraisal is essential given that these kinds of imbalances can intensify employee time theft (Koehn, 2005). Thus, an integrity-based approach will address the neglected issue of employer time theft in practice and hopefully generate greater attention in empirical research and other scholarly works.

An honesty approach, of itself, in the form of implementing rules and regulations, is unlikely to prove a panacea. One reason for this is that avoiding dishonesty and negative consequences by complying with rules does not mean an individual is more moral, honest, or virtuous (Carr, 2014, p. 11; Gössling, 2003, p. 122; Koehn, 2005, p. 126). Under these circumstances, an employee may be functionally honest (e.g., accurately record the time in office)—and perhaps this is the extent of some managers' or organization's interest in the matter—but it would not automatically follow that an employee would be honest in all other contexts, perhaps where no rules or controls have been developed (e.g., recording time taken when visiting remote sites of the organization). If one accepts that all humans are at some point or another faced with dilemmas in situations where honesty and self-interest appear to be at odds, focusing on the "bad apple" who engages in dishonest and unethical behavior may be less effective than attending to those factors that sway otherwise "good apples" (Xu & Ma, 2015). An integrity-based approach enables this shift in focus. It extends beyond single instances (Gosling & Huang, 2009) as an honesty-based approach cannot and does this by adopting a more holistic assessment of time theft behaviors and their sustainable management.

An integrity-based approach requires deep and genuine engagement at all organizational levels both in planning and in implementation. It is likely to be facilitated in a variety of ways that operate collectively and in an integrated manner. Some of the strategies, discussed in this chapter include questions that probe ethical issues during an interview and professional development.

One challenge in the process of implementing an integrity-based approach may prove to be the "ambiguity" or "vagueness" that surrounds integrity as a concept (Audi & Murphy, 2006, p. 11) that makes it difficult for individuals to envision its operationalization in practical contexts. So, the question, "What counts as conduct that expresses integrity?" (Audi & Murphy, 2006, p. 10) with respect to time theft, is useful in exploring practical situations where integrity is important. For example, discussion of integrity as a hyper-norm (see Gosling & Huang, 2009) may assist in providing employees with strategies to avoid time theft behaviors that are tacitly and widely accepted in the organizations and how to combat any opposition from that community. Those situations and discussions about them should be presented in case studies rather than expecting individuals to be forthcoming about their own experiences, especially in organizations where trust relationships appear to have deteriorated. Investing time in thinking through ethical dilemmas concerned with time theft will assist in creating an organizational culture of integrity as it sensitizes participants to the implications of perspectives and actions.

The identification of employer time theft, where it exists, is vital to implementing an integrity-based approach because, as we have argued in this chapter, employer and employee time theft are related to one another. As Audi and Murphy (2006) have cautioned, however, organizations need to resist paying lip service (pp. 10–11) to integrity, or "hijacking" the virtue, in order to serve their own purposes or interpretations—for example, by management making appeals to employee integrity in order to manipulate them into carrying out, "more work than can be reasonably expected of them" (p. 11).

A link between integrity and reflective processes has been noted in the literature (Goodstein, 2000) and indeed, genuine reflection embedded in an integrity-based approach by senior management in reviewing employer time theft, suggests little room for self-deception or hypocrisy. Carr's (2014, p. 11) observation of Rousseau's work, that injustice is rooted in a misguided belief in superiority that justifies treating others as socially inferior in order to fulfil desirable ends, is useful. Reflective practice exploring these possibilities and their influence on employer time theft could help organizations to address any self-deception that Smith (2006) suggests has no place in honesty or, indeed, integrity. Given the complex nature of time theft, critical reflection at all levels of the organizations is necessary for an integrity-based approach to flourish.

Conclusion

Linking an integrity-based approach to time theft management partly responds to a call, many years ago, for business ethicists to pay greater attention to organizational norms rather than focusing almost exclusively on individual employee behavior (Quinn et al., 1997). As this chapter has outlined, time theft is a complex issue, suggesting that its effective management requires a flexible, holistic approach to the problem and one that encompasses both individual and organizational aspects of the issue. This perspective resonates with the conclusions of a recent study, championing a holistic approach to trust repair through a business ethics lens following integrity violation by engaging all stakeholders, including those with little power in the organization, in restoring a positive culture with desired values and behaviors (Gillespie, Dietz & Lockey, 2014).

This chapter, in reviewing the complexities around time theft and relevant theories, concludes that an integrity-based approach to time theft would serve as a powerful strategy to address the issue of both employee and employer time-theft in their dynamic interaction. An integrity-based approach brings to the table a capacity for holism, inclusivity, sustainability, flexibility, and proactivity. Its implementation within an organization, however, is not for fainthearted managers who seek simple and quick solutions to complex, ethical issues. Further modeling of an integrity-based approach, as a tool to facilitate its implementation, and empirical research in the form of case studies present some opportunities for the future direction in addressing time theft.

Note

1. The authors wish to acknowledge the work of Dr. Stacey Bradley in her thesis on petty theft. Discussions with Stacey about what constitutes petty theft inspired them to explore the issue of time theft, through a business ethics lens.

References

Ajzen, I. (1991). The theory of planned behavior. *Organizational Behavior and Human Decision Processes, 50*(2), 179–211.
Ajzen, I. (2011). The theory of planned behavior: Reactions and reflections. *Psychology & Health, 26*(9), 113–127.
Ajzen, I. & Fishbein, M. (1980). *Understanding attitudes and predicting social behavior*. Englewood Cliffs, NJ: Prentice-Hall.
Applebaum, S., Cottin, J., & Molson, J. (2006). Employee theft: From behavioral causation and prevention to managerial detection and remedies. *The Journal of American Academy of Business, 9*(2), 175–182.

Arel, B., Besudoin, C., & Cianci, A. (2012). The impact of ethical leadership, the internal audit function, and moral intensity on a financial reporting decision. *Journal of Business Ethics, 109*(3), 351–366.

Arjoon, S. (2006). Strike a balance between rules and principles-based approaches for effective governances: A risk based approach. *Journal of Business Ethics, 68*(1), 53–82.

Atkinson, W. (2006). Stealing time. *Risk Management Magazine, 53*(11), 48–52.

Audi, R. & Murphy, P. (2006). The many faces of integrity. *Business Ethics Quarterly, 16*(1), 3–21.

Badaracco, J. J. & Ellsworth, R. R. (1991). Leadership, integrity and conflict. *Journal of Organizational Change Management, 4*(4), 46–55.

Bailey, A. (2006). Retail employee theft: A theory of planned behavior perspective International. *Journal of Retail & Distribution Management, 34*(11), 802–816.

Baker, D. (2014). When moral awareness isn't enough: Teaching our students to recognize social influence. *Journal of Management Education, 38*(4), 511–532.

Baltes, B., Briggs, T., Huff, J., Wright, J., & Neuman, G. (1999). Flexible and compressed workweek schedules: A meta-analysis of their effects on work-related criteria. *Journal of Applied Psychology, 84*(4), 496–513.

Bandura, A., Barbaranelli, C., Caprara, G., & Pastorelli, C. (1996). Mechanisms of moral disengagement in the exercise of moral agency. *Journal of Personality and Social Psychology, 71*(2), 364–374.

Beck, L. & Ajzen, I. (1991). Predicting dishonest actions using the theory of planned behavior. *Journal of Research in Personality, 25*(3), 285–301.

Becker, T. (1998). Integrity in organizations: Beyond honesty and conscientiousness. *Academy of Management Review, 22*(1), 154–161.

Bowers, J. (2010). Legal guilt, normative innocence, and the equitable decision not to prosecute. *Columbia Law Review, 110*(7), 1655–1726.

Bowling, N., Burns, G., & Beehr, T. (2010). Productive and counterproductive attendance behavior: An examination of early and late arrival to the departure from work. *Human Performance, 23*(4), 305–322.

Brock, M., Martin, L., & Buckley, M. (2013). Time theft in organizations: The development of the time banditry questionnaire. *International Journal of Selection and Assessment, 21*(3), 309–321.

Carr, D. (2014). The human and educational significance of honesty as an epistemic and moral virtue. *Educational Theory, 64*(1), 1–14.

Casper, W., Weltman, D., & Kwesiga, E. (2007). Beyond family-friendly: The construct and measurement of singles-friendly work culture. *Journal of Vocational Behavior, 70*(3), 478–501.

Cohen, T., Gunia, B., Kim-Jun, S., & Murnighan, J. (2009). Do groups lie more than individuals? Honesty and deception as a function of strategic self-interest. *Journal of Experimental Social Psychology, 45*(6), 1321–1324.

Cohen, T., Panter, A., Turan, N., Morse, L., & Kim, Y. (2014). Moral character in the workplace. *Journal of Personality and Social Psychology, 107*(5), 943–963.

Conway, N. & Sturges, J. (2014). Investigating unpaid overtime working among the part—time workforce. *British Journal of Management, 25*(4), 755–771.

Crossman, J. & Doshi, V. (2014). When not knowing is a virtue: A business ethics perspective. *Journal of Business Ethics, 131*(1), 1–8.

Crossman, J. & Noma, H. (2013). Sunao as character: Its implications for trust and intercultural communication within subsidiaries of Japanese multinationals in Australia. *Journal of Business Ethics, 113*(3), 543–555.

Curphy, G., Gibson, F., Macomber, G., Calhoun, C., & Wilbanks, L. (1998). Situational factors affecting peer reporting intentions at the U.S. Air Force Academy: A scenario-based investigation. *Military Psychology, 10*(1), 27–43.

Dineen, B., Tomlinson, E., & Lewicki, R. (2006). Supervisory guidance and behavioral integrity: Relationships with employee citizenship and deviant behavior. *Journal of Applied Psychology, 91*(3), 622–635.

Faraz, M., Shamsi, A., & Bashir, R. (2014). Working off the clock and its impact. *Journal of Business Ethics, 122*(3), 395–403.

Fenn, D. (1995). Preventing employee pilferage. *Inc., 17*(2), 112.

Fine, S. (2013). Practical guidelines for implementing preemployment integrity tests. *Public Personnel Management, 42*(2), 281–291.

Fishbein, M. & Ajzen, I. (1975). Belief, attitude, intention and behavior: An introduction to theory and research. Reading, MA: Addison-Wesley.

Fishbein, M., Hennessy, M., Yzer, M., & Douglas, J. (2003). Can we explain why some people do and some people do not act on their intentions. *Psychology Health & Medicine, 8*(1), 3–18.

Frey, B. (2000). The impact of moral intensity on decision making in the business context. *Journal of Business Ethics, 26*(3), 181–195.

Gillespie, N., Dietz, G., & Lockey, S. (2014). Organizational reintegration and trust repair after an integrity violation: A case study. *Business Ethics Quarterly, 24*(3), 371–410.

Goodstein, J. (2000). Moral compromise and personal integrity: Exploring the ethical issues of deciding together in organizations. *Business Ethics Quarterly, 10*(4), 805–819.

Gosling, M. & Huang, H. (2009). The fit between integrity and integrative social contracts theory. *Journal of Business Ethics, 90*(3), 407–417.

Gössling, T. (2003). The price of morality. An analysis of personality, moral behavior, and social rules in economic terms. *Journal of Business Ethics, 45*(1), 121–131.

Greenberg, J. (2010). *Managing Behavior in Organizations.* Upper Saddle River, NJ: Prentice-Hall.

Greenberg, L. & Barling, J. (1996). Employee theft. In C. L. Cooper & D. M. Rousseau (Eds.), *Trends in organizational behavior* (pp. 49–64). Hoboken NJ: John Wiley and Sons.

Gross-Schaefer, A., Trigilio, J., Negus, J., & Ro, C. (2000). Ethics education in the workplace: An effective tool to combat employee theft. *Journal of Business Ethics, 26*(2), 89–100.

Gruys, M. & Sackett, P. (2003). Investigating the dimensionality of counterproductive behavior. *International Journal of Selection and Assessment, 11*(1), 30–42.

Henle, C., Reeve, C., & Pitts, V. (2010). Stealing time at work: Attitudes, social pressure and perceived control as predictors of time theft. *Journal of Business Ethics, 94*(1), 53–67.

Hollinger, R. & Clark, J. (1982). Formal and informal social controls of employee deviance. *The Social Quarterly, 23*(3), 333–343.

Hollinger, R. & Clark, J. (1983). *Theft by employees.* Boston, MA: Lexington Books.

Imbrisevic, M. (2010). Why is (claiming) ignorance of the law no excuse? *Review Journal of Political Philosophy, 8*(1), 61–73.

Jackson, M. (2008). May we have your attention, please? *BusinessWeek, 4089*, 55–56.

Jacobs, D. (2004). A pragmatic approach to integrity in business ethics. *Journal of Management*, 13(3), 215–223.

Jones, T. (1991). Ethical decision making by individuals in organizations: An issue-contingent model. *The Academy of Management Review*, 16(2), 366–395.

Joosten, A., Dijke, M. van, Van Hiel, A., & Cremer, D. (2014). Feel good, do-good! On consistency and compensation in moral self-regulation. *Journal of Business Ethics*, 123(71), 71–84.

Kelloway, E., Francis, L., Prosser, M., & Cameron, J. (2010). Counterproductive work behavior as protest. *Human Resource Management Review*, 20(1), 18–25.

Ketchen, J., Craighead, C., & Buckley, R. (2008). Time bandits: How they are created, why they are tolerated, and what can be done about them. *Business Horizons*, 51(2), 141–149.

Kidder, D. (2005). Is it 'who I am', 'what I can get away with', or 'what you've done to me?' A multi-theory examination of employee misconduct. *Journal of Business Ethics*, 57(4), 389–398.

Koehn, D. (2005). Integrity as a business asset. *Journal of Business Ethics*, 58(1), 125–136.

Kulas, J., McInerney, J., Rachel, F., & Jadwinski, V. (2007). Employee satisfaction and theft: Testing climate perceptions as a mediator. *The Journal of Psychology*, 141(4), 389–402.

Langner, D. (2010). *Employee theft: Determinants of motive and proactive solutions*. Masters dissertation. University of Nevada Las Vegas, Las Vegas USA, Retrieved from http://digitalscholarship.unlv.edu/thesesdissertations/543/.

Leitsch, D. (2004). Differences in the perceptions of moral intensity in the moral decision process: An empirical examination of accounting students. *Journal of Business Ethics*, 53(3), 313–323.

Lipman, M. & McGraw, W. (1988). Employee theft: A $40 billion industry. *Annals of the American Academy of Political and Social Science*, 498(1), 51–59.

Lim, V. (2002). The IT way of loafing on the job: Cyberloafing, neutralizing and organizational justice. *Journal of Organizational Behavior*, 23(5), 675–694.

Liu, Y. & Berry, C. (2013). Identity, moral and equity perspectives on the relationship between experiences injustice and time theft. *Journal of Business Ethics*, 118(4), 73–83.

Lombardi, R. (2013). Death, time and psychosis. *Journal of the American Psychoanalytic Association*, 61(4), 691–726.

Lorsch, J. W. & McTague, E. (2016, April). Culture is not the culprit. *Harvard Business Review*, 94(4), 97–105.

Maak, T. (2008). Undivided corporate responsibility: Towards a theory of corporate integrity. *Journal of Business Ethics*, 82(2), 353–368.

Marshall, B. & Dewe, P. (1997). An investigation of the components of moral intensity. *Journal of Business Ethics*, 16(5), 521–529.

Martin, L., Brock, M., Buckley, R., & Ketchen, D. (2010). Time banditry: Examining the purloining of time in organizations. *Human Resource Management Review*, 20(1), 26–34.

McClurg, L. & Butler, D. (2006). Workplace theft: A proposed model and research agenda. *Southern Business Review*, 31(2), 25–34.

McKenzie, P. (2004). Theft includes stealing time. *Engineering News Record*, 257(17), 47.

Marx, K. (1893/1971). *Capital* (Vol 2). Moscow, Russia: Progress Publishers.

McGee, M. K., & Fillon, M. (1995, March 20). Honesty is still the best policy. *InformationWeek*, *519*, 156.

Merritt, A., Effron, D., & Monin, B. (2010). Moral self-licensing: When being good frees us to be bad. *Social and Personality Psychology Compass*, *4*(5), 344–357.

Monga, M. (2016). Meaning of integrity from the upper echelons perspective, *The Journal of Developing Areas*, *50*(6), 333–340.

Monin, B. & Miller, D. (2001). Moral credential and the expression of prejudice. *Journal of Personality and Social Psychology*, *81*(1), 33–43.

Moore, A. (2000). Employee mentoring and computer technology: Evaluation surveillance v privacy. *Business Ethics Quarterly*, *10*(3), 697–709.

Murphy, K. (1993). *Honesty in the workplace*. Pacific Grove, CA: Brooks/Cole.

Niehoff, P. & Paul, R. (2000). Causes of employee theft and strategies that HR managers can use for prevention. *Human Resource Management*, *39*(1), 51–64.

O'Fallon, M. & Butterfield, K. (2011). Moral differentiation: Exploring boundaries of 'monkey see monkey do' perspective. *Journal of Business Ethics*, *102*(3), 379–399.

Palanski, M. & Yammarino, F. (2007). Integrity and leadership: Clearing the conceptual confusion. *European Management Journal*, *25*(3), 171–184.

Palanski, M. & Yammarino, F. (2009). Integrity and leadership: A multi-level conceptual framework. *The Leadership Quarterly*, *20*(3), 405–420.

Perrow, C. (1986). *Complex organizations: A critical essay* (3rd ed.). New York: McGraw-Hill.

Poulston, J. (2008). Rationales for employee theft in hospitality: Excuses, excuses. *Journal of Hospitality and Tourism Management*, *15*(3), 49–58.

Promislo, M. & Giacalone, R. (2013, Janaury–February). Sick about unethical business. *BizEd*, 20–26.

Quinn, J., Reed, J., Browne, M. N., & Wesley, J. H. (1997). Honesty, individualism, and pragmatic business ethics: Implications for corporate hierarchy. *Journal of Business Ethics*, *16*(12), 1419–1430.

Robinson, S. & Bennett, R. (1995). A typology of deviant workplace behaviors: A multidimensional scaling study. *Academy of Management Journal*, *38*(2), 555–572.

Robinson, S. & O'Leary-Kelly, A. (1998). Monkey see, monkey do: The influences of work groups on the antisocial behavior of employees. *Academy of Management Journal*, *41*(6), 658–672.

Robinson, S., Wang, W., & Kiewitz, C. (2014). Coworkers behaving badly: The impact of co-worker deviant behavior upon individual employees. *Annual Review of Organizational Psychology and Organizational Behavior*, *1*(1), 123–143.

Salancik, G. & Pfeffer, J. (1978). A social information processing approach to job attitudes and task design. *Administrative Science Quarterly*, *23*(2), 224–253.

Shalvi, S., Eldar, O., & Bereby-Meyer, Y. (2012). Honesty requires time (and lack of justifications). *Psychological Science*, *23*(10), 1264–1270.

Siegel, P., Post, C., Brockner, J., Fishman, A., & Garden, C. (2005). The moderating influence of procedural fairness on the relationship between work-life conflict and organizational commitment. *Journal of Applied Psychology*, *90*(1), 13–24.

Smith, T. (2006). *Ayn Rand's normative ethics: The virtuous egoist*. Cambridge, UK: Cambridge University Press.

Snider, L. (2001). Crimes against capital: Discovering theft of time. *Social Justice*, *28*(3), 105–120.

Snider, L. (2002). Theft of time: Disciplining through science and law. *Osgoode Hall Law Journal, 40*(1), 89–111.

Sparks, P. & Shepard, R. (2002). The role of moral judgments within expectancy-value-based attitude-behavior. *Ethics & Behavior, 12*(4), 299–321.

Stevens, A. & Lavin, D. (2007). Stealing time. The temporal regulation of labour in neoliberal and post-Fordist work regime. *Democratic Communiqué, 21*(2), 40–61.

Swanberg, J., Pitt-Catsouphes, M., & Drescher-Burke, K. (2005). A question of justice: Disparities in employees' access to flexible schedule arrangements. *Journal of Family Issues, 26*(6), 866–895.

Taylor, F. (1911/2005). *The principles of scientific management.* Boston, MA: IndyPublish.com.

Ünal, A. (2013). Teachers' deviant workplace behaviors scale development. *Social Behavior and Personality, 41*(4), 635–642.

Verhezen, P. (2008). The (Ir)relevance of integrity in organizations. *Public Integrity, 10*(2), 133–149.

Verhezen, P. (2010). Giving voice in a culture of silence. From a culture of compliance to a culture of integrity. *Journal of Business Ethics, 96*(2), 187–206.

Weatherbee, T. (2010). Counterproductive use of technology at work: Information & communications technologies and cyberdeviancy. *Human Resource Management Review, 20*(1), 35–44.

Weber, J., Kurke, L., & Pentico, D. (2003). Why do employees steal? Assessing differences in ethical and unethical employee behavior using ethical work climates. *Business and Society, 42*(3), 359–380.

Woiceshyn, J. (2008). 'Ayn Rand's normative ethics: The virtuous egoist by Tara Smith' [book review]. *Business Ethics Quarterly, 18*(1), 117–126.

Xu, Z. & Ma, H. (2015). Does honesty result from moral will or moral grace? Why moral identity matters. *Journal of Business Ethics, 127*(2), 371–384.

Yang, F., Tsai, Y., & Liao, W. (2014). Examining the mechanisms linking behavioral integrity and affective commitment: The moderating role of charismatic leadership. *International Journal of Organizational Innovation, 6*(3), 153–173.

4 Financial Motives for Integrity and Ethical Idiosyncratic Credit in Business

A Multilevel Conceptual Model

Carolyn Predmore, Janet Rovenpor, and Frederick Greene

Introduction

Although many people believe that "nice guys finish last" (Durocher, 1975), this chapter demonstrates that a relationship between integrity, ethical idiosyncratic credit, and profitability exists and that higher levels of integrity and ethical idiosyncratic credit lead to greater long-term profitability. We provide examples that indicate that well-intentioned individuals perform better in today's business world than do individuals who cut corners and seek easy ways to move ahead over a long-term time frame. It is important to understand that the benefits of an integrity-based focus are not immediate and require time to accrue.

Recent events, including the 2008 financial crisis that started with the fall of Bear Stearns and Lehman Brothers, have shown that the pursuit of short-term profits can have disastrous effects on society. Nonetheless, there has yet to be any serious legal or judicial indictments of the masters of the financial world who managed to foist another "new economy" on us (McGrew, 1999) or to introduce risky financial instruments into the investment portfolios of their clients. In its examination of 156 criminal and civil cases against 10 of the largest Wall Street banks since 2009, the *Wall Street Journal* reported that in 81% of those cases, individual employees were neither identified nor charged with a crime (Eaglesham & Das, 2016).

Those financiers that created subprime mortgages and credit default swaps do not seem to be the same people who felt the pain of a worldwide economic downturn. Over a short time frame, it is possible for unethical, shameful behavior to appear to be rewarded with profits. It is our argument that these profits will not be sustainable because of the reemergence of someone's conscience or the loss of support from customers, investors, and other stakeholders, which causes the business to decline. The Ponzi scheme, the illegal business deal, and the unethical strategic plan do not stand a test of time over the longer term.

Legislators and politicians have tried to enact laws, such as the 2002 Sarbanes–Oxley Act, that require and/or enhance the integrity and ethical behavior on the part of the corporation. CEOs and CFOs must attest to the veracity of the financial statements that a corporation files with the Securities and Exchange Commission (SEC). If the financial statements prove to be inaccurate or false, then the CEO and CFO are personally liable (Predmore, Manduley, Abdulahad & Goma, 2005). Despite these laws, companies continue to engage in fraudulent practices. The SEC, for example, did not detect the securities fraud occurring at Bernard Madoff's securities firm. Madoff's Ponzi scheme went undetected for years, until it was no longer sustainable. The fraud came to light only when Madoff confessed his crimes to his sons, who turned him over to the authorities (Kakutani, 2009).

Madoff had been a role model and a well-respected leader in the financial services industry. Through his hard work as a lifeguard and as a sprinkler installer, he saved enough money to help start up his own firm. Madoff's computerized trading systems were very innovative and became the technology used by the NASDAQ. The years as founder of his own securities firm and his work as chair of the board of directors of the NASDAQ, however, became mere footnotes to his nefarious dealings in perpetuating a fraud upon hundreds of people and taking their money. Madoff's soaring ambition, overconfidence, and lack of self-control led him down a "slippery slope" in which small infractions grew into large infractions and his true self was revealed (Nobel, 2016). Madoff lacked the integrity and ethical behavior that contribute in the long term to positive financial outcomes (Kakutani, 2009).

This chapter proposes that integrity is an internal quality that is composed of several constituent parts and is not just another word for honesty. The critical elements of integrity are wholeness or completeness, consistency of word and action, consistency in the face of adversity, and ethics and morality (as defined by Gosling & Huang, 2009). Integrity results in reliable ethical behaviors that build over time. An individual who consistently "does the right thing" can accumulate ethical idiosyncratic credit (Predmore & Greene, 2008). Integrity can be enhanced or diminished through subsequent behavior. It is hard to build a solid reputation for above-average ethical behavior, but it is easy to lose it.

If many individuals within a firm possess integrity, they are likely to implement codes of conduct, training programs in ethics, and anonymous hotlines for whistle-blowers. These systems, processes, and programs will help the firm create an ethical culture. The business attributes that result from an ethical culture for a firm are the long-term strategic orientation of managers, favorable stakeholder perceptions, enhanced public reputation, shared governance within the business, and attraction of talented employees with high-level moral values to support the continuation of integrity and ethical behavior. The higher the level of a positive ethical culture within a company, the more likely the company will have a positive net income or profit.

Our model is a multilevel model with five stages. It follows individual behavior as it agglomerates within a firm to create organizational behavior. Integrity begins with individual decisions based on consistency in word and action, acting within a framework of wholeness, consistency in the face of opposition, and a desire to engage in ethical and moral behaviors. It is not enough for a manager to possess integrity; he or she must instill trust within others and acquire a strong reputation for ethical behavior. As a manager builds ethical idiosyncratic credit, he or she acts as a signal for others in the organization. It is the accumulation of the myriad actions of the employees of the company that creates the ethical culture of the company. One individual may promulgate the ethical culture, usually the creator of the business, but the ethical culture must be integrated into the actions of many and supported by many in order to exist and be recognized.

When the model is examining integrity and ethical idiosyncratic credit, the model is at the individual level. It focuses on collective group behavior when lower level executives take their cues from a firm's top manager and use values to guide everyday decision making. Once the model begins to evaluate ethical culture and the resulting business profit, then the model has moved to the organizational level.

Our model, depicted in Figure 4.1, melds these definitions of integrity with ethical idiosyncratic credit and illustrates how an increase in integrity leads to an increase in ethical idiosyncratic credit, which, in turn, supports a positive ethical culture within a corporation. A positive ethical culture that permeates a firm creates the foundation for five favorable outcomes: shared governance, the attraction of talented employees, enhanced reputation, the long-term strategic orientation of managers, and favorable stakeholder perceptions. The emergence of these outcomes creates an environment for profitability for a company, which incorporates integrity as a guiding principle within its internal structure. If, at any point, there is a choice to turn away from integrity or ethical behavior, then the long-term profitability of the company is in jeopardy.

Model Development

In the course of doing business, managers face considerable pressure to conform to the existing standards within their particular industry. Until the financial crash of 2008, investment bankers traded risky financial instruments, including mortgage-backed securities and collateralized debt obligations, to some extent because everyone was doing it. Brokers were earning large commissions and year-end bonuses based on their performance. The economy was booming, and everyone believed that housing prices would continue to soar. Beaumier and DeLoach (2011) remarked that ineffective risk management, lax regulation, poor underwriting standards, financial innovation that went awry, and a short-term focus on incentive compensation programs all contributed to the financial crisis. Yet, they also noted that

> the tipping point was the sheer volume of activity by mortgage brokers, lenders, mortgage insurers, investment banks, credit default issuers, and

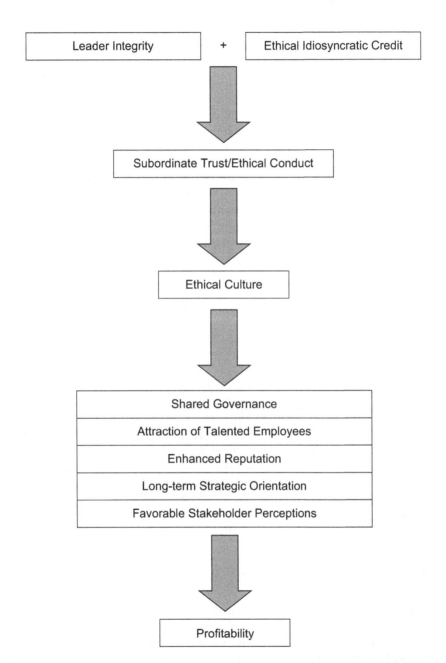

Figure 4.1 Multilevel Model of the Impact of Integrity and Ethical Idiosyncratic Credit on Profitability

institutional investors. Not enough players knew when to stop. It is one thing to engage in legitimate business activity. It is quite another to know when the risks of doing so have reached an unacceptable level. Too much of a good thing can become a bad thing when following the herd.

(Beaumier & DeLoach, 2011, p. 48)

In approximately the same time frame, between 2006 and 2007, but in a different part of the world, Chinese companies were manufacturing children's toys with lead-based paints for sale in the United States ("Mattel issues new massive China toy recall," 2007). It is illegal to use lead-based paints on children's toys sold in the United States, but the inspections were carried out in China, and the toys had been certified as being safe. Part of the reason that these companies continued to manufacture toxic toys was the "anything goes" mentality in Chinese production, which encourages manufacturers to lower their costs and push as many items through the supply chain as they can (McBride, 2009). Toy companies such as Mattel, who had used Chinese manufacturing plants, had a very poor sales season that Christmas, and China saw some of the production of toys move to other countries. More than half of China's 3,631 toy exporters went bankrupt in the first 7 months of 2008 (Pomfret, 2008).

Who is going to stand up and see the risks associated with the "crowd" mentality that affected the financial services industry in the United States and toy manufacturing in China? Who will dare to take a contrary position and argue that things must be done differently? Not many individuals have the insight or the courage to do so. It takes an outstanding individual who has a considerable amount of confidence in him- or herself to go against conventional wisdom. We believe that this kind of individual possesses integrity, and therefore, integrity is the first stage in our model. As our model shows, managers at the middle-level ranks as well as those who are managing from the top who act in an ethical and moral fashion and show consistency in their words, actions, and business dealings will put their firms on a steady and more certain path toward profitability (Gentry et al., 2013; Simons, Leroy, Collewaert & Masschelein, 2015; Monga, 2016).

Integrity and Ethical Idiosyncratic Credit: The First Stage in the Model

Integrity, or its absence, is a concept that has been around for a long time and can be applied to many different situations. In our model, integrity begins at the individual level rather than the company level. A few examples will indicate why. Between 2000 and 2009, there was a severe food crisis in Zimbabwe. A woman in the impoverished village of Dongamuzi bartered a cow for 6 buckets of maize to feed her family. She knew that the deal was not fair, but she had no choice since there was no grain available in her community ("Zimbabwe: Farm animals bartered to stave off hunger," 2008). According to Famine Early Warning System Network (FEWSNET), the expected normal terms of trade were 1,000 kg of maize for a beast (Misa, 2010). Meanwhile, the woman's trading partner was prospering by exchanging farm animals for maize and then selling the livestock to city butcheries and slaughterhouses. He may have lacked integrity because he did not consider the woman's plight or engage in an equal exchange.

In 2011, a farmer in Kansas purchased future's contracts so that he would receive a guaranteed price for the 35,000 bushels of wheat he expected to deliver at harvest time. His broker worked with a third party, MF Global Holdings (MF), to process the trades. At the time of MF's collapse, the farmer had $30,000 in his account. He was able to retrieve only 20% of his funds. And he may have been among the lucky ones! The accounts of hundreds of other farmers were frozen. This included $400,000 belonging to the owner of an Iowa hog farm who was unable to finish construction on a new equipment shop (DiColo & Strumpf, 2011). Jon Corzine, the CEO, invested in short-term, high-yield sovereign bonds of financially troubled European countries. His reckless behavior, which affected farmers, employees, and investors, may have resulted from a lack of integrity.

An article published in *The Manufacturer and Builder* in 1881 explained why it is so important for integrity to prevail during business transactions:

> No merchant, however persistent and shrewd he may be in his commercial operations, can build up a great and prosperous business without integrity. Integrity is the link that holds the great financial world together; it is the basis upon which all great commercial operations are founded. When business men lose faith in one another, mercantile interests are immediately affected, industries become paralyzed, and the great laboring world complains of poverty, of hunger and hard times. The great rush and struggle to win immediate wealth, bankrupts many a reputation and ingloriously ends many a brilliant business career.
>
> ("Integrity in Business," 1881, p. 19)

This excerpt has several implications. First, integrity is the building block for outstanding success in the business world. It is needed in addition to continuous effort, smart strategies, and innovation. It differentiates between mediocre companies and excellent companies. Second, managers must overcome their desire for short-term gains and immediate profit. They must devote their energy to building long-term, reciprocal and trusting relationships with customers and trading partners. Third, business transactions fall apart if one of the parties fails to keep his or her promise or if the goods/services being exchanged are of poor quality. It takes just a few bad deals and corrupt individuals to poison an entire industry and to send an economy into a downward spiral.

A Working Definition of Integrity

Integrity is a subject under great debate in management literature due to its subjective meaning. As indicated by the 1881 article, integrity is most often defined by Western European/American Judeo-Christian values. When that was the world of commerce as China turned on itself with early communism and the Red Guard under Mao and Russia instituted a cold war behind its own walls as exemplified by the Berlin Wall, it was easy to rely on those commonly shared cultural and societal values. Now that China is embracing more private ownership within its business environment, as is Russia and former Soviet states, and the Arabic world is advancing on the business world with Dubai entrenching itself as a Middle Eastern commercial hub, the definition of integrity may have to become more objective in its nature (Noelliste, 2013). Researchers that stress commonality to unify an integrity framework refer back to "moral principles," but those certainly would have a societal underpinning which would have to be referenced which in this situation would again be Western European Judeo-Christian (Monga, 2016). At a basis, it has meant that the person would not lie, cheat, or steal in business or in one's personal interactions (Gentry et al., 2013).

Despite its widespread use and importance, *integrity* is a term that has not been well defined. It is easily confused with other similar terms, such as *honesty, morality,* and *ethics.* It is unclear if integrity is a unidimensional or multidimensional construct. There is considerable debate regarding whether the standards used to judge whether an individual possesses integrity should be based on the standards operative within a specific community or culture or on a set of high-level moral and universally accepted standards.

Palanski and Yammarino (2007) reviewed the scholarly literature on integrity and found that it has been used in five different ways. Integrity means (1) wholeness or completeness, (2) consistency between words and actions, (3) the ability to hold true to one's beliefs despite adversity and temptation, (4) being authentic and true to oneself, and (5) acting in accordance with high moral and ethical standards. Most of these dimensions, however, need to be placed within a framework in which "doing the right thing" is paramount.

Several researchers have pointed out that defining integrity as *consistency between words and actions* (i.e., keeping one's promises and behaving in a way that is consistent with one's beliefs) becomes problematic when one considers individuals like Adolf Hitler (Becker, 1998; Gosling & Huang, 2009). Hitler had strong beliefs and values and acted on them by trying to eliminate non-Aryans from modern society. No one would claim, however, that Hitler possessed integrity or that genocide was an example of "doing the right thing." Similar concerns can be raised about *wholeness, consistency in the face of adversity,* and *authenticity.* What if the values a person holds are immoral but he or she truly believes in them, acts on them, and persists even though it is difficult or costly?

Palanski and Yammarino (2007) get around this issue by proposing that *integrity* is one of the virtues which comprise good character. It is unidimensional and relates to "consistency of an acting entity's words and actions." Some researchers think that this definition does not convey the full, rich meaning of integrity. It becomes almost synonymous with "behavioral integrity" or the "perceived congruence between the values expressed by words and those expressed through action" (Simons, 1999, p. 89).

Gosling and Huang (2009) make the case for treating integrity as a multidimensional construct and understanding it within an integrative social contracts theory. "Authentic norms" in local communities need to be tested against universal standards or *hypernorms*. Hypernorms are "principles so fundamental to human existence that they serve as a guide in evaluating lower level moral norms" (Donaldson & Dunfee as quoted in Gosling & Huang, 2009, p. 412). So, even if Hitler's words and actions were consistent and sanctioned by the Nazi Party and/or Germany, they violated universally held human rights principles. He, therefore, lacked integrity.

In the post–World War II era, hypernorms can be found in such documents as the *United Nations Universal Declaration of Human Rights* (www. un.org/en/documents/ udhr/). The 30 articles in the declaration include such statements as "No one shall be held in slavery or servitude; slavery and the slave trade shall be prohibited in all their forms" (article 4); "no one shall be subjected to arbitrary arrest, detention or exile" (article 9); and "everyone has the right to freedom of opinion and expression; this right includes freedom to hold opinions without interference and to seek, receive, and impart information and ideas through any media and regardless of frontiers" (article 19).

Gosling and Huang (2009) concluded that integrity consists of four dimensions: wholeness, consistency in the face of adversity, consistency of word and action, and ethics and morality. *Wholeness* refers to individuals whose thoughts, words, attitudes, and behaviors are mutually consistent across time and situations. If a government official refuses to accept a bribe from a company seeking new business, then he or she will not engage in an extramarital affair or cheat on his or her personal income taxes. The official has demonstrated consistency in all the different roles she plays in society. This holds true, as long as the society in which the official operates, strongly values level playing fields, fidelity, and civic duty. Plus, most countries have laws prohibiting bribe taking, politicians have been sanctioned for sex scandals and affairs with interns, and citizens are penalized for not paying income taxes.

Consistency in the face of adversity means that an individual will do the right thing even if it is difficult, costly, or unpleasant (Gosling & Huang, 2009). Thus, an employee will stand up for what he believes in and blow the whistle on wrongdoing even if he could lose his job. Often, an individual will espouse a universally held norm even though it may not be endorsed by the local community. For example, members of the Occupy Wall Street movement believed in the right to congregate and to protest even though their efforts were not supported by local mayors, businesses, and residents; they violated rules and regulations governing public spaces; and they suffered the discomfort of cold weather, time away from jobs/families, and, sometimes, police arrests.

Consistency of word and action means that a manager "walks the talk." He does what he says, lives by his values, and keeps his promises. If his values are in accordance with local norms and universal norms, he is said to have integrity. Finally, integrity will lead to better than expected ethical and moral behaviors (Palanski & Yammarino, 2007, p. 174).

An individual with integrity should incorporate all four dimensions into his or her everyday life. The person should possess wholeness, consistency in words and actions, consistency in the face of adversity and demonstrate ethical and moral behaviors. An overabundance of one does not compensate for an underabundance of the other. Also, there is a hurdle rate, or a minimum acceptable level for each component. For an individual to possess integrity, for example, he or she would have to "do the right thing" more than once and always act according to his or her promises to his or her constituencies.

The individual should not only talk about doing the "right thing" but also needs to do the" right thing" as it is leading by example that has the most influence on others (Simons et al., 2015). Within the global business environment where there is less commonality between the variety of social and cultural norms, the terms of appropriate behavior may need to be detailed within the business contract to forestall the majority of misunderstandings about business behavior expectations.

Jon Corzine and the Bankruptcy of MF Global

Now that we have a better idea of what is meant by integrity, let's examine more closely the words and deeds of Jon Corzine, as reported by the media. Corzine has had a long career, spanning business and politics. He started out as a bond portfolio manager at BancOhio National Bank in Columbus, worked his way up from government-bond desk trainee to co-CEO of Goldman, Sachs and Company, served as a Senator and then as Governor of NJ, and returned to the private sector when he became the CEO of MF Global. A few examples taken from different points in Corzine's career will attest to his integrity, or lack thereof.

As senator from 2001 to 2006, Corzine was responsible for several progressive initiatives. He was one of 23 senators to vote against the Iraqi War, was the first to speak out against the genocide occurring in Darfur, and was in favor of universal health care and free day care (Daly, 2011). It seems that Corzine stood for important moral values (e.g., peace, freedom, equal access to health care). He also fought for stricter regulations on 401(k)s and hedge funds and wanted to grant greater enforcement powers to the SEC. Along with Senator Christopher Dodd, Corzine introduced legislation in 2003 that would impose Sarbanes–Oxley-like reforms on mutual funds, such as a Fund's audit committee must be composed of independent directors (Hume, 2003). It is clear that he knew how important it was to protect customers from fraud.

When Corzine became the CEO of MF in 2010 he turned his attention to making as much money for the firm as he could. He intended to transform it from a small commodities broker to a full-service investment banking powerhouse (Lucchetti & Spector, 2011). As senator, he fought for greater federal regulation of financial institutions but as head of a financial institution himself, he exploited an easing of rules that did not necessarily benefit customers or business partners. Traditionally, accounts with customer assets were segregated from a firm's assets so that customers could retrieve their funds if something happened to the firm. The firm could invest a customer's cash in excess of the returns promised in safe investments such as U.S. treasuries. Then, investments in the sovereign debt of other countries were allowed. In 2000, they seemed like safe investments, but starting in early 2010, countries like Greece, Ireland, and Portugal encountered great difficulty in paying their debt. Corzine's investments became risky. Moreover, under his watch, $1.2 billion of customer funds from segregated accounts went missing. We conclude that Corzine did not fulfill the "wholeness" component of integrity. He should have known better about what was happening in the eurozone and in his own company's back offices. His actions were not consistent across time and across situations.

Associates of Corzine noted that his unusual trades were driven by desperation (Lucchetti & Spector, 2011). As soon as he became head of MF Global, Corzine was notified by Moody's Investors Services, Standard and Poor's, and Fitch Ratings that he would have to boost the firm's earnings rapidly or face downgrades on the firm's debt. MF had been losing money for 3 years straight. Corzine turned to a quick fix by investing in European sovereign bonds with high yields. These investments were structured as "repurchase to maturity agreements," which enabled MF to show profits up front on the difference between the interest rate on the bond and the interest rate it was paying to its lender. When the size of these investments rose to $6.3 billion, counterparties began to worry that if market prices for the bonds declined, MF would not have enough money to pay the interest on the loans. They demanded more collateral, which MF did not have. We use this as evidence to indicate that Corzine did not engage in proper behaviors when faced with adversity. He violated the second standard of integrity.

During his career, Corzine exhibited several instances in which his words did not match his actions (the third dimension of integrity). He got into trouble at Goldman Sachs when he held secret merger negotiations with Mellon Bank and failed to inform Hank Paulson, his co-CEO, even when asked by Paulson specifically (Burrough, Cohan, & McLean, 2012). As the newly elected governor of New Jersey, Corzine failed to keep his campaign promises when he submitted a state budget in 2006, which would increase taxes (Chen & Jones, 2006). When asked if MF had any exposure to the debt of European countries in a survey of financial firms distributed by the Financial Industry Regulatory Authority, an industry-funded watch group, Corzine said no (Lucchetti & Spector, 2011).

In the end, MF was shut down and became the eighth-largest bankruptcy in the United States. Corzine insists that he had no idea where the $1.2 billion in customer funds went (Daly, 2011). He did not exhibit moral and ethical behaviors (the fourth dimension of integrity).

Blake Mycoskie and the Launch of TOMS Shoes

In 2002, while competing on the reality show *The Amazing Race* with his sister, Blake Mycoskie witnessed global poverty for the first time. On a subsequent vacation in Argentina, he met a group of community workers who were organizing a drive to deliver discarded shoes to poor children who went barefoot. He was further inspired by a local shoe, the alpargata, worn by farmers. In 2006, Mycoskie returned home and launched TOMS Shoes to manufacture a slip-on shoe made from vibrantly dyed and lightweight fabrics (Friday, 2007). He developed a unique "One for One" model (Prois, 2011). For every pair of shoes that the company sold, it would donate a second pair of shoes to a child in need. In its first year, the company sold 10,000 pairs of shoes. Mycoskie later extended this model to an eyewear line of sunglasses. Every time a consumer buys a pair of sunglasses, the company will give someone in need prescription lenses or eye-related medical treatment (Prois, 2011).

Mycoskie is an example of a social entrepreneur who keeps things simple and comfortable. This pertains not just to the shoes he sells but also to the way he lives his life. Mycoskie refers to himself as "chief shoe giver," not "chief executive officer," and has opted to reside on a sailboat docked in Marina Del Rey, California (McDonald, 2011). From time to time, he opens his closets to contribute items he no longer wants to an "office garage sale." He regularly blogs about such companies as FreeRice.com (which donates 10 grains of rice to the World Food Program for every trivia question subscribers answer) and Movember (a group which raises awareness and funds for men's health issues, especially prostate cancer, by growing mustaches during the month of November).

Mycoskie's passion for blending business with philanthropy may have stemmed from an early interest in world religions and spirituality, which began in a high school theology class and continued during his studies as a philosophy major at Southern Methodist University in Texas. Plus, his mother instructed him to "be nice to everyone" (Ramirez, 2010). We conclude that Mycoskie passes the integrity test that requires "wholeness." Doing good and helping others seem to have been a long-term commitment, which is woven into every aspect of his life.

One of Mycoskie's favorite quotes is from Gandhi: "Be the change you wish to see in the world" ("Blake's bio," 2012). To spread his message,

Mycoskie recently wrote a book titled *Start Something That Matters*, which provides readers with ideas on how to improve the world around them. The book's publisher, Random House, agreed to keep the one-for-one model. For every book it sells, it gives a book to a child in need. Furthermore, Mycoskie takes 50% of the proceeds from the book and offers grants to individuals who want to launch a community project or incorporate a social component into a business. In an interview, Mycoskie said, "With the grants, I wanted to put my money where my mouth is. It's my way of giving back to readers and asking them to start something" (as quoted in Prois, 2011). He shows consistency between words and actions and satisfies the second dimension of integrity.

Mycoskie reported that his biggest challenges occurred during the start-up. No one thought that his one-for-one idea would work. His college professor anticipated that he would need $1 million to launch his shoe company. His peers in the business world believed he would be much better off giving away a percentage of any profits that a new venture might generate. So, Mycoskie started with a modest goal and vowed to give away 250 shoes in the first year of operations. Neither Mycoskie nor his colleagues knew how to make shoes or how to market them. They did not have enough money to hire experienced managers or to advertise in traditional media outlets. Instead, they learned about production, quality control, and inventory the hard way through trial and error. They relied on social media and on word of mouth to keep consumers excited about their products (Lerman, 2009). Mycoskie persevered through difficult times and held true to his beliefs during adversity (the third dimension of integrity).

The outcomes that resulted from Mycoskie's work at TOMS are indicative of moral and ethical behaviors (the fourth dimension of integrity). By 2010, the company had given away 1 million shoes. It received the Secretary of State's 2009 Award for Corporate Excellence, which celebrates companies committed to corporate social responsibility, innovation, exemplary practices and democratic values ("Blake's bio," 2012).

A Working Definition of Ethical Idiosyncratic Credit

Another important concept in our model, which is still at the personal level, is ethical idiosyncratic credit. It is based on the idea of idiosyncratic leadership, which suggests that one can accumulate the positive perceptions of employees around oneself. These credits then allow the person some latitude in acting within social norms and mores. The more idiosyncratic credit that has been saved, the more one can stage outside of the societal norms for a short period (Christman, 1963).

Ethical capital is the reserve of respect that a person has been accorded by his or her compatriots through following high moral/ethical codes and acting in an ethical manner (McTiernan, 2003). However, people are not perfect. One can have a lapse in judgment and make an unethical decision, perform an unethical act, and ruin one's reputation. Some researchers believe that once ethical capital is spent, then it is gone, and there is little to be done to find redemption. However, ethical idiosyncratic credit is posited as creating a bridge between idiosyncratic credit and ethical capital wherein a person may build a collection of ethical idiosyncratic credit and spend it either willingly or thoughtlessly.

The important difference lies in the evaluation of the extent of harm that has been done to the community. It may be possible to rebuild a reputation through a long, slow process of again acting consistently in an ethical manner at all times. Reputations are ruined in an instant (Predmore & Greene, 2008). It happens in the time it takes to assign blame when there are negative outcomes.

Good behavioral acts result in enhancing the balance. Predmore and Greene (2008, p. 132) take this concept a stage further by stating that ethical idiosyncratic capital and its resulting credits "operate within ethical and trust environments in which credits may be accumulated, spent and re-accumulated over time, albeit exceedingly slowly." These credits must represent behavior "considered ethical by both the professional and the interacting referent exogenous groups" (Predmore & Greene, 2008, p. 132) who give the person their trust.

It is our belief that unintentional errors can more quickly mended than can intentional wrongdoing. The spending of the ethical idiosyncratic credits is a result of behavior that is considered to break the bounds of trust, company moral/ethical code and societal norms, putting the actor beyond what is normally excusable accidental behavior (Predmore & Greene, 2008). However, even after an unethical act, it is possible for a person to devote a large portion of his or her career to doing good for others, thereby rebuilding his or her reputation through the accumulation of ethical idiosyncratic credit.

Examples of unintentional errors from which decision makers can rebound can be found in the private and public sector. Consider the actions of Jon Corzine during his early career in politics and the decisions of Japanese officials when they determined that it was safe to build the Fukushima Daiichi nuclear plant. Following his successful service in the Senate, Corzine was able to be governor of New Jersey for one term. There were some glimmers of a risk predilection during that time. He was severely injured in a high-speed car accident and was not wearing a seatbelt during the drive. Because he was being chauffeured by a police officer, it is assumed that Corzine encouraged the officer to drive well above the speed limit in order to be on time for the next meeting. The decision to not wear a seatbelt would appear to be only a personally reckless decision, except for the fact that Corzine had responsibility for the State of New Jersey and his disappearance from state government would have made a difference in the management of the state. Nonetheless, the public disregarded this incident and continued to imbue him with trust and legitimacy. He was able to return to the private sector when he took over the management of MF Global (until it went bankrupt because of its abuse of customer funds and overly risky investments).

Sometimes the decision maker decides that the odds for a poor outcome are so unlikely, that it is close to impossible for a plan to fail. In the design of the nuclear plants at Fukushima, there was evidence on the rocks of previous tsunamis at levels higher than the level of the nuclear plants, but those events had occurred more than 1,000 years ago, so the likelihood that another tsunami would track on that same path and be as tall as that ancient wave was perceived to be very small. Plus, the country needed power ("Study: Japan nuclear plant chiefs downplayed evidence of tsunami risk," 2011).

In the immediate aftermath of the earthquake–tsunami–flooding and nuclear disaster, Japan's leaders decided to reverse their move toward nuclear power and look to creating power using less potentially harmful methods. Although this action may seem an extreme reaction to the natural disaster, researchers have found that human error or human hubris played a significant role in the siting of the Fukushima Daiichi nuclear plants in that particular location. In the years between 800 CE to date, there have been two previous "mega earthquakes," which should have served notice to the engineering planners that this area was known to experience infrequent but severe tectonic shifts (Nöggerath, Geller, & Gusiakov, 2011).

Initially, the Japanese government moved away from using nuclear power for several reasons, one of which may have been a need to begin to accumulate ethical idiosyncratic credits in order to instill trust in the government again. It may be a long road for Japan as embedded in bureaucracy is a desire to keep the status quo. There remains a desire to hide the underlying reasons for the poor strategic modeling that was the foundation for the Fukushima Daiichi nuclear plants (Matsumura, 2012). There was an opportunity for true leadership and integrity in the march away from nuclear power, but the ethical behaviors of many have to become the ethical culture of the nation. Lately it appears, however, that Japanese officials are losing the trust of the public. Data from a 2012 Edelman Trust Barometer showed that the level of trust in civil servants fell from a high of 63% to 8% after the 3/11 disaster (as reported in Aldrich, 2013).

An example of an intentional unethical act, made for personal gain or professional profit, is the creation of the largest Ponzi scheme to date by Bernard Madoff. Here was a man who had helped create the quote system for the NASDAQ and had been respected for 50 years in the financial world of Wall Street (Chapman, 2009). However, there had been some warnings that were ignored for several years that there might be a problem with the investment company run by Madoff because of Madoff's standing within the financial community (Kakutani, 2009). The Ponzi scheme had worked well for decades, but in the summer and fall of 2008, it was getting difficult to keep getting more people to invest enough to payout the overly generous quarterly dividends that his investors had come to expect. The economic meltdown of Wall Street made it impossible for Bernard Madoff to continue to deceive regulators and investors.

Subordinate Trust and Ethical Conduct: The Second Stage in the Model

Business leaders who possess integrity and have built ethical idiosyncratic credit gain the respect and loyalty of their subordinates. They become role models from whom subordinates take their cues. Subordinates adopt their leaders' values and begin to emulate their ethical behaviors. A meta-analysis has shown that a leader's behavioral integrity (measured by alignment of words and deeds) has a strong effect on follower trust, in-role task performance, and organizational citizenship behavior (Simons et al., 2015). In their review of the literature, Sosik, Gentry, and Chun (2012) pointed out that individuals who act with integrity experience positive moods, garner high levels of trust, and engage in effective workplace relationships. Moreover, the "character strengths of top managers often cascade down the ranks and influence the organization's ethical climate" (Sosik et al., 2012, p. 367).

Ethical Culture: The Third Stage in the Model

Integrity is evidenced by the ethical behavior of the employees of the firm as well as upper management. No one should be exempt from the clear moral and ethical path that the company should be following. With the building of ethical idiosyncratic credit by individuals within the firm, the company creates an ethical culture, which is a macro level of ethical consideration having developed from the micro level of personal integrity focus and ethical behavior.

Trevino and Weaver (as cited in Kaptein, 2009) defined *ethical culture* as those aspects of the organizational context that impede unethical conduct and promote ethical conduct. It reflects a company common mindset and a collection of shared values that encourage employees to "do the right thing." It is associated with attitudes, processes, procedures, and systems that can be identified as critical to maintaining an ethical culture. Ethical behavior within ethical cultures, for example, calls for giving equivalent value in business transactions, in treating stockholders and stakeholders well, and in understanding that within a community one company's actions have a billowing effect on the people and business in the area. It is not sufficient to be able to drive a hard bargain or to be a tough competitor. One should be fair within business dealings and consider the effects of the business processes that are being used.

It is certainly possible that a business process in use today may prove to be harmful in the future. An ethical company would take responsibility for the unintended consequences of its actions and make reparations where needed. A company that finds out about a problem and sounds an alert is given the benefit of the doubt by its customers and regulators. Managers who implement company mandated recalls are held in higher regard by the consumer public than are managers who wait to be required by a legal decision to recall a product. For example, Corning Glass personnel discovered that its new method for attaching handles to its coffee makers was flawed. The high temperature of a full pot of coffee was enough to melt the glue used. The handles were falling off, and the pots of coffee were dropping and spilling hot coffee in the process. The company called in all of the newly designed coffee pots and replaced them with the older design of a metal-banded handle. It was more important for Corning to ensure the health of its customers than to save money and wait to see if the government would mandate a recall (Trausch, 1981).

Other examples point to the dangers of unethical cultures, especially when they permeate through many companies within a particular country. Iceland was the first country to encounter a severe credit crunch during the financial crisis of 2008. Its three largest banks had grown rapidly over the years by borrowing and lending money abroad (Forelle, 2008). The banks were unable to refinance their debt and were seized by the government. The Icelandic stock market lost 80% of its value. Iceland received loans of approximately $10 billion from the International Monetary Fund and other countries, including Sweden, Denmark, Germany, the Netherlands, and Great Britain.

Vaiman, Sigurjonsson, and Davidsson (2011) suggested that a weak business culture was one of several factors that contributed to the economic crisis in Iceland. The country's weak business culture suffered from a "lack of tradition and consideration toward the set of explicit and implicit rules that facilitate business interactions in society" (Vaiman et al., 2011, p. 98). Businesspeople exhibited strong optimism, excessive risk taking, and adventurism, as well as a lack of self-discipline. These problems were exacerbated by a lack of diversity, cross-ownership, and nepotism that were characteristic of Icelandic businesses. When an unethical business culture is rampant within a particular society, the potential for corruption and poor decision making is much greater.

We suggest that there are five important outcomes of an ethical culture— shared governance, the attraction of talented employees, enhanced reputation, the long-term strategic orientation, and favorable stakeholder perceptions—which, in turn, lead to higher company profits.

The Outcomes of an Ethical Culture: The Fourth Stage in the Model

Shared Governance

The firm benefits from acting with integrity in its business philosophy, decisions, methods, and behaviors. One consequence of using integrity in business is realizing that good information and decisions can come from many different areas in the company. Firms have seen that a good way to encourage multiple viewpoints within the company is through shared governance. Shared governance allows staff, line and upper management to come together to develop new ideas, new products, and methods for working with challenges that develop over time. With top-down management styles, there is a likelihood that plans will get approved by CEOs and their staff with little negative feedback from other employees within the organization. It is easy for a poor idea to gain momentum within a company if there is no mechanism in place for a person to state potential problems with the intended plans. Shared governance offers an open forum for alternative ideas to enter into discussions and strategic plans.

Within a business environment, further evidence of a solid integrity-based company philosophy would be noted by a company having a shared governance structure. That shared governance structure is important for encouraging divergent views into company planning and for avoiding the likelihood of one opinion or one person being able to redirect a company's philosophy and actions without agreement from multiple constituencies. The view that integrity will be evidenced by shared governance permeates managerial thought. In an address to the country, President Obama announced in November 2008 that he intended to help create a presidency that would hold integrity as one of its highest values along with leveraging technology to build our economy. Shared governance was to be evidence of opening the door to new ideas and plans for incorporation into legislation for moving the United States forward (Houston, 2008). The president of the American Association of University Professors, Cary Nelson, has written a book that examines the reduction in shared governance and the concomitant lessening of integrity perceived within U.S. institutions of higher education (reviewed by Jacobs-Lustig, 2011). Shared governance opens the doors to an examination of policies, procedures, plans, and strategies and reduces the likelihood that unethical standards are being used to evaluate present and future actions (Collier & Esteban, 1999; Iwu-Egwuonwu, 2011; Rok, 2009). Nursing has also seen the emergence of shared governance as a method for underscoring the necessity for integrity in health care and employee/management behaviors. Shared governance is important in maintaining the integrity of the programs that are developed for improving health care (Brenner, Dambaugh, Hill, Roberts, & Vollers, 2008).

Attraction of Talented Employees

Talented employees are critical to the efficient operation of an organization. These employees are "productive" and have a positive influence on the company culture and profits in ways that any potential replacement employee might not be able to replicate (Sigler, 1999). An integrity-based company philosophy should lead to the company being able to attract very talented employees who understand the importance of continuing ethical behavior. The ethical culture of a company should also encourage greater numbers of talented and skilled potential employees to apply to work for a firm with an ethical culture. "Labor, operating, and overhead costs may increase if the enterprise is perceived to be so unprincipled in its conduct toward employees that its recruiting and retention of skilled personnel are at risk" (Young & Hasler, 2010, p. 37).

Talented employees want to work for companies that will appreciate their skills and work. Talented employees want to be treated fairly and are more likely to perform better for a company that not only rewards output but also the methods used for achieving that output. Corporate ethical/moral behavior is rewarded by more employees wanting to work for the company. The firm can then choose to hire those whose personal ethical codes match the ethical philosophy of the company. Companies with a good ethical culture have no problem in stating their moral codes and remaining firm on those principles. That is true of all companies, whether they are large or small. It is especially important for small businesses to act with integrity as their profits rest more on their local community and their reputation within the community than do large firms operating in a much larger environment.

An enhanced public reputation for the firm is another result of using integrity as a focus for business methodology. Scott (2011) reported that ethical behavior in a company resulted in a much greater employee retention rate for those companies rated as being ethical from within the Standard & Poor's top 500 companies. The attraction of talented employees is intimately entwined with the ethical reputation of the company. Talented employees want to know that they will be contributing to a company whose stated goals can be trusted, which values its employees, rewards ethical behavior, pays a living wage for a day's work, and understands work–life balance.

The Millennial generation has been noted as prizing a balance in their work–career life, which is a continuation of the concern for a good work–life balance that the Baby Boomers had after watching their parents jump to the wishes of the organization. The World War II generation was grateful for any job after returning from the war and eagerly acceded to the demands of the organization. This led to impersonal production lines, seemingly unending workdays, and transferring people to different jobs in different geographic regions in the company in order to add to the breadth of their work experience. There was usually only one head of household working so that there was no concern given to the comfort of the transferred spouse in the moving experience. Baby Boomers found that accepting those working conditions meant that a parent would miss the softball game or the school concert, and that was not perceived as an equitable exchange for the Baby Boomers. That generation began to ask and expect more accommodations for family life needs and responsibilities.

The Millennial generation has the Baby Boomers as parents and continued to see work intrude (from the children's perspective) into family life. The Millennials have also grown up during a period of economic prosperity within the global economy and expected until the financial collapse in 2008 to be able to have a good career and a balanced family life. While this desire for a satisfying career and a good home life may seem antithetical, companies that foster an ethical culture will be companies that come the closest to providing the flexibility for their employees to have an equitable work–life balance.

Enhanced Reputation

The U.S. Supreme Court found in a 1995 decision that reputations were to be valued above all else and that one's good reputation in the local community was the highest prize to achieve in one's lifetime (Rolph, 2008). In 1929, Sir Frederick Pollock (as cited by Rolph, 2008) wrote about the importance of reputation in business in the early part of the 20th century, stating that reputation was almost more important than life itself, especially in local retailing. These few examples of legal expert opinion on reputation show that the instillation of a positive ethical culture within an organization is critical to the enhanced trust between a company and its stakeholders—the stockholders, customers, employees, and neighbors. Arguably, the firm's market value is enhanced over the long term as its reputation continues to grow. It is important for customers to believe that they can trust the company that they want to buy from. If a company will misrepresent some of its products and services, then what else is not true? As the reputation for being ethical grows, more stakeholders are drawn to the company and want to engage in business with the firm. This leads to a more constant stream of revenue, which encourages management to stay longer with a company. As management perceives a reason for remaining with one company over a longer period, managerial decisions will become more focused on the health of the company for the long term, leading to a focus on long-term sustainability, viability, and profitability.

Long-Term Strategic Orientation

Integrity encourages a company to plan for the long-term life of the firm and thereby have long-term profitability in order to sustain itself over the years. Firms have traditionally been responsive to shareholder desires for maximum returns on investments. However, that view has led to poor strategic decisions that could bring a financial return in the short term, but financial hardships in the long term. The invention of credit default swaps is one example of a business strategy that sought to reduce the amount of capital a company had to have on reserve to hedge its risks. It was thought that the financial house, which was rising at a very fast pace in 2008, was strong enough to withstand the vagaries of some poor-risk mortgages as the market was so large and the likelihood of default by many was so unlikely. The credit default swap was considered to be a promise that on demand from the certificate holders, the issuing company would be able to produce the amounts required from money set aside to cover the value of the underlying assets ("S&P Asgns STEERS Credt Bkd Tr Ser, 2002–4 KO Certs Rtg," 2002). Businesses relied on that promise. It was not a promise kept in the early fall of 2008. From the disintegration of the business markets in 2008 through 2009, many broken promises and reputations were uncovered.

Allio (2011) found that corporate misbehavior, top management hubris, and general short-term profit strategies have caused many in the public to think that re-regulation is the only way to maintain ethical cultures within business. Allio (2011) suggested, however, that a long-term strategy of "satisficing key stakeholders" (customers, employees, investors and suppliers) is a much better long-term strategy both for survival and profitability.

Favorable Stakeholder Perceptions

The company's good reputation, talented employees, and long-term strategic orientation contribute to favorable stakeholder perceptions. Stakeholders include not only employees, but also business partners, suppliers, distributors, customers, and the public.

Companies are run by people who sometimes make the wrong decision; an error is made in the manufacturing process or in the provision of service in such a way that the reputation of the company may very likely be damaged. In situations like this, Young and Hasler (2010) found that

> a reputation for poor ethics can lead to costs of replacing lost business partners or going it alone. . . . Similarly, purchasing, logistics, and overhead costs may increase if suppliers judge the enterprise to be unfair or dishonest. . . . Unethical conduct puts reputational capital—and economic value—at risk. . . . [It is important] to elicit stakeholder judgments about a company's commitment to principled ethical behavior in their relationship [with the company].
>
> (p. 37)

Young and Hasler (2010) believed that it is critical for managers to encourage their stakeholders to evaluate the ethical behaviors of their companies with a goal of helping them improve their decision making in the future.

Companies cannot consider only their stockholders and the earnings per share as the measurement by which their business acumen will be judged. That view supports a short-term, quarter-by-quarter evaluation of how the firm is doing business. That type of shortsighted business philosophy has led many a business into bankruptcy like Enron, Waste Management, and Lehman Brothers. Even with strong balance sheets, if the company doing business is not conducting its affairs within an ethical culture, it will lose its working partnerships as well as its customers and a good relationship with its surrounding communities.

Sometimes, the potential future use of a stakeholder analysis of company actions is considered to be possibly financially hard on small firms (Belal & Roberts, 2010). What must be taken into account are the relationships that continue to build the company that may not reside on the balance sheet.

Good company reputations give the firm the potential for eliciting government support when they seek favorable business conditions in which to grow. Public hearings offer a pulpit for the community to voice its approval or negativity. Acting on behalf of the good of its stakeholders, a business is much more likely to receive community support for these requests. A view to enhancing the well-being of all of the company stakeholders adds to long-term positive business conditions and profitability of the company.

Haigh and Brubaker (2010) have found that even though bad things can happen to good companies even when management believes it is prepared to handle adversity, "consumers expect organizations to act responsibly" during the ordeal. It is important that the company take ownership of the problem, be truthful about the conditions that resulted in the negative event, and state what the company will do going forward in order to keep the public's perception of the company's reputation and ethical culture intact.

Profitability: The Fifth Stage in the Model

While it is comforting to suppose that acting according to ethical principles and moral standards in business would reap profits, it is even more reassuring when research underscores this precept. Scott (2011) reported that a culture of integrity increases shareholder value. A study by the Corporate Executive Board (CEB) examined the records of 130 companies over a 10-year period. Companies in the top 25% for a culture of integrity generated shareholder returns of 8.8%, while companies in the bottom 25% experienced losses of 7.4%, illustrating that it is not only good for the individual spirit to act in a moral fashion, but it is good for the company as a whole.

A CEB survey of half a million employees in more than 85 countries found that companies with strong ethical cultures experienced 10 times fewer incidents of employee misconduct than do companies with weak ethical cultures ("Research reveals," 2010). In addition, firms with cultures that encouraged open communications with employees realized greater shareholder returns by an average of 5% than firms with cultures that did not encourage open communications with employees. Finally, managers that were able to lead in an ethical fashion and cultivate trust improved employee performance by 12%. The CEB identified seven key attributes that formed an integrity index: comfort in speaking up, trust in colleagues, direct manager leadership, tone at the top, clarity of expectations, openness of communication, and organizational justice ("See something, say something," 2012; "How corporate integrity helps your bottom line," 2012).

Conclusion

If profitability is king, then integrity, as our model shows, is the path for companies to follow in order to retain excellent employees and return higher profits to the company and to stockholders. As noted by Becker (2009, p. 80), integrity "functions as a benchmark for business by setting consistent ethical standards for individual, corporate, and market performance. . . . It sharpens our views for the dangers of a free-market economy detached from the ethical basis of the society within which it operates." In the aftermath of the largest financial nightmare since the Great Depression, where the world has seen century old companies wither under the spotlight of financial misdeeds (e.g., Lehman Bros.) and business strategies that satisfied the consumer, but were ignorant or dismissive of environmental costs (e.g., Chrysler and General Motors), companies must take a long-term view of what is best for their stakeholders and how to give those stakeholders value for the actions, products, and services that they deliver.

It is not just the stockholders who support the company, as they are usually not the majority of the customers of the company. It is the network of business partners, the suppliers, distributors, customers, communities, and the public, which have needs that must be carefully considered. Although one stakeholder group may wish for a certain type of good or service, if that good or service is not good for the community or the environment in a long-term view, that would not be a good exchange to make as a major proportion of the company's business activities. While it is important to listen to the consumer, it is also important to educate the consumer on products that may be better for the long-term health and well-being of all. "When workers take pride in their profession and find value and meaning in the mission of the firm, they inevitably do a better job of innovating, pleasing customers, and meeting the needs of the community and other stakeholders" (Allio, 2011). The company survives and gains profitability.

References

Aldrich, D. P. (2013). Rethinking civil society-state relations in Japan after the Fukushima accident. *Polity*, *45*(2), 249–264.

Allio, R. J. (2011). Reinventing management purpose: The radical and virtuous alternatives, *Strategy and Leadership*, *39*(4), 4–11.

Beaumier, C. & DeLoach, J. (2011). Ten common risk management failures and how to avoid them. *Business Credit*, *113*(8), 46–48, 50–52.

Becker, G. K. (2009). Integrity as moral ideal and business benchmark. *Journal of International Business Ethics*, *2*(2), 70–84, 88.

Becker, T. E. (1998). Integrity in organizations: Beyond honesty and conscientiousness. *Academy of Management Review*, *23*(1), 154–161.

Belal, A. R. & Roberts, R. W. (2010). Stakeholders' perceptions of corporate social reporting in Bangladesh. *Journal of Business Ethics*, *97*(2), 311–324.

Blake's bio. (2012). Toms.com. Retrieved from www.toms.com/blakes-bio.

Brenner, Z., Dambaugh, L., Hill, E., Roberts, C., & Vollers, D. (2008). The evolution of clinical nurse advancement. *Nursing Management*, *39*(10), 28.

Burrough, B., Cohan, W.D., & McLean, B. (2012, February). Jon Corzine's riskiest business. *Vanity Fair*, 95–101, 149–153.

Chapman, P. (2009). Before the fall. *Traders Magazine*, *22* (292), 30.

Chen, D. W. & Jones, R. G. (2006, March 22). Corzine proposes increased taxes and cost cutting. *New York Times*, 1.

Christman, L. (1963). Small group behavior: As applied to nursing in the hospital setting. *Nursing Forum*, 2(2), 98–111.

Collier, J. & Esteban, R. (1999). Governance in the participative organisation: Freedom, creativity and ethics. *Journal of Business Ethics*, 21(2) 173–188.

Daly, M. (2011, December 12). Where's the money, Jon? With the collapse of MF Global, Jon Corzine stands in the middle of the missing-billion-dollar crossfire. *Newsweek*, 158(24), 57.

DiColo, J. A. & Strumpf, D. (2011, December 7). MF Global collapse felt in farm country; hedging positions caught up in firm's bankruptcy filing. *Wall Street Journal*, C1.

Durocher, L. (1975). *Nice guys finish last*. Simon and Schuster. New York.

Eaglesham, J. & Das, A. (2016, May 26). 7 years, 156 cases, few convictions. *Wall Street Journal*, C1.

Forelle, C. (2008, October 25). The financial crisis: Iceland borrows $2 billion from IMF. *Wall Street Journal*, 9.

Friday, N. M. (2007, January 26). A shoe that fits so many souls *Time Magazine*. Retrieved from www.time.com/time/magazine/article/0,9171,1582305-1,00.html

Gentry, W. A., Cullen, K. L., Sosik, J. J., Chun, J. U., Leupold, C. R., & Tonidandel, S. (2013). Integrity's place among the character strengths of middle-level managers and top-level executives. *Leadership Quarterly*, 24(3), 395.

Gosling, M. & Huang, H. J. (2009). The fit between integrity and integrative social contracts theory. *Journal of Business Ethics*, 90, 407–417.

Haigh, M. M. & Brubaker, P. (2010). Examining how image restoration strategy impacts perceptions of corporate social responsibility, organization-public relationships, and source credibility. *Corporate Communications*, 15(4), 453.

Houston, B. (2008). Transition 'innovation team' agenda, Inside the Beltway, American Ceramic Society. *American Ceramic Society Bulletin*, 88(1), 50.

How corporate integrity helps your bottom line (2012). Gelman, Rosenberg & Freedman. Retrieved from www.grfcpa.com/resources/articles/corporate-integrity-helps-your-bottom-line

Hume, L. (2003, November 14). Senator's bill to aim for fund reform: Measure follows Sarbanes-Oxley. *The Bond Buyer*, 346(31762), 1.

Integrity in Business. (1881). *The Manufacturer and Builder*, 13(1), 19. Retrieved from http://lcweb2.loc.gov/cgi-bin/query/r?ammem/ncps:@field(DOCID+@lit(ABS1821-0013-57))::.

Iwu-Egwuonwu, R. (2011). Behavioral governance, accounting and corporate governance quality. *Journal of Economics and International Finance*, 3(1), 1–12.

Jacobs-Lustig, M. (2001). *No University Is an Island: Saving Academic Freedom* [book review]. *Libraries and the Academy*, 11(3), 872–873.

Kakutani, M. (2009, August 23). Man of steal, two authors attempt to explain what went wrong with Wall Street's Superman. *South Florida Sun-Sentinel*, G3.

Kaptein, M. (2009). Ethics programs and ethical culture: A next stage in unraveling their multi-faceted relationship. *Journal of Business Ethics*, 89(2), 261–281.

Lerman, E. (2009, April 15). PhiLAnthropist Interview: TOMS shoes founder Blake Mycoskie plans to give away 300,000 pairs in 2009. *Laist*. Retrieved from http://laist.com/2009/04/15/what_happens_when_you_travel.php

Lucchetti, A. & Spector, M. (2011, December 31). The unraveling of MF Global—with $1.2 billion still missing, Corzine's aggressive strategy comes in focus. *Wall Street Journal*, B1.

McBride, S. (2009). Something wicked this way comes: The United States Government's response to unsafe imported Chinese toys and subsidized Chinese exports. *Texas International Law Journal, 45*(1), 233–295.

McDonald, P. R. (2011). Is Blake Mycoskie of TOMS an evangelical? *LA Weekly News.* Retrieved from www.laweekly.com/2011-07-28/news/is-blake-mycoskie-of-toms-an-evangelical/.

McGrew, D. (1999). Engineers & the new economy. *Prism Online,* 1–5.

McTiernan, S. (2003). *Stakeholder perceptions of the effectiveness of nonprofit organizations.* White Paper, Weatherhead School of Business, Case Western University, Cleveland, OH.

Matsumura, A. (2012). *Why nuclear scientists have missed the danger of the spent fuel pools.* Finding the Missing Link, Scientific blog. Retrieved from http://akiomatsumura.com/2012/01/lack-of-training-on-the-catastrophic-accident-potential-at-spent-fuel-pools.html.

Mattel issues new massive China toy recall (2007, August 14). *Associated Press.* Retrieved from www.msnbc.msn.com/id/20254745/ns/business-consumer_news/t/mattel-issues-new-massive-china-toy-recall.

Misa. (2010, October 2). Villagers barter goats for bag of maize. *The Zimbabwean.* Retrieved from http://thezimbabwean.co/2010/10/villagers-barter-goats-for-bag-of-maize/

Monga, M. (2016). Integrity and its antecedent: A unified conceptual framework of integrity. *The Journal of Developing Areas, 50*(5), 415–421.

Nobel, C. (2016, October 24). Bernie Madoff explains himself. *Harvard Business School Working Knowledge.* Retrieved from http://hbswk.hbs.edu/item/bernie-madoff-explains-himself.

Noelliste, M. (2013). Integrity: An intrapersonal perspective. *Human Resource Development Review, 12*(4), 474.

Nöggerath, J., Geller, R. J., & Gusiakov, V. K. (2011, September 1). Fukushima, the myth of safety, the reality of geoscience. *Bulletin of the Atomic Scientists, 67*(5). Retrieved from http://thebulletin.org/2011/september/fukushima-myth-safety-reality-geoscience.

Palanski, M. E. & Yammarino, F. J. (2007). Integrity and leadership: Clearing the conceptual confusion. *European Management Journal, 25*(3), 171–184.

Pomfret, J. (2008, December 14). Chinese toy factories take hit; signs of sharp economic slowdown everywhere. *The Province,* 46.

Predmore, C. E., Manduley, A. R., Abdulahad, F., & Goma, A. (2005). Management of product augmentation in the legal environment: Impact of Sarbanes Oxley. *Proceedings of the 13th Annual International Conference of the Association of Employment Practices and Policies,* October 6–8, Baltimore, MD.

Predmore, C. E. & Greene, F. D. (2008). Ethical idiosyncratic credit-don't waste that rosy evaluation: Balancing beliefs and value. In S. Natale (Ed.), *Beatitudes past utterance: Balancing life, career, values, ethics* (Vol 12, pp. 129–134). New York: Global Scholarly Publications.

Prois, J. (2011). *TOMS Founder, Blake Mycoskie, discusses new book 'Start Something that Matters', posted 9/16/11.* Retrieved from www.huffingtonpost.com/2011/09/ 16/toms-founder-blake-mycosk_n_966452.html.

Ramirez, K. (2010). *TOMS shoes entrepreneur Blake Mycoskie talks about his passions, posted 11/8/10.* Retrieved from www.dallasnews.com/lifestyles/style/fashion/20101103-TOMS-shoes-entrepreneur-Blake-Mycoskie-talks-7600.ece.

Research reveals that integrity drives corporate performance: Companies with weak ethical cultures experience 10x more misconduct than those with strong one;

Corporate Executive Board uncovers key drivers of cultural integrity and its role in risk; outlines corrective actions to increase corporate performance and shareholder return. (2010, September 15). *PR Newswire.*

Rok, B. (2009). Ethical context of the participative leadership model: Taking people into account. *Corporate Governance, 9*(4), 461–472.

Rolph, D., (2008). *Reputation, celebrity and defamation law.* Abingdon, Oxon, UK: Ashgate Publishing Group.

S&P Asgns STEERS Credt Bkd Tr Ser 2002–4 KO Certs Rtg. (2002, March 8). *Business Wire*: 1.

Scott, M. (2011, June 2). Is your company building 'integrity capital? *Corporate Secretary: Governance, Risk and Compliance.* Retrieved from www.corporatesecretary.com/ articles/compliance-and-ethics/11914/your-company-building-integrity-capital/.

See Something, Say Something (2012). *NYSE Magazine.* Retrieved from www.nyse magazine.com/ backpage

Sigler, K. J. (1999). Challenges of employee retention. *Management Research, 22*(10), 1–5.

Simons, T. L. (1999). Behavioral integrity as a critical ingredient for transformational leadership. *Journal of Organizational Change Management, 2*(2), 89–104.

Simons, T., Leroy, H., Collewaert, V., & Masschelein, S. (2015). How leader alignment of words and deeds affects followers: A meta-analysis of behavioral integrity research. *Journal of Business Ethics, 132*(4), 831–844.

Sosik, J. J., Gentry, W. A., & Chun, J. U. (2012). The value of virtue in the upper echelons: A multisource examination of executive character strengths and performance. *Leadership Quarterly, 23*(3), 367.

Study: Japan nuclear plant chiefs downplayed evidence of tsunami risk. (2011, March 27). *Associated Press.* Retrieved from www.haaretz.com/news/international/ study-japan-nuclear-plant-chiefs-downplayed-evidence-of-tsunami-risk-1.352189.

Trausch, S. (1981, January 25). Search for quality; demanding more and getting less from US products. *Boston Globe*, 1.

Vaiman, V., Sigurjonsson, T., & Davidsson, P. (2011). Weak business culture as an antecedent of economic crisis: The case of Iceland. *Journal of Business Ethics, 98*(2), 259–272.

Young, G. & Hasler, D. S. (2010). Managing reputational risks: Using risk management for business ethics and reputational capital. *Strategic Finance, 92*(5), 37–47.

Zimbabwe: Farm animals bartered to stave off hunger (2008, September 30). *IRIN Africa.* Retrieved from www.irinnews.org/report.aspx?ReportId=80674

5 The Role of Family Values in the Integrity of Family Business

Claire Seaman and Richard Bent

Introduction

Business integrity is a key area for 21st century research (Verschoor, 2004; Werhane, 2015). This is, in part, highlighted by recent ethical failures and the consequent regulatory reforms and, in part, a much wider debate about the role of business in society that is sometimes expressed in economic terms and sometimes defined by a broader set of parameters including the social good (Brown, 2006). Similarly, the role of the family in developing values and a sense of integrity within individuals is relatively well researched in a psychological context, with distinct *foci* on the development of values in children, work values in parents, and the links between early family experience and the development of socially undesirable, sometimes criminal, behavior (Johnson, 2005). Furthermore, organizational research that has focused on the interaction between family and business has tended to focus on the relationship between the individual's work values and their family commitments out with the business (Rothausen, 1999). While there is certainly evidence that family has an impact on the work values of individual employees (Johnson, 2005; Rothausen, 1999), the influence of the family within the business on the development of business integrity remains a current gap.

The economic and social backdrop to this chapter, however, is relatively well established: Families run businesses. Indeed, family businesses are the most common form of business worldwide, contributing to economies across communities, countries, and geopolitical boundaries (Poutziouris, Smyrnios, & Klein, 2006; Seaman, Bent, & Unis, 2015, 2016). While the values of the individuals who lead businesses have a general importance in the development of business integrity, in a family business there are commonly a number of individuals whose family values have some degree of commonality and hence are likely to exert greater combined influence on the development of business integrity within the organization. This chapter proposes that the combined influence of a number of different family members may contribute to the development of business integrity and would usefully merit further research.

Research that considers the influence of family values in the development of business integrity in a family business context is at an early stage, but by linking work from a number of different fields and developing a model that includes the influence of family values on the development of business integrity in a family business setting, this chapter considers the area as one ripe for future research. The heterogeneous nature of family business is acknowledged as one challenge, although the extant literature has found ways to include values within scales such as the Family: Power— Experience—Culture (F-PEC) scale, which is widely used to quantify family influence (Astrachan, Klein, & Smyrnios, 2004). Providing similar frameworks to link the family influence with business integrity builds on Petrick and Quinn (2000) and is proposed here as a fruitful area for future research. This chapter sets out, therefore, to provide a theoretical contribution, drawing on literature from a variety of fields to propose a model that integrates family values into the development of business integrity. Drawing on the work of Petrick and Quinn (2000), the four dimensions of the integrity construct (process, judgment, development, and system) are extended to bridge a gap that currently exists between business integrity research and family systems theory. As part of this process we will consider four broad ideas: business integrity, its definitions and importance, family business, extant research on family business values, and existing models of business integrity. By incorporating the family business dimension into models of business integrity, we allow scope for future researchers to accommodate the family within future empirical research that considers business integrity in a family business context. As a prelude to the more substantive discussion, therefore, some family business context is merited.

Family Businesses and Integrity

Family Business

The importance of family businesses, in economic terms, has been researched worldwide. Family businesses form a cornerstone of the economies of most developed countries and appear to provide a degree of community and social stability (IFB, 2008; Kets de Vries, Carlock, & Florent-Treacy, 2007, p. xiii; Poutzioris, 2006). Estimates of the predominance of family business vary, in part because of a lack of definitional clarity, but numerous authors have estimated that somewhere between 65% and 80% of businesses have families at the core of the business (Collins & O'Regan, 2010; Collins, O'Regan, Hughes, & Tucker, 2010; Seaman, McQuaid, & Pearson, 2014, Seaman et al., 2015, 2016).

This lack of clarity or agreement about what a family business actually is, merits some consideration in the context of the links between family values and the development of business integrity. In trying to define a family business, Sharma, Chrisman, and Chua (1997) and Chua, Chrisman, and Sharma (1999) identified no less than 34 operating definitions (Getz, Carlson, & Morrison, 2004), albeit with common themes that included the definition of a business as a profit making operation, at least in intent (Getz et al., 2004, p. 4) and the construct that one family has a predominant level of control and may also be employed within the business (Getz et al., 2004, pp. 4–5). Subsequent work by Sharma (2004) and Collins and O'Regan (2011) only served to reinforce the challenge presented by definition. Indeed, researchers have tried to circumvent the definitional issues by developing scales that focus instead on levels of family engagement (Astrachan et al., 2004), including such constructs as familieness and familiarity, but in the context of the current discussion the definitional challenges appear to be less important than the precept that where one family has a predominant level of control over the business, the values of that family will contribute to perceived business integrity and acceptable behavior within that business (Phan & Butler, 2008).

Business Integrity: Definitions and Importance

Although the importance of business integrity is relatively widely acknowledged and indeed has generated a certain media profile in recent years, defining *business integrity* has provoked some debate. Koehn (2005) highlights the interpretation of integrity as a consistent set of behaviors that have a relationship with moral worth, drawing on a number of different religious frameworks as possible platforms for the development of values that lead to individuals behaving with integrity. Importantly, however, Koehn (2005) also highlights that one reason why it is not sufficient to define integrity as meaning consistent behavior: Behavior can be consistently "bad" or can consistently fall short of the ethical standards regarded as normal within the societal context. There is a strong parallel here with some of the discussion within family business writing where the assumption that a family business is in some way inherently superior in terms of moral or social behavior terms is surprisingly common. In arguing that family values influence the development of business integrity in a family business context it should in no sense be assumed that a family business will always behave with greater integrity than its corporate equivalent. Rather, and more simply, the family values influence business integrity for better or worse. In this context, also, business integrity is distinct from family integrity. Family integrity, discussed in the context of later life by King and Wynne (2004), is a construct focused on multigenerational relationships past, present, and future and the degree of relationship satisfaction felt by family members. While family integrity may be felt by individuals engaged with family businesses, this is distinct from the integrity frameworks that influence their business behavior, albeit an area where exploring the potential links would be an interesting area of research.

Family, Family Values, and Family Business Integrity

Defining a family also presents some challenges for researchers. Social historians, anthropologists, and psychologists have described a wide variety of forms and norms for that entity described as "family," over a wide variety of historical periods and social settings (Bloch & Harrari, 1996; Doherty & Boss, 1991). Indeed, the word *family* is derived from the Latin *familia*, meaning "household servants, family" and closely linked to *famulus* (servant). In more recent times, there is some evidence that the word *family* was used to mean a group of slaves (Coontz, 1993), but more recent commentary has reached general agreement that a family is

> a group of individuals linked by blood, living arrangements, marriage or civil partnership who consider themselves to be family, who often choose to spend time together and may live together.
>
> (Adapted from: *Family: Business Dictionary*, 2016)

While the historical perspective is interesting, there are also a variety of different contexts where the word *family* is used in the 21st century, including the familial analogy in business (Seaman et al., 2014) and, indeed, varying social structures in countries where religion or tribal affiliation form a core societal unit. This definitional debate is critical, however, because it provides a backdrop to the understanding that family norms and values can only be fairly considered in the context of the time and place in which they are formulated (Bloch & Harrari, 1996) and lends weight to ongoing discussion in the family business literature about the importance of context in family business research (Seaman et al., 2016).

Values are defined as the "principles or standards of behavior; one's judgment of what is important in life" (Oxford Dictionaries, 2016), but family business values initially received scant attention in family business research that, in its early stages, focused heavily on economic contribution, definitional challenges, and the interactional systems between the family and the business (Davis & Stern, 1981; Distelberg & Blow, 2010; Distelberg & Sorenson, 2009; Taguiri & Davis, 1982). However, as the theoretical basis for family business research developed, an increasing understanding of the heterogeneous nature of family businesses worldwide (Distelberg & Blow, 2010) and the importance of the context in which the family and the business exist (Seaman et al., 2016) has developed and the importance of family values in business comes to the fore (Phan & Butler, 2008). The heterogeneity of family businesses is in part a function of their context; by considering the context in which the family business operates, questions such as why the family are in business and, indeed, whether they perceive being in business as a good thing come to the fore and offer insight into the wide range of family circumstances that underpin the family in business (Seaman et al., 2015, 2016). The study of family business context among Asian-owned family businesses in Scotland, for example, was developed, in part, as a response to research findings that indicated that some smaller family businesses did not see business growth as their primary objective and, indeed, did not always view succession by a family member as a desirable outcome

(Seaman et al., 2015, 2016). Clear evidence has been identified that within certain communities the family felt they had been pushed into starting a business through lack of alternative opportunities and that the purpose of the business was to support the family so that the next generation could have a wider range of educational and career choices (Seaman et al., 2015; Welsh, Seaman, Ingram, & Bent, 2006). This research links to work on migrant entrepreneurship (Chapanti & Greene, 2002; Jamal, Penaloza, & Laroche, 2015) and stands parallel to an understanding that for many family businesses succession remains a highly desirable goal (GGiS, 2014) highlights the importance of family values in business decision making.

In terms of business integrity research, there is a dearth of research-based evidence that links directly to family business. Research that focuses specifically on family business ethics is also sparse, but there is some comparative work from the United States that considers the mission statements of family businesses and corporate entities from within and outside of the United States (Blodgett, Dumas, & Zanzi, 2011). The results from Blodgett et al. (2011) suggest that there is a distinctly higher "ethical" flavor to the mission statements of family businesses; the challenge in integrating this research lies in the presumed link between the mission statement of an individual business and the likely behavior in which that business might engage. Distinct differences in the foci between family businesses from different countries also emerged that, while of less direct relevance here, might reasonably prompt future researchers to explore the contextual links between business culture, fashion, the development of mission statements, and the links to family business in a wider sense.

Modeling Business Integrity

Business integrity is a social construct that exists within the culture and communities within which the business operates and probably varies over time and due to the influence of key individuals. However, within this, attempts have been made to model factors that contribute to the development of business integrity, including an initial model presented by Petrick and Quinn (2000). The initial modeling work carried out by Patrick and Quinn (2000) regarded business integrity as an intangible strategic asset, viewing the integrity capacity as part of the process for continual process alignment that achieves balanced judgment. Key here is the timeframe within which competitive advantage is viewed. Where short-term competitive advantage is desired, Petrick and Quinn (2000) argued, appealing to customers in external targeted markets is a reasonable approach. However, where a longer term view is taken of sustainable strategic competitive advantage, the core capability differentials incorporated by the long-term responsible management of tangible and intangible capital become essential (Petrick & Quinn, 2000). Family businesses have been shown to take a longer term strategic view in a variety of research (Braidford, Houston, Allinson, & Stone, 2008;

Phan & Butler, 2008) and this may in part explain their differences from corporate-focused entities. Looking at the initial model of global competitive advantage from Petrick and Quinn (2000, Figure 5.1), the absence of family within the core capability differentials would appear to represent an area where adaptation of the model would be useful (Figure 5.2).

The key focus of Figure 5.2, in this context, is the perception that family forms a key capability differential that should be factored into future research. How this family dimension manifests itself can be evidenced from research in a variety of areas, including family capital (Sorenson & Bierman, 2009), networks (Seaman et al., 2014), the influence of family on business governance and decision making (Chami, 2001), and, indeed, values per se (Phan & Butler, 2008). When those capability differentials are considered in the wider context of the integrity constructs (Figure 5.3), the potential for the extension of the model from Petrick and Quinn (2000) that factors in the family business research dimension becomes apparent (Figure 5.4).

Key here is that there are four dimensions to business integrity: character, systems, rules, and results. The challenge for incorporating family business into the four dimensions is that the evidence suggests that all four dimensions will be influenced by family values, albeit to differing and largely unresearched extents. We propose here that family business values are likely to

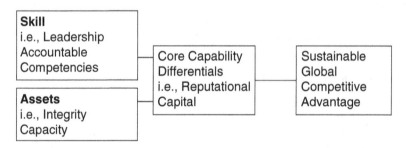

Figure 5.1 The Strategic Resource Model of Global Competitive Advantage

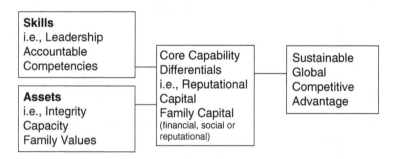

Figure 5.2 The Family Business Strategic Resource Model of Global Advantage

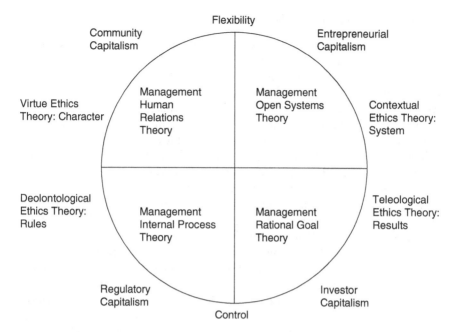

Figure 5.3 Judgment Integrity: Balanced Economics, Management, and Ethics Theories

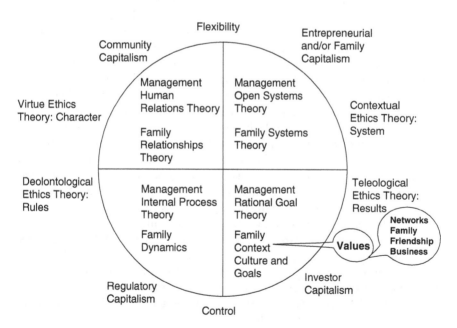

Figure 5.4 Judgment Integrity: Balanced Economics, Management, Ethics, and Values in Family Business

have their greatest impact on the development of goals within the family and the business. It is likely that an impact will also be seen on the internal rules developed within the business but that the impact of the family on the external rules with which the business must comply is likely to be far less. The exception here is around succession where specific rules (laws) for family business succession and inheritance may apply in certain countries. Similarly, an impact of the family business values on the results a business achieves cannot be ruled out, but the direct effect may be less obvious and, indeed, more difficult to quantify. Furthermore, the impact of family business values on the business may not always be an obviously positive effect. Family values that mitigate against, for example, short-term approaches (Braidford et al., 2008; Ernst & Young, 2014) or unsustainable approaches (Ernst & Young, 2014) may actually have a negative effect on short-term profitability, although the longer term impact on stakeholder value may be positive. A reworking of the original model of integrity constructs to include key areas of family business theory, therefore, is presented as Figure 5.4.

If business integrity is viewed as the decision-making process that develops from aspects covered in the wider field of business and management research, it follows that family business-specific research should be factored in a similar manner. In addition, values have been researched in family business and organizational contexts in their own right (Aranof, 2004; Aranof & Ward, 2001; Brown & Toyoki, 2013; Brundin, Florin, & Melin, 2014; Chirico & Salvato, 2014; Garcia-Alvarez & Lopez-Sintas, 2001; Koiranen, 2002; Yan & Sorenson, 2006) and research highlights both the impact of the individuals' values on the organization and the importance of family business values to the family business in a wider sense.

Family values have been defined as those values commonly learned within a traditional family unit, typically those of high moral standards and discipline (Oxford Dictionaries, 2016), but the capacity for families' behaviors that range from the highest moral standards to the depths of depravity is well established. Within family business research, history is replete with examples of spectacular ascents of family businesses, alongside numerous accounts of family businesses brought down by bitter feuds among family members, disappointed expectations between generations, and tragic sagas of later generations unable to manage their wealth (Bertrand & Schoer, 2006). A useful perspective in the family business values debate is added by García-Álvarez and López-Sintas (2001), who highlight that although family firms are commonly associated with a traditional way of doing business, the heterogeneity of first-generation family firms can be explored by building a taxonomy of four groups of founders based on values. By examining heterogeneity of family business through the prism of family values, García-Álvarez and López-Sintas (2001) also highlight the possibility that family values may diverge from that of the first generation as new generations are born into the family and, indeed, the partners of second and subsequent generations exert their influence. In part, this acceptance of the heterogeneity of family businesses and indeed of family values serves as a useful starting point in adopting a distinct part of the definition of values from Oxford Dictionaries: "Principles or standards of behavior; one's judgment of what is important in life: they internalize their parents' rules and values."

By applying the definition of values as the internalization of priorities learned from the parents, the potential role of family values in the development of family business integrity becomes clearer. The questions that remain include where within current models family values are best positioned, and the evidence to date suggests that they form part of the family context and culture (Seaman et al., 2015), which in turn contribute to the development of family business goals. The role of the family in developing values can be expressed in a number of ways, but in this context it is helpful to view the family as a network of individuals with varying levels of influence, building on early work on family structure by Sussman and Burchinal (1962).

Viewing the family as a kinship network highlights the mutual assistance provided by kin, which we would regard here as a contributor to the family business dimension. The influence exerted by the family network is also useful because it reminds us that within many family businesses, especially smaller and medium-sized enterprises, family, business, and friendship networks are not distinct (Seaman et al., 2014). While the extant literature alerts us to the vital importance of family in the development of values, the role of business contacts and social/friendship networks should not be overlooked. As we consider the development of values and their contribution to 21st-century business integrity, networks deserve a special mention simply because of the fast pace of change within network development, often facilitated by technology. Networks, within the family, business and friendship dimension, have always existed, usually characterized as a series of nodes (individuals) linked by ties. What modern technology has offered is often characterized as an extension of the number of individuals with whom regular contact and information sharing is available (Lin & Lu, 2011). The expansion of networks and the relative ease with which contact can be maintained with geographically remote family and friends may well act as an influencer in terms of value development, but this is an area where further research would be valuable. Including values within the current model of judgment integrity can identified as Figure 5.4.

By identifying values as a key contributor to the development of business integrity within a family business context and highlighting the possible contributing role of networks in the developing those values, an area of research is opened up that has the potential to contribute to our understanding of the development business integrity as a practical manifestation of ethics.

Conclusion

This chapter has set out the case for the inclusion of family values and, indeed, research that includes the family business dimension within current models of business integrity and the revised models presented here reflect this. The testing of those models within empirical research would merit further research and is currently being planned in the context of family businesses in Scotland, but the literature reviewed allows a number of preliminary conclusions to be drawn.

One conclusion is that, if we accept that family values are an internalization of parental/family influence, the potential for these values to exert either a positive or negative force is clear. The adage that "one person's ethical objection is another person's artificial barrier" probably carries some weight here, but by acknowledging how much ethical values vary we should not lose sight of the impact a number of individuals from the same family, commonly with variations of the same value system, may have on the business. Furthermore, formalized governance structures that seek to ensure that the next generation joins the business when they have sufficient experience and are likely to work well within the business may reinforce this effect as the values of the next generation are effectively screened before they join the business.

A second conclusion and area for future research would be around the potential spheres of influence that contribute to family values, including interaction with networks. Again, accepting that family values are an internalization of parental/family influence, the changing patterns of family influence in the 21st century are notable. In many communities, rising levels of divorce and remarriage, alongside higher levels of geographical mobility, have fundamentally changed the pattern of family life. Different patterns of family life may result in larger numbers of family members being part of the immediate circle of influence and contact with the wider family circle has been facilitated via different online routes and media. Furthermore, the widespread use of technology probably means that for many individuals within the family business checking facts has never been easier, although checking the veracity of those facts may well prove more challenging.

A further conclusion can be drawn from the links highlighted between the initial constructions of business integrity and family values and we propose that, in a family business setting, the role of the family values is likely to be of major importance. This should not be confused with the assumption that family businesses are in some way better than their corporate equivalents. Although some of the business and professional dialogue around family businesses is prone to the assumption that a business with a family component will in some way be morally or socially superior to corporate business, there would appear to be limited robust evidence for this. Rather, it is more likely the family business and its constructs of integrity will reflect, to some extent, the core family values, for good or ill. Although constructs of business integrity may vary widely between and within families, and may be tacitly reinforced by formalized governance mechanisms, the family in business plays a role in 65% to 80% of businesses worldwide. That alone should merit further research, using the models developed as the basis for future empirical research with family businesses as a mechanism for factoring family business values into future research on business integrity. As awareness of business integrity and its role in the development of the future business environment develops, so too should an evidence-based understanding of the manner in which ideas of business integrity are socially constructed within family businesses, as well as within corporate organizations where the role of family influence on individuals in the workplace is considered.

References

Aranof, C. E. (2004). Self-perpetuation family organization built on values: Necessary condition for long-term family business survival. *Family Business Review*, 17(1), 55–59.

Aranof, C. E. & Ward, J. L. (2001). *Family business values: How to ensure a legacy of continuity and success*. Marinetta, GA: Family Enterprise Publishers.

Astrachan, J., Klein, S. B., & Smyrnios, K. X. (2004). The F-PEC scale of family influence: A proposal for solving the family business definition problem. *Family Business Review*, 15(1), 45–58.

Bertrand, M. & Schoer, A. (2006). The role of family in family firms. *The Journal of Economic Perspectives*, 20(2), 73–96.

Bloch, S. & Harrari, E. (1996). Working with the family: The role of values. *American Journal of Psychotherapy*, 50(3), 274–288.

Blodgett, M. S., Dumas, C., & Zanzi, A. (2011). Emerging trends in global ethics: A comparative study of U.S. and international family business values. *Journal of Business Ethics*, 99(2), 29–38.

Braidford, P., Houston, M., Allinson, G., & Stone, I. (2008). *Research into family businesses*. BIS Research Paper 172. London, UK: Department of Business and Innovation.

Brown, A. D. & Toyoki, S. (2013). Identity, work and legitimacy. *Organization Studies*, 34(5), 875–896.

Brown, M. T. (2006). Corporate integrity and public interest: A relational approach to business ethics and leadership. *Journal of Business Ethics*, 66(4), 11–18.

Brundin, E., Florin Samuelsson, E., & Melin, L. (2014). Family ownership logic: Framing the core characteristics of family businesses. *Journal of Management & Organization*, 20(7), 6–37.

Chami, R. (2001). *What is different about family businesses?* IMF Working Paper. Washington, DC: International Monetary Fund.

Chapanti, R. & Greene, P. G. (2002). Who are the ethnic entrepreneurs? A study of entrepreneurs, ethnic involvement and business characteristics. *Journal of Small Business Management*, 40(2), 126–143.

Chirico, F. & Salvato, C. (2014). Knowledge internalization and product development in family firms: When relational and affective factors matter. *Entrepreneurship Theory and Practice*, 40(1), 201–229.

Chua, J., Chrisman, J. J., & Sharma, P. (1999). Defining the family business by behavior. *Entrepreneurship Theory and Practice, 23*(4), 19–39.

Collins, L. & O'Regan, N. (2010). The evolving field of family business. *Journal of Family Business Management, 1*(1), 5–13.

Collins, L., O'Regan, N., Hughes, T., & Tucker, J. (2010). Strategic thinking in family businesses. *Strategic Change, 19*(1–2), 57–76.

Collins, L. & O'Regan, N. (2011). Editorial: The evolving field of family business. *Journal of Family Business Management, 1*(1), 5–13.

Coontz, S. (1993). The way we never were: American families and the nostalgia trap. New York: Basic Books.

Davis, P. & Stern, D. (1981). Adaptation, survival, and growth of the family business: An integrated systems perspective. *Human Relations, 34*(3), 207–234.

Distelberg, B. & Blow, A. (2010). The role of values and unity in family business. *Journal of Family Economic Issues, 31*(1), 427–441.

Distelberg, B. & Sorenson, R. (2009). A systematic examination of family business: A focus on values, resource flows and adaptation. *Family Business Review, 22*(4), 65–81.

Doherty, W. J. & Boss, P. G. (1991). Ethics and values in family therapy. In S. Gurman & D. P. Kniskern (Eds.), *Handbook of family therapy* (2nd ed., pp. 606–637). New York: Brunner/Mazel.

Ernst, & Young (2014). *Built to last: Family businesses lead the way to sustainable growth.* Retrieved from www.ey.com/Publication/vwLUAssets/EY-Built-to-last-family-businesses-lead-the-way-to-sustainable-growth/$FILE/EY-Built-to-last-family-businesses-lead-the-way-to-sustainable-growth.pdf.

Family (2016, October 13). *Business Dictionary.com.* Retrieved from Business Dictionary.com website: www.businessdictionary.com/definition/family.html.

García-Álvarez Ercilia & López-Sintas, J. (2001). A taxonomy of founders based on values: The root of family business heterogeneity. *Family Business Review, 14*(3), 209–230.

Getz, D., Carlson, J., & Morrison, A. (2004). *The family business in hospitality and tourism.* New York: Cabi.

GGiS (2014). *Sustainability: The challenges facing Scotland's SMEs.* Report from the Goodison Group in Scotland in partnership with Scotland's Futures Forum. Retrieved from http://scotlandfutureforum.org/assets/library/files/application/Family%20Business%20SME%20-%20Report.pdf.

Institute for Family Business (IFB) (2008). *Emotional ownership: The critical pathway between the next generation and the family firm.* Westminster, UK: Institute for Family Business Report.

Jamal, A., Penaloza, L., & Laroche, M. (Eds.) (2015). *Routledge companion to ethnic marketing.* London, UK: Routledge.

Johnson, M. K. (2005). Family roles and work values: Processes of selection and change. *Journal of Marriage and Family, 67*(2), 352–363.

Kets de Vries, M. F. R., Carlock, R. S., & Florent-Treacy, E. (2007). *Family business on the couch.* London, UK: Wiley and Sons.

King, D. A. & Wynne, L. C. (2004). The emergence of 'family integrity' in later life. *Family Process, 43*(1), 7–12.

Koehn, D. (2005). Integrity as a business asset. *Journal of Business Ethics, 58*(2), 125–136.

Koiranen, M. (2002). Over 100 years of age but still entrepreneurially active in business: Exploring the values and family characteristics of old finnish family firms. *Family Business Review, 15*(3), 175–187.

Lin, K. & Lu, H. (2011). Why people use social networking sites: An empirical study integrating network externalities and motivation theory. *Computers in Human Behavior, 27*(3), 1152–1161.

Oxford Dictionaries (2016). Definition of Family. Retrieved from https://en.oxford dictionaries.com/definition/family ; definition of Values. Retrieved from https://en.oxforddictionaries.com/definition/value ; definition of Family Values. Retrieved from https://en.oxforddictionaries.com/definition/family_values.

Petrick, J. A. & Quinn, J. F. (2000). The integrity capacity construct and moral progress in business. *Journal of Business Ethics, 23*(1), 3–18.

Phan, P. H. C. & Butler, J. E. (2008). *Theoretical developments and future research in family business: A volume in research in entrepreneurship and management.* Charlotte, NC: IAP.

Poutzioris, P. Z. (2006). The structure and performance of the UK family business PLC economy. In P. Z. Poutziouris, K. X. Smyrnios, & S.B. Klein (Eds.), *Handbook of research on family businesses* (pp. 552-574). Cheltenham, UK: Edward Elgar.

Poutzioris, P. Z., Smyrnios, K. X., & Klein, S.B. (Eds.). *Handbook of research on family businesses.* Cheltenham, UK: Edward Elgar.

Rothausen, T. (1999). 'Family' in organizational research: A review and comparison of definitions and measures. *Journal of Organizational Behavior, 20*(4), 817–836.

Seaman, C., Bent, R., & Unis, A. (2015). The future of family entrepreneurship: Family culture, education and entrepreneurial intent in Scottish Pakistani communities (Special Issue on the 'Futures of Family Entrepreneurship'). *Futures, 75,* 83–91. Retrieved from www.sciencedirect.com/science/article/pii/S0016328715300458.

Seaman, C., Bent, R., & Unis, A. (2016). The role of context: South Asian family firms in Scotland and the succession paradox (Special Issue on 'The Role of Context in Family Firms'). *International Journal of Management Practice, 9*(4), 433–447.

Seaman, C., McQuaid, R., & Pearson, M. (2014). Networks in family business: A multi-rational approach. *International Entrepreneurship and Management Journal, 10*(3), 523–537.

Sharma, P. (2004). An overview of the field of family business studies: Current status and directions for the future. *Family Business Review, 27*(1), 1–36.

Sharma, P., Chrisman, J., & Chua, J. H. (1997). Strategic management of the family business: Past research and future challenges. *Family Business Review, 10*(2), 1–35.

Sorenson, R. L. & Bierman, L. (2009). Family capital, family business and free enterprise. *Family Business Review, 22*(3), 192–195.

Sussman, M. & Burchinal, L. (1962). Kin family network: Unheralded structure in current conceptualizations of family functioning. *Marriage and Family Living, 24*(3), 231–240.

Taguiri, R. & Davis, J. A. (1982). Bivalent attributes of the family firm. *Family Business Review, 9*(3), 199–208.

Verschoor, C. (2004, July). Integrity is a strategy for performance. *Strategic Finance,* 15–17.

Welsh, R., Seaman, C., Ingram, A., & Bent, R. (2006, July 9–12). Minority ethnic business in Edinburgh: Micro-retailing, research and the development of a framework for business support systems. Budapest, Hungary: European Institute of Retailing and Services Studies.

Werhane, P. H. (2015). Competing with integrity: Richard De George and the ethics of global business. *Journal of Business Ethics*, 2(2), 737–742.

Yan, J. & Sorenson, R. (2006). The effect of Confucian values on succession in family business. *Family Business Review*, 19(3), 235–250.

6 "Doing the Right Thing" in the Banking Sector

Integrity from an Upper Echelons Perspective

Manjit Monga

Introduction

A string of corporate scandals and recent global financial crisis (GFC) stunned the world with the magnitude of ethical lapses on the part of the upper echelon executives. As the world deals with the consequences of the GFC, there is a growing public concern about business behavior, and increasingly stakeholders and the wider society expect businesses to act responsibly. In a highly competitive and complex business environment, the onus is on the senior management to navigate the organization in the right direction, and integrity appears as a vital element in responsible and effective leadership (Palanski & Yammarino, 2009; Parry & Proctor-Thomson, 2002; Peterson, 2004). Although integrity is a pervasive and sought-after attribute among managers and employees alike, there is no consensus in the management literature on the meaning of integrity and the implications of acting with integrity (Becker, 1998; Koehn, 2005). For example, De George (1993) defines integrity as actions that demonstrate high moral and ethical standards, and there are others like Jensen (2009) who see integrity as normatively neutral. The definitions of *integrity* often vary in scope and perspective across professional disciplines (see Chapter 1 in this volume) and even among scholars within the same academic field of study (Noelliste, 2013). The definitional opacities and uncertainties make integrity in management a contested topic (Monga, 2016).

In the management literature, the various definitions and meanings of integrity can be categorized under two broad streams: One incorporates morality and ethics as an essential ingredient for the achievement of integrity—the normative view—while the other views integrity as a morally and ethically neutral term—the Objectivist view. The moral meaning specifically describes an individual's integrity as a person's uncorrupted moral character and has been expressed in a variety of ways such as honesty, moral trustworthiness, justice, respect, fairness, caring, being true to oneself, empathy/compassion, and moral courage (Palanski & Yammarino, 2007, 2009). Some other meanings assigned to integrity in management literature are authenticity, consistency of words and deeds, wholeness, and consistency in adversity

(Palanski & Yammarino, 2007, 2009, 2011). Authenticity is described as being true to your values, or consistency between espoused and enacted values. It suggests an intrinsic quality/dimension of integrity that reflects on the intention behind the manifest actions, and implies that even though a person may appear to be acting in accordance with his or her beliefs and values, it may not necessarily be the case (Batson, Thompson, Sueferling, Whitney, & Strongman, 1999). For example, a CEO may implement environmental sustainability initiatives because he or she actually values the environment or as a covert strategy to build stock value, profit, and bonus for him- or herself under the guise of "I value the environment." Integrity as "consistency in adversity" implies the presence of adverse circumstances, temptations, or choices that may challenge a person's integrity (McFall, 1987, Carter, 1996). According to this meaning, a person of integrity will maintain moral steadfastness and not get swayed by temptations or choices even at a personal cost. McFall (1987) suggests that integrity is only exhibited in adverse circumstances. Integrity as "wholeness" denotes that there are multiple dimensions or facets, which when integrated form a whole person—a person of integrity (Badaracco & Ellsworth, 1992). In the organizational context, the notion of wholeness points toward a person's overall consistency of behavior, across time and situations. Solomon's (1992, 1999) description of integrity as a supervirtue, and a synthesis of virtues that form a coherent character, an identifiable and trustworthy personality, resonates well with the notion of wholeness.

Integrity as consistency between words and actions is used in a variety of ways. According to the normative view, the nature of the word given needs to be moral/ethical, whereas the Objectivists disregard the content of the word/commitment and focus only on the consistency between the words and actions. Simons (1999, 2002) calls it behavioral consistency and includes both the perceived fit between espoused and enacted values and the perceived promise-keeping. However, integrity purely as consistency between words and actions or explicit promise keeping means that the word given or the promise made can be of unethical or immoral nature (Audi & Murphy, 2006; Bauman, 2013). Jensen (2009; see also chapter 2 in this volume) defines *integrity* as "honoring your word." According to Jensen, integrity is morally and ethically neutral like the law of gravity. However, he also explains that honoring your word leads the way to trustworthy relationships which may result in high productivity.

Similarly, Locke and Becker (1998) define integrity as loyalty in action, to a morally justifiable code of principles and values, which promotes the long-term survival and well-being of individuals as rational beings. They argue that the criterion for moral justification is *reality*—and not merely the acceptance of the values by an individual, group, or society. They further explain integrity as practicing what one preaches regardless of emotional or social pressure and not allowing any irrational consideration to overwhelm one's rational convictions. The Objectivist view of integrity has been challenged by a few scholars (Orlitzky & Jacobs, 1998; Barry & Stephens, 1998; Jacobs, 2004)

While scholarly and practitioner interest in integrity is on the rise, the definitional inconsistencies and disagreements also make it a very complex construct for empirical studies. Unsurprisingly, there is a paucity of empirical literature research on integrity. The scant empirical research focuses on the perceptions of leader integrity by a range of follower groups, for example, Simons (1999, 2002) Simons and McLean-Parks (2000) and Craig and Gustafson (1998). Simons's (2002) behavioral integrity (BI) study uses the BI scale to investigate the integrity of leaders/managers as the perceived pattern of the alignment of their words and deeds and promise-keeping and the alignment of espoused and enacted values by the followers. Craig and Gustafson (1998) developed perceived leader integrity scale (PLIS) to study the role of ethical integrity in leader effectiveness. The PLIS scale relies on the followers' perception of the presence or absence of unethical behavior of their leaders. In the main, both scales are designed to measure managers' or leaders' integrity as perceived by their followers. There are few other studies, for example, Vogelgesang, Leroy, and Avolio (2013) who studied the relationship between leader behavioral integrity and individual follower work engagement and performance and found that leader behavioral integrity played a positive mediating role. Gentry et al. (2013) examined integrity as character strength among middle-level managers and top executives and its impact on their performance. Moorman, Darnold, and Priesemuth (2013) investigated perceived leader integrity and its impact on followers' performance and job engagement using Simons's BI Scale and added moral behavior to it in order to capture how followers make judgments of their leaders' integrity. Martin et al. (2013) conducted a cross-cultural study of how leaders demonstrate integrity in their behavior across six societies. Despite a strong agreement on the critical importance of integrity in leader effectiveness and the repeated calls for businesses to act with integrity, there is very little known about what the business leaders themselves think integrity to be and how it translates into action in the organizational context.

Although perceptions of leader integrity are important, and the body of empirical research on the employees'/followers' perceptions of their leaders is growing, the meaning of integrity from the leader's perspective is largely overlooked. It is vital that practitioners' understanding of the concept is taken into consideration because they are tasked with the implementation of integrity in the workplace. It is within this context that the current study aims to draw from senior executives' conceptualization, understanding, and application of integrity in leading their organization and decision making in the workplace. The study is was designed to generate an understanding of how senior executives actually construct integrity cognitively and (inter) subjectively, while making organizational decisions, and to uncover how they deal with integrity challenges in their industry context. This chapter reports the findings of the research conducted on the banking sector in the finance industry and elicits the informants understanding of the meaning of integrity. This study advances a better understanding of the elusive concept of integrity from a business leader's perspective, a largely unknown and unstudied topic.

In the next section I detail the research design and the methodology used. After that, I present the findings and discussion in order to answer the following research questions: *What does integrity mean to the participating senior executives in the banking industry? How do they foster and implement integrity in their organizations?*

Method

An interpretive approach was appropriate to conduct this study in order to ensure an emic understanding of integrity. Interpretivism is based on the assumption that human understanding and action are based on the interpretation of information and events by the people experiencing them (Gioia & Chittipeddi, 1991). An emic approach investigates how local people think, how they perceive and categorize the world, their rules for behavior, what has meaning for them, and how they imagine and explain things (Kottak, 2006). I wanted to understand the senior executives' view of integrity with the basic assumption that the organizational world is socially constructed by its members. The executives participating in the research construct their organizational realities and act as "knowledgeable agents" who know what they are trying to do and can explain their thoughts, intentions, and actions (Gioia, Corley, & Hamilton, 2012).

The finance industry was chosen because it is under intense scrutiny after a spate of corporate scandals like Enron, WorldCom, Lehman Brothers, and Arthur Anderson—even more so after the global financial crisis (hereafter referred to as GFC). Some observers deem moral deficiencies on part of market parties to be the cause of the recent credit crisis (Graafland & Ven, 2011). The *Greycourt White Paper* attributed the financial crisis to the collapse of moral and ethical behavior in the majority of activities within the finance industry:

> The root cause of the crisis was the gradual but ultimately complete collapse of ethical behavior across the financial industry. Once the financial industry came unmoored from its ethical base, financial firms were free to behave in ways that were in their—and especially their top executives'—short-term interest without any concern about the longer term impact on the industry's customers, on the broader American economy, or even on the firms' own employees.
>
> (*Greycourt White Paper*, 2008, p. 1)

Findings like these have resulted in increasing pressure on financial institutions worldwide to operate with extreme care and act in a responsible manner. The finance industry is a service industry and includes a range of activities such as banking, insurance, mutual funds, private equity firms, credit agencies, and so on. Broadly speaking, their role is to take part in transactions essential for economic activity by optimizing the use of available capital. Therefore, traditionally their performance has been measured by their capacity to maximize their financial assets.

Interestingly, the financial system in Australia has performed much better than the rest of the world during the GFC. In the 2010 *World Economic Forum Financial Development Report*, Australia was ranked fifth among the world's leading financial systems and capital markets.[1] The financial sector is one of the largest contributors to Australia's national output according to the Australian Bureau of Statistics (2010). By the same token, with the ever-changing economic environment and technological advances, there are new challenges and opportunities. Recognizing the need for change, the Federal Treasurer of Australia appointed a committee to undertake the financial system inquiry in November 2013, aimed at looking into how to best position Australia's financial system to meet its evolving needs and support economic growth. The final report into the inquiry was submitted to the treasurer in November 2014 with a list of recommendations to promote resilience, efficiency, and fairness of the system (Murray, Dunn, Hewson, & McNamee, 2014). The committee identified the need to enhance the credibility of the financial system and emphasized on the need to run the financial system fairly. A recommendation in the report was that the financial firms can enhance the confidence and trust by creating an environment in which financial firms treat customers fairly. It indicated that all participants must act with integrity, honesty, transparency, and nondiscrimination. Another important recommendation was to enhance the regulator independence and accountability and minimize the need for future regulation. It is important for a market economy to run effectively where participants enter into transactions with confidence that they will be treated fairly (Murray et al., 2014).

The finance industry includes a range of sub-industries such as the conventional banking, credit agencies, insurance companies, pension funds, hedge fund companies, venture capital firms, and so on. Each of these sub-industries operates in its own unique regulatory environment, with a varied set of expectations arising from the business environment.

The banking industry was purposely chosen for this study for a number of reasons. First, it has been in existence for the longest time and is well established, so it can be expected to have a rich heritage of changing practices. Second, the need to adapt to the new complex and volatile business environment would place intense pressure on the executives to be competitive and to succeed. Third, after the pre-GFC corporate disasters and the GFC, it has been under intense scrutiny by various stakeholders in the field, including the social activists. In this context, the executives can be expected to face challenges to their integrity in their everyday work life.

Purposive sampling method was applied, and current and recently retired senior executives in the banking industry in South Australia were contacted. Senior executives were chosen because of their potential to influence and shape employees behavior and to set the direction for their organization (Gioia & Chittipeddi, 1991; House, Javidan, Dorfman, & Gupta, 2004; Scandura & Dorfman, 2004). The process involved making initial phone contacts with the potential participants in 12 large banks in South Australia. Those who expressed interest in participating were followed up by e-mails providing detailed and specific information about the project with the invitation to participate.

Five senior executives from three banks expressed interest in participating in the study. The senior executives (hereafter referred to as informants) participating in the study were experienced and knowledgeable people (Gioia et al., 2012). Informant 1 is a senior executive in an organization which is a government-owned financial institution. Informant 2 had recently quit the banking industry after nearly three decades' long career and had joined a not-for-profit organization. Informant 3 is a senior executive in a large bank in Adelaide, South Australia. Informant 4 had recently taken retirement from the banking industry after a long career spanning 35 years as a bank executive. Informant 5 is the CEO of a Credit Union in Adelaide. The interviews were held in a place convenient to the informants. I met either in the official premises of the informants or in a meeting room on university premises. The interview protocol was signed by both the researcher and the research participants before the commencement of the interviews. The protocol included an undertaking by the researcher that the identity of the organization would be kept confidential, and all information provided would be kept anonymous. The informants would not be identified in any research reports or publications. The informants had the right to withdraw from the project or the interview at any time they wished to. All the informants gave the consent for the interviews to be audio recorded.

The interviews were semistructured and open-ended. Each of the interviews evolved organically. Depending on the way the conversations went, I restructured the questions to obtain the information required to answer the research question. The conversations typically started with the researcher asking the informants how they felt being in an industry which is under intense scrutiny and spotlight for irresponsible behavior. The conversation continued with the open-ended core question: "For you what is the meaning of integrity?" This was followed by a set of probes:

- "Have you ever felt that your integrity was challenged?"
- "Please describe an incident where you felt there was an integrity challenge?"
- "Give an example of integrity breach you have seen or heard about in your firm or industry."
- "How would you deal with it?"
- "How do you foster integrity in your organization?"

- "Please describe various ways you ensure that your staff act with integrity."

Each interview lasted between 60 and 90 minutes, with an average of 70 minutes. The interviews were transcribed verbatim by a professional transcription company. The informants expressed their confidence in the integrity of the process and did not wish to verify the content of the transcribed interviews.

The transcribed interviews were analyzed using thematic analysis to identify emerging themes from the conversations in order to understand the informants' view of integrity in the context of their organizations (Braun & Clarke, 2006). The process involved careful reading and rereading of the conversations by the author to identify patterns within the data and emerging themes for analysis (Braun & Clarke, 2006). The data were then analyzed by an independent researcher in order to ensure accuracy and rigor in identifying the patterns and themes in the data (Maree, 2015).

Findings and Discussion

I present the findings of the study and discussion together in this section. The purpose of this study was to understand the meaning of integrity as conceptualized by the informants in their organizational context.

The Meaning of Integrity

Integrity Is an Organizational Value

The informants perceived integrity as an element of organizational culture and claimed their organizations generally maintained high levels of integrity. The complexity in describing the meaning of integrity and multiple facets of integrity was illuminated in the conversation with the informants, for example:

> I don't think there's one single thing that would define it, I think it is behaviors, actions, ethics, connection, DNA, culture that you build with your staff, it's all those things.

All the informants viewed integrity as a vital part of their organization's values. Integrity was seen as very highly valued in their organizations and an integral element of organizational culture. Informant 1 replied that the organization was going through the review of its core values at the time of the interview, and integrity was one of the core values:

> We're doing an exercise at the moment to look at our organizational values, and integrity is one of the ones that's actually in the mix as a value, and that's something we take quite seriously. We stand and represent government, and integrity is very core to what we do and how we operate.

It was perceived as deeply engrained in the organizational culture and embedded in the work culture. One informant used DNA as a metaphor to illustrate that integrity was so deeply embedded in the organizational culture that acting with integrity is a natural part of the decision-making process for the staff in his organization:

> At the end of the day integrity is about people who run the organization and it's part of DNA and culture of business in my opinion. It's part of organizational values and we hold it very strongly. We as an organization have a set of values, they are corporate values, and we consider those values as values that are enduring, they are not values that you change because the environment no longer supports those values and it happens that integrity is actually one component of our value statement including honesty, financial prudence, and service. So, we hold those values as fundamental components that drive our decision making and there's an expectation and the tone at the top is set by the board and by me and my leadership team that we expect people to adhere to those fundamental values, integrity is one of those values.

Informants emphasized that integrity was not just talked about in their organizations but was also documented as being important. The value statements and codes of conduct of organizations substantiated the assertions of the informants. Because of reasons of confidentiality of the identity of the organizations, these value statements cannot be provided here.

Integrity Means "Doing the Right Thing"

"Doing the right thing" was the commonly used phrase by the informants to explain what the meaning of integrity was to them. The analysis of the conversations with the informants strongly indicated that integrity was seen as actions that are ethically and morally sound. For example,

> I mean integrity in my view is sort of the business ethics—your framework of how you work. It's about taking the right action which ethically sounds right to you is what integrity you think is about. It's taking the right action along with your conscience and everything.

Integrity was seen as distinct from morality and ethics yet inseparable. According to the informants, one cannot be a person of integrity if their actions are not ethically right; for example,

> "Morality, ethics and integrity. I think they are different. I think if someone lacks integrity, then their morality—they're parallel . . . If someone lacks integrity then their morality is low. Their ethics or their preparedness to live by ethics is lower. Equally if someone's integrity is very high

their morality tends to be much higher and their tendency to live by ethics is higher."

My integrity that you do the right thing. It would seem to have a pretty close relationship in my mind, really; integrity and ethics, generally if you believe you're acting with one you'd generally think you're acting with the other in mind.

The analysis of the conversations showed that for the informants, ethics and morality were positively related to integrity. Arguably, acting with integrity means ethically and morally sound behavior. The values that were consistently used as expressions of acting with integrity by all the informants were honesty, fairness, transparency, accountability, being true to your word, consistency, standing up for your values, being true to yourself, not putting your personal interest first, and being considerate toward others. For example,

> It is about transparency at the start. I think I'd add another word to that [. . .] and that would be accountability. Honesty kind of seems to go without saying, but probably should be said, as a part of it. I think you'd generally boil down integrity to be partly, if you say you're going to do something you do it, it's about your intention, and that if you're acting with integrity you're acting with the best intentions, but that doesn't always mean you're doing the right thing.
>
> I think that's really the crux of it not putting yourself first is a really important part of it. Accountability, transparency at the start. Honesty kind of seems to go without saying. Consistency. Mindfulness of impact on the wider group and putting that ahead of individual gain or individual benefit.

This analysis of the conversations strongly indicated that integrity underpins ethics and does not support the morally and ethically neutral notion of integrity suggested in the Objectivist literature. Within the Objectivist literature, Jensen (2009) has argued that integrity is morally neutral and is a matter of "a person's word—nothing more and nothing less." According to Jensen, honoring your word makes the person complete or whole and paves the way to the development of trustworthy relationships. However, the findings of this study strongly suggest that the ethicality of actions takes precedence over every other parameter to ensure integrity. For the informants, if one's actions are not ethically sound, then one cannot be acting with integrity; for example,

> Integrity, I guess you can say is being true to your word, but I say your word has to be honest as well, so there's no point in having integrity to do something, unless it's honest and ethical. And that is probably one of the dilemmas that you face that stuff is legal but is it ethical.

The expressions of the "right thing" (honesty, transparency, honoring your word, being consistent, being accountable, and being true to your values) are present in the normative stream of the management literature on integrity. It is interesting to note that the etymological meaning of integrity—*oneness* or *wholeness*—as such did not appear in any of the conversations with the informants. However, there was implicit presence in various forms such as being consistent in the way people are treated, standing up for your values, and acting in accordance with personal and organizational values. The "intentions behind actions" is an additional expression that I found in this study, which emphasizes the coherence of espoused and enacted values or beliefs of the person. In the current management literature, "intention behind the action" is also expressed as "authenticity," "being true to yourself," and "standing up for your values" (Calhoun, 1995; Baccilli, 2001; Cox et al., 2003; Howell & Avolio, 1995; Koehn, 2005; Lowe, Cordery, & Morrison, 2004; McFall, 1987; Morrison, 2001; Paine, 2005; Peterson & Seligman, 2004; Posner, 2001; Rawls, 1971; Yukl & VanFleet, 1992). "Consistency of words and actions" or "honoring your word" (Bews & Rossouw, 2002; Jensen, 2009; Kirkpatrick & Locke, 1991; Paine, 2005; Simons, 1999, 2002; Tracey & Hinkin, 1994; Worden, 2003), integrity as "ethical and moral behavior" (Newman, 2003; Posner, 2001; Trevino, Hartman, & Brown, 2000), and "consistency in adversity" or moral steadfastness (Carter, 1996; Duska, 2005; McFall, 1987; Paine, 2005; Posner, 2001; Worden, 2003) are some of the other meanings of integrity currently found in management literature. Clearly, standing alone, any of the meanings does not fully capture the essence of the etymological meaning of integrity—wholeness (Monga, 2015). The meanings assigned to acting with integrity by the informants strongly suggest that in order for a person to act with integrity, a person must be committed to a set of sound ethical and moral principles or ethical ideology and act in accordance with them consistently. Integrity is the continued enactment of ethically sound behavior that results in unbroken completeness or wholeness. For example,

> It is your own value systems and decision-making frameworks. Being true to your own value systems and not wavering, not being, not exploring exceptional behavior or, it's being, it's about consistency and being true to your own values.

The data presented suggest that at the heart of integrity is a person having strong moral and ethical reflectiveness, someone committed and adherent to the ethical values and beliefs (moral and ethical steadfastness) recognized as sound moral and ethical principles or ideology. One must be unwaveringly committed to sound ethical and moral principles and values and remain steadfast on them in all circumstances in order to achieve integrity. Conversely, if a person is not committed to sound ethical and moral principles, then he or she cannot be a person of integrity. Thus, it is plausible to argue that commitment to sound ethical and moral principles is a prerequisite to achieving integrity. Commitment signals that a person prescribes to a set of values and beliefs that they follow and these can be used to evaluate and sanction their conduct. These moral principles or ideologies can be described as an integrated system of beliefs, values, standards, and self-images that define an individual's orientation towards discerning the right and wrong (Schlenker, 2008). A person must not only act in accordance with his or her ethical and moral principles but should be perceived to be acting in compliance with his or her moral and ethical value systems. As one informant said,

> I think until you get to the core of that (what is the right thing to do), all the maths in the world and all the geography in the world is not going to help your cause if you can't distinguish between right and wrong.

Thus, this study supports the normative meaning of integrity in literature, which is moral and ethical behavior. Two propositions emerge from the findings and discussion for developing further research on the topic:

1. Integrity is a normative concept.
2. Commitment to a set of sound ethical and moral principles is a precondition to achieving the state of integrity.

Due Care of Customer Interest

"Doing the right thing" is an interesting expression in itself because it lends itself to a number of questions like, "Doing the right thing by whom?" "Is it about doing the right thing by yourself, or by the customers, or by the principals/ shareholders, or by the employees, or by the community, or by everyone?" and "In an organizational setting, is it really possible to do the right thing by everyone, given that there are competing stakeholder interests?" The banks play an important role in creating productive and prosperous societies. Banking being a service industry, customer service was thought to be at the heart of its operations. All the informants held a sharp focus on customer service, "service being the absolute key delivery." Building strong and trusting relations with their customers was an emergent theme. The expression "doing the right thing" also included acting in the best interest of the customers. Customers were seen as key stakeholders whose interest was to be prioritized:

> Doing the right thing by our customers and how we report externally is of the utmost integrity for me, and therefore you ask me to do something that's outside of it I won't do it, to stand up for what I think is right.

Effective communication between the customers and the bank personnel was seen as a key in providing high-quality service and developing strong relationships with them. There was concern expressed that there can be perceived conflict of interest between the bank and the customer if the customers' needs were not met by the bank. There was a view that the organizations do not only need to be doing the right thing, but must also be perceived to be doing the right thing. This can be illustrated by the following quote:

> Some of our people would struggle with, would be people come to us with a view that they need to borrow money to buy a house, or they need to borrow money for their business, and is saying yes to them is doing the right thing by them, and that comes into some of the judgement because you can put people into situations that, really they can't afford it or they don't understand the situation that they're being put into, and I guess that's probably some of the—a couple that I've had to deal with in my life as a banker is saying no to people, and then giving them the reason of why I'm saying no to their lending right upfront so that they understand that by saying yes, I'm actually not doing the right thing by them.

Rejection of a loan application by the bank could be interpreted by a customer as acting against his or her interest. There was strong emphasis laid on the critical importance of explaining to the customers why the bank has decided against lending the requested amount. Effective communication means full and honest product disclosure, explaining the potential associated risks and implications for the customer to facilitate informed decision making. It was seen as organization's duty of care toward the customer, and it leads to positive outcomes for the organization in the form of referrals by the satisfied customers:

> I still believe service is the best sales outcome, because in that industry if my—my involvement with customers is when a customer really finds someone they think they get great service from, you actually get more of that person's business and you get referrals from that person. So, I still maintain it's the key factor to success. But the dollar was, certainly became important in banking, particularly when the margins started to reduce in banking.

Thus, due care of the interest of customers was seen as the top priority and a critical factor in acting with integrity. The informants believed that acting in the best interest of the customers over self-interest was the right thing by the organization.

The next section addresses the question, "How do the informants foster conditions for integrity in their organizations?" "Doing the right thing" emerged as an overarching theme of integrity in action. How is "doing the right thing" operationalized in behavior in the workplace?

Strategies to Foster Conditions for Integrity in Organizations

Organizational Socialization Through Leadership

Organizational socialization sets up role expectations for individuals, communicates which organizational goals are important, and establishes appropriate ways to achieve those goals (Moore & Gino, 2013). All the informants talked about setting standards of behavior as a starting point for building a culture in the organization where integrity is a core value. The informants believed that, as senior executives, it was their responsibility to set behavioral expectations and be a role model for their staff. Reflecting on their own career experiences, they believed that role models and mentors are an important source of inspiration and guidance for other staff in the organization. The role of a mentor was seen critical in helping people seeking guidance around how one should operate. Reflecting on his own experience, one informant said that he had a boss during the early years of his career whom he admired for his integrity and who became his role model and mentor. He gained a lot of insight through working with him and developed his capability to identify issues which had ethical connotations and resolving them in the organizational settings:

> I'd certainly use integrity to describe him every day of the week, and the way that he role models that it is, he's consistent, he's transparent with his decision making, he invokes integrity frequently, so it's not a hidden topic. It's something that we talk about and he talks a lot about the right thing, so again it's that crossover with ethics, as well.

Support for Social Learning Theory

Social learning theory explains why the informants' strategy to provide a role model to emulate could be an effective approach to foster integrity (Bandura, 1986; Crittenden, 2005; Thyer & Myers, 1998). Social learning theory states that individuals can learn through direct experience or through observing behaviors of others. The importance of walking the talk was expressed often during the conversations:

> If I'm seen to be willing to compromise my integrity then what I believe will happen is that others will interpret that as acceptable behavior and I think it goes across.

Most individuals look outside themselves to other individuals for ethical guidance (Kohlberg, 1969; Trevino, 1986; Brown & Trevino, 2006). Senior executives are the most likely sources of guidance because their power, position, authority, and status enhance their attractiveness as role models (Bandura, 1986). However, this attractiveness is not determined by power and authority only, but there is more to it. Brown and Trevino (2006) argue that leaders who show care and concern and treat others fairly garner positive attention. For them, ethical leaders are credible because they are trustworthy and they practice what they preach. Social learning theory postulates that learning can also occur vicariously. It can be argued that, if people are exposed to unethical behavior, they may align their behavior with it because it is deemed to be appropriate behavior. Research has shown that when people are already aware of the normative behavior in a given situation because of the presence of a role model, they follow the role model's actions automatically (Gino & Galinsky, 2012). Studies by Eibach, Libby, and Ehrlinger (2009) and Fitzsimons and Bargh (2003) found that priming of a role model also helps people regulate their behavior and influences their judgment. The consequences of having the wrong leader, described as one who lacks ethical values and principles, was regarded as a traumatic experience:

> I've only had, I guess one occasion where I had a leader that I didn't think was very ethical, and that was very traumatic, and it sets a bad tone for the organization, you find that people are prepared to do anything to anyone to get to the next job and get a promotion and walk all over people and whatever, so it sets a bad tone for the whole organization.

The informants also emphasized the need to have appropriate incentives and rewards in place for encouraging behavior with integrity and disciplinary action to curtail undesirable behavior:

> [Acting with integrity] that's just the way I wish to operate and I expect everyone in our organization to follow those behavioral attributes at all times. And that's not meant to sound draconian either, it's not, it's seriously not, I think it's an example that I set and I expect my leadership team to do the same and I expect behaviors in the organization to emulate the example that we set.

Thus, the conversations with the informants strongly affirm the positive role appropriate role models and mentors can play in fostering integrity in the organizations supported by social learning theory and organizational socialization.

Communication, Alignment, and Enforcement

In addition, there was strong emphasis on the importance of clearly communicating the organizational values to the staff and management teams and to encourage them to use them as a guide in decision making and dealing with customers:

I would always talk about the vision and the values of the organization, and my experience within the framework of that, and if you always default back to—if you are ever challenged—default back to the values of the organization and look those as your guiding principles. [. . .] For the last 30 years in particular have always had the vision, the values of the organization, above the line and below the line behavior—those sorts of things so I think it is a good frame of reference.

The alignment of policies and guidelines with the organizational values for staff to refer to, the role of positive reinforcement of desired behavior for motivating their staff to "do the right thing" was also emphasized. The structure of the code of ethics and its consistent enforcement and the code of conduct were cited as useful means of driving desired behaviors. Detailed explanations of desirable and undesirable behavior were a critical part of the enforcement of the code of conduct and code of ethics; for example,

> So, we have a code of ethics and that is a broad policy and we communicate that and update all of our staff every year and reinforce that to our staff every year so they understand what ethics mean. They understand conflict of interest, they understand the honesty around representation of a product and disclosure of whether it be commissions or disclosure of information that's required so that the consumer can make their decision on fully informed basis so we go down to that level of detail to help. And even examples of if a client gives you a box of chocolates that's actually okay that's just a thank you. If a client gives you a gold bracelet that's is not okay and so we use real live examples so people don't just interpret for themselves the issue of conflict of interest, the issue of accepting gifts and the relevance of accepting a gift.

Strict enforcement of codes of conducts was deemed instrumental in shaping desirable behavior within organizations.

Risk Management and Business Case

Acting with integrity as a risk management strategy emerged as a strong theme. The informants believed that acting ethically and responsibly produces goodwill and builds reputational capital for the organizations. Otherwise, the survival of the organization can be at risk because it will have negative impact on the brand value and erode their customer base:

> I think honest organizations that have integrity and are ethical will ultimately benefit from that in terms of the strength of their brand in the long term. Not doing the right thing will challenge the brand the strength of your brand and the goodwill attached to your brand in the long term and I think poor ethics and poor behaviors and lack of integrity will

diminish the value of your brand in the long term. I believe that if you make the right decision, you will not live to regret it. If you do the wrong thing, it will eventually catch up with you. I believe in karma.

So, it appeared that the informants viewed acting with integrity as a risk management strategy, and there was a business case. The informant working in the government-owned financial institution believed that because the organization is a government agency, employees are expected to act with integrity that is critical to the organization's brand:

We represent the government, and our brand, and we would certainly want to hold ourselves up as operating with a high level of integrity and we'd see that as critical to our brand and to our organizational values.

An example of acting with integrity was an incident where a longtime customer tried to defraud the bank by forging the guarantor's signature to avail a loan and was picked up during document scrutiny by the assessment team. Upon asking his team what they would do, he said he was very pleased to hear that they will report the case to the police because it did amount to deceit and fraud. He said these are the times when the staff may struggle to resolve the conflict between losing a customer and business and doing the right thing. Leaders must be supportive and appreciative of decisions made in line with the values of the organization by the staff.

The rising expectations of transparency by the key stakeholders, the public, and the media were envisaged as a concern because and the implications of not meeting those expectations were far-reaching. The power of the social media was also a cause of concern because it had the capacity to vitiate the reputation and brand value of the organization. It has provided a platform for free expression of opinion to everyone who has access to it. The public and activists can now hold organizations accountable for not behaving in responsible manner. There was a sense of fear of losing the license to operate and putting the reputation of the brand at risk by not doing the right thing and acting irresponsibly:

I think we live in an era of high levels of expectation in terms of transparency. I also think, with the virility of the digital age we live in, organizations are held to account more often and they are more interested in their reputation and their reputation risk, so when they do something wrong it's not just one person that I don't know tweets it, one person might tweet it and then 20,000 might see it and then it might spread to half a million and all of a sudden they've got a problem on their hands. So I think the degree of transparency in the world we live in today has the capacity to hold organizations to account when they do the wrong thing. In doing business you have to protect the brand value and you don't want to jeopardize or compromise the corporate brand name.

So, you really can't afford to be seen to be acting without integrity in that space because you're going to hear about it very quickly and it just whips up a storm and the media loves picking up on what's happening on social media because it's easy fodder, I suppose. But it can snowball very quickly, so you have to be very, very careful, and this is why companies are spending a lot to protect their brands on social media.

Building reputational capital and strengthening the brand value through doing the right thing was certainly seen as a business case and a win-win situation for the organization and the stakeholders.

Removing Moral Hazards

The industry structure was seen as the strongest barrier to integrity in the banking and other services in the finance industry due to the presence of many moral hazards. The banks develop their financial products and services, and a fair service to the customers will be that the products perform in a way that consumers expect or are led to believe. However, there need to be appropriate processes, policies, and frameworks designed to ensure that the products work effectively. The reality was seen to be the opposite by the informants. Poorly designed incentive programs and compensation schemes were seen to create moral hazards that encouraged unethical behavior. The informants believed that there was a shift from a services-based to a sales-based culture in the finance industry, including banks. As the industry became sales driven and rewards became linked to the volume of sales, questionable services started to get offered to consumers:

> Sales became sales for sales' sake, the balance sheet became absolutely critical in the behaviors and that started a drive for much greater focus around sales—different to how it had been perceived previously in the finance or banking industry in particular. So, it became heavily oriented toward making that upfront sale, and then rewards linked to that. The brokering industry became particularly significant, then on the financial planning side, the financial planners became particularly important around selling that next major financial asset transaction. That was a significant shift in the finance industry, particularly banking. And it's the behaviors that went with that that became challenging for me, more than anything. The dollar has become certainly more important in banking, particularly when the margins started to reduce in banking. The increased prominence of the balance sheet showed the impact on behaviors.

This statement points to problems related to shortcomings in product disclosure and financial advice given to the customers. The operational environment created by the incentive systems clouded moral reflectiveness and encouraged some staff to prioritize their own best interest over the interest of the customers, which was not the right thing to do. The informants gave examples to illustrate how there are times when consumers are sold products that are not suitable to their needs and not in their interest but that could fetch bonuses for the staff for meeting sales target. For example,

> The root cause is what incentives are there for people to act or not act. And if you look at things like commissions, and you look at how mortgage brokers and financial planners might refer products, the commission structure is a real barrier to acting in the best interest of the client. So the way that these people are rewarded doesn't necessarily reward them for acting with integrity.

According to socialization theory, people can get socialized into unethical behaviors consciously and unconsciously (Moore & Gino, 2013): consciously, when an individual resists objectionable practices until finally surrendering to them as inevitable, and unconsciously, when an individual becomes seduced by the positive material or psychological benefits of participating in immoral behavior (Moore, 2009; Moore & Gino, 2013). This illuminates the importance of moral leadership in an organizational setting where the external environment can easily entice staff into undesirable behaviors. It also sheds light on the critical role policies and practices that encourage, support and reward doing the right thing.

Self-Regulation—or the Inefficacy of Regulatory Systems

The need for a cultural shift towards self- regulation and away from regulations and compliance was raised by the informants. The conversations indicate the presence of an "ends justify the means" mentality in the industry which rendered external compliance systems ineffective. The informants gave examples of instances where they witnessed questionable behaviors being knowingly overlooked as innocent human error. For example,

> I have seen situations where—I can't go into explicit details about these things—but I've seen situations where a produced results despite behavior being inconsistent is ignored, because it produces a better result. So, I've seen that, is that widespread, I hope not but I don't know. And there's no question in my mind behaviors reflect the income someone can get, and if there's a slight bending of their rules, then it seems to be acceptable for some people. And then your compliance factors have to address it. So, the compliance factors keep going up in cost.

When regulations and compliance systems are porous enough to be used as a veil for dubious actions to cover up the unethical or wrong decisions, it becomes imperative that self-regulation is exercised at an organizational level. The informants discussed the highly regulated banking sector in

Australia, and yet there were ongoing unethical practices in news. Banking is a highly regulated industry sector, and banks in Australia have performed rather well on the basis of their financial performance throughout the GFC as compared to the rest of the world.

The Australian Prudential Regulation Authority (APRA) and Australian Securities and Investments Commission (ASIC) are the two main bodies that regulate the finance sector. APRA is the key prudential regulator of the financial system. It mainly takes a risk-based approach to ensure that the risks are assessed rigorously and consistently, and warning signs are identified and flagged early. It has strong statutory powers to regulate and intervene in the operations of financial institutions (Australian Trade Commission, 2011). ASIC is an independent statutory body that is Australia's corporate, markets, and financial services regulator. ASIC is also responsible for administering the market misconduct provisions of the Corporations Act, which covers market manipulation, insider trading, and misleading or deceptive conduct. In addition, Reserve Bank of Australia is responsible for maintaining stability of the overall financial system and monetary policy and provides banking services for the government of Australia, along with managing nation's official reserve assets (Australian Trade Commission, 2011).

The informants expressed concerns about the capability and effectiveness of the regulatory systems. The need for the regulatory agencies was not undermined, but was not believed to be the answer to curb the ongoing unethical practices in the industry. For example,

> We obviously operate in a highly regulated industry so financial institutions are regulated by APRA and ASIC and under the Banking Act and the Reserve Bank so we are very, very highly regulated. Notwithstanding that, that doesn't necessarily mean that integrity exists in organizations that happen to be regulated. The regulators were toothless tigers who did not have enough power to crack down on the bad practices and take action.
>
> I don't believe in prescriptive regulation or legislation. It is not going to make anyone more honest or ethical or anyone to maintain higher levels of integrity.

The perceived inadequacy of the regulators meant that the individual organizations themselves were deemed to be largely responsible for their own behavior. All the informants emphasized that, as business leaders, they needed to take responsibility for guiding and directing their organizations and employees in the right direction. They could not only rely on the external regulatory agencies. The importance of the role of organizational leaders and senior management was a prominent theme in the conversations; for example,

> It's always going to come down to leadership; who's leading these organizations, who's leading the sales teams, and you're thinking about

some of the root causes I've identified, if you have the right leaders in place and the right culture in place, then you shouldn't have a problem with integrity, and if you couple that with incentive systems, then it really shouldn't be an issue, should it—and that's where I think the issues crop up.

I think in my mind a lot of it gets back to the leadership of the organization, so who are the leaders of the organization and what are their values; what do they stand for and if those things line up, are they able to influence how far does their reach go down the organization.

The code of ethics and the integrity rests a lot with the leader of the organization, and you need to make sure that your leader has got strong moral values.

The views expressed by the informants on the critical role of leadership in organizational behavior are consistent with a growing body of literature on authentic leadership, responsible leadership, and ethical leadership. Although some theorists like Minkes, Small, and Chatterjee (1999) have questioned how much leaders can influence the behaviors of subordinates, most theorists are supportive of the view that the authority and power bestowed on leaders in organizations provide them with the capability of setting the tone at the top and ethical atmosphere of the organization (Trevino, 1986; Trevino et al., 2003). These theorists assert that leaders have the ability to establish and communicate organizational values as well as rewards and sanctions to ensure compliance with organizational policies (Paine, 1997; Peterson, 2004; Sims, 2000; Sims & Brinkman, 2002).

The spectacular collapse of Enron led to a number of investigations set up by the U.S. Congress. William C. Powers led one such investigation and among other reasons he attributed the failure to "a fundamental default of leadership and management." He further stated that "leadership and management begin at the top with the CEO" (Trevino et al., 2003, p. 6). In the aftermath of these corporate debacles, leadership has once again come to the forefront, and there are calls from all fronts to recruit leaders who are known for their integrity and can provide ethical and responsible leadership to the businesses. Integrity has emerged as an essential characteristic of business leaders. In their study of 25,000 profiles of managers and leaders, Zenger and Folkman (2003) found that honesty and integrity were seen as essential for the business leaders who were perceived very highly by their peers, subordinates, and bosses. Success factors for corporate leaders included integrity, as the third most important factor after the essential functional and technical skills in a survey of chief finance officers conducted by *Financial Executive Magazine* in 2010. According to these studies, business leaders play a critical role in leading the organization in the direction they set up and the informants were in agreement with it. They considered themselves to be responsible for setting the tone at the top, set expectations, and ensure that the staff behaviors were in line with the standards set by them:

I don't think regulation is the answer—it's always going to be cultural. If the organization rewards and recognizes the demonstration of integrity, then yes there's a fair chance that it will happen because the person will see that's my pathway.

So, it is critical that structures are put in place to reward desired behavior and punish undesirable behavior:

I guess the code of ethics that we've got and the procedures that we've got around those things, and the willingness and the desire of the managers supported by HR department to make sure that we follow those things and that when someone breaks the code of conduct they are issued with written formal warnings, and/or dismissed, and making sure you set that integrity benchmark.

This points toward the fact that there are discrepancies in the levels of integrity of two individuals. It is the leader's responsibility to foster a climate in which integrity is valued and rewarded (Palanski & Yammarino, 2009). As Grojean et al. (2004) state, it is important for leaders to be aware that there are differences among subordinates with respect to such things as values and personality; thus, integrity alignment may require investment in time and effort.

Protecting Integrity

The informants told us they had devised their own methods to determine what was the right thing to do and protect their integrity. One of them was the newspaper test:

What I've always tried to do at a personal level was- is it going to appear on page 1 of the paper? And am I comfortable with it to appear on page 1? If I am that's fine. If I'm not, I have to query my own set of values that sit around that decision or decisions that's made. If I'm comfortable for it to be known by a journalist and I did a lot of media for a company at a radio, TV and press. If not, I really said that doesn't pass the common-sense test. Sometimes, you're overruled because of the profitability aspect or the shareholder's return—the people are trying to push for.

One informant detailed his "social filters" that were developed over time and experience. He explained that he filtered his decisions through his value systems and beliefs and had a set of questions which he asks himself to determine the right thing to do. He believed it had worked well for him and saved him from breaching his integrity and described the process as follows:

I have a value system that tends to—tends to firstly put a filter on these things to make a judgment, and that judgment is am I getting a direct benefit, so my value system says am I getting a direct benefit, and if I am, then I feel it's wrong. They tend to be social based filters and it's around impacts on people generally. So if I take a particular stance around integrity, so if I get an offer on the table and say how about you do this, the filters I use are very much, well is it right, but then that comes from, is anyone hurt by me doing this. So, if I accept that offer where I'm benefiting firstly, so that's the first filter that goes through, Do I benefit personally? If the answer's yes I do, then I start to get down to this next level of integrity which is, Is it fundamentally right? If I'm benefiting is someone, yin and yang argument, if I'm benefiting is there an equal and opposite non-benefit for someone else, and if I arrive at a view anywhere along that stage that says, or continuum that says, someone is negatively impacted by virtually me accepting this, then I won't do it. And it's around consideration for others. So, it's a social, largely a social filter.

So, the benefit level is am I benefiting above and beyond what my value system says is reasonable. If I sense that the value I'm receiving is beyond what I put back in that's where I draw my own value systems, and that's essentially the way I try to assess my own application with integrity, what am I getting out of it in aggregate, and if it's more than I've put in, I sense it's more than I'm being paid for and then I doubt the integrity if I said yes because that implies that I'm, I'm potentially being influenced to behave a certain way that is contrary to what I believe was what I put in.

Exit Strategy—Distancing From the Issue or Situation

Exiting the organization or distancing yourself from the issue or situation were found to be the strategies to protect personal integrity. The informants gave examples of how they dealt with the situations when they encountered situations where their own integrity was challenged. However, the examples were related to the early stages of their careers. Four of the five informants said that they had decided to leave their employing organizations when they felt they are unable to act in alignment with their integrity:

> It goes right back early in my career, and I was working in a sales-based organization and I had a particular view about a product, and this was a financial services organization as well. I had a particular view on a particular situation that didn't fit the view of the entity I was working with. They wanted a different view. I was quite young at that point and I didn't roll over, but I also didn't put a stop to it, so it was a case of absenting myself from that situation, really. So, providing factual information, not providing any recommendation one way or the other, just saying here it is, I'm not giving you the recommendation that you want, but I'm also not putting a stop to it either. [. . .] I probably would say I would stand up for it more strongly now than I did back then. As I

said, I was pretty young back in. Early career type stuff. Now I'd be very comfortable taking a really strong stand.

Another informant described a similar situation he faced at the very early stage of his career when he felt he had to compromise his integrity because he was financially dependent on the organization:

> My values were in conflict at the earlier part of my career, there were other drivers, I was producing a living, I had life goals that I was trying to achieve and, to be blunt, I was caught between a breach of my personal values and still achieving the things that were important to me at the time. So, they were in conflict in that sense. So, I didn't feel financially I was in a position to do something about it immediately. Over time I could, but I couldn't on the spot. So no, that discomfort just, I sat with it, lived with it for the period that I had until I had an opportunity to do something about it. But at the same time I had goals from a family perspective that I was attempting to achieve, and my job was important to me, and I quite frankly couldn't afford to just turn my back on it at the time. So, it's something I had to live with. Don't get me wrong it wasn't difficult, because I—I could reconcile that I wasn't—that I wasn't hurting anyone directly by doing that. But in the long run, it didn't sit right, still doesn't sit right today.

He said he was able to rationalize his decision because he was not causing anyone direct harm by his decision. So, he did not spend sleepless nights but had discomfort about it and still continues to feel the discomfort even though he left the organization long ago.

The conversations underscored the evolving nature of capability to deal with matters related with their ethics and integrity with experience:

> When you're young and green and that, you tend to be a lot more naïve to what's going on around you and you don't actually understand what are the kick-backs and bribes that go on in the organizations around you, and making sure that you don't—so, as you grow in terms of you see more, you learn how to influence people more, and you look for the good role models as well, and I think that would probably be the greatest thing that I got out was finding the good role models that I had and how they handled situations, and learning to manage those, and like I said, you make mistakes, and you know, the non-early intervention with customers and things like that, you learn from those mistakes when you make them, and you don't make them yourself if you've seen them happen by someone else, you go, I won't let myself into that position.

One informant said that he felt very disappointed with himself and the organization and started questioning himself if he wanted to be in an organization whose values were not in alignment with his personal values. He said he ultimately decided to quit the organization as soon as he got an opportunity because he felt he did not want to be a part of it. He said that he temporarily removed himself to another part of the organization when he thought it was not the place to be because his values were not aligned with his other senior managers' values:

> I did vacate the position; I actually went back out and did commercial lending for a period of time. So, I did remove myself from the situation, but was able to remove myself from the situation without removing myself from the organization completely, so I went out and did some commercial lending for a period of four or five years, and then came back after we'd been taken over by someone else.

There is an underlying theme that acting with integrity in organizational settings is a learned skill that strengthens with experience. It also brings to light the fact that our decisions are influenced by numerous forces including social forces more than we realize, as argued by Van Lange (1991) and Van Lange and Sedikides (1998) in the context of moral decision making. And rationalizing morally uncertain behaviors through self-verification may facilitate moral justification (Moore & Gino, 2013). Competing priorities, complexities of organizational life, and personal situations and personal issues may sometimes result in interim integrity concessions even for people who consider themselves to be highly ethical.

Conclusion

Managing with integrity is a topic much in demand in the business world and wider society. There is continuing debate in scholarly literature about the meaning of integrity, but there is no agreement on its meaning. The scant empirical research on integrity focuses on the followers' perceptions of their managers' or leaders' integrity, but there is not much known about what the organizational leaders themselves think about the meaning and implications of acting with integrity. This interpretive study was designed to understand the meaning of integrity from the perspective of senior executives in the banking sector and explore how they foster integrity in their organizations. The qualitative data were collected in semistructured, openended interviews with senior executives of banks in South Australia in order to elicit the meaning, conceptualization, and application of integrity in the workplace. Asking the informants to describe instances where they felt their integrity was challenged and give examples of when they believed they themselves or someone else acted with integrity generated a rich source of data to identify the themes and concepts. This approach also helped provide some empirically grounded explanations of the abstract concepts found in the literature (Martin et al., 2013; Palanski & Yammarino, 2007).

The thematic analysis of the conversations confirms the normative, yet imprecise, meaning of integrity found in management literature. The meaning of integrity was described as "doing the right thing." "Doing the right thing" in action had a wide range of meanings:

- Honoring your word or promise-keeping and the word or promise must be honest and ethical, consistent in word and actions
- being honest, being upfront
- being transparent in decision making
- being mindful of the impact of actions on the people around you, being fair, upholding social relationships, upholding stakeholder interest
- being morally reflective
- authentic, or staying true to who you are, consistent with espoused and enacted values
- consistent in adverse circumstances, accepting negative consequences of doing the right thing for yourself, unwaveringly adhere to espoused values and ideologies, morally steadfast

Each of the preceding manifestations of acting with integrity reflects a central tenet of ethically or morally appropriate behavior. Although the difference between morality, ethics, and integrity was mentioned, they were seen to be intertwined and positively related. Thus, it is argued that if a person does not hold ethical or moral values, then they cannot be a person of integrity. In other words, ethicality of action determined whether the action was the right action. Two propositions, which could be explored further in future research, were highlighted:

1. Integrity is a normative concept.
2. Commitment to a set of sound ethical and moral principles or ideology is a prerequisite to the achievement of integrity.

In addition, a duty of care to act in the best interest of customers was seen as a top priority in a service sector like banking. A cultural shift away from a compliance-based mindset to self-regulation at the organizational level was emphasized, as the informants believed that regulation and compliance cannot guarantee responsible behavior. However, an effective regulatory system was seen to be essential as a broad framework to facilitate enforcement of at least a minimum level of responsibility at organizational level. The highly competitive business environment, rising expectations of transparency, and the increasing power of social media suggested a compelling business case for acting with integrity in order to sustain and enhance brand value and strength. This goes somewhat against Koehn's (2005) argument that integrity is worthwhile because of its intrinsic value and not as a business asset. It appears that, currently, integrity (whatever its meaning) is also viewed as a business imperative which can provide an edge over the competiters. It is a necessity to meet the stakeholders' expectations. It is little wonder that there is a widespread desire to identify public and corporate leaders who bring integrity to their work, who operate in a transparent manner, who espouse courage and optimism in the face of challenge, and who are guided by an enduring internal moral compass (Avolio & Gardner, 2005; Diddams & Chang, 2012; May, Chan, Hodges, & Avolio, 2003).

Career stage can have an impact on a person's integrity in the workplace. It was found that, during early stages of their careers, the informants faced challenges to their integrity, which they were unable to address to their satisfaction. As their career progressed, they gradually learned how to deal with integrity challenges from their role models and mentors. The conversations reflect that they felt confident that at present they would be able to deal with any such challenges in a far more effective way. Acting with integrity is a learned skill in organizational settings, which can be acquired through various interventions, for example, business leaders being role models to emulate. Socializing integrity through role modeling, mentoring, and supportive policies, which act as guidelines for expected behavior, help foster integrity in organizational settings. The informants also believed that acting with integrity should be incentivized in reward systems to shape the behavior of staff.

Limitations

The nature and design of the study suggest that it is subject to limitations. The first limitation of this study is the sample of informants as the results are based on a relatively small number of respondents. Although the sample size was small, the information obtained through the semistructured interviews has provided rich data for future theoretical advances. Second, an element of self-selection should be kept in mind. The informants who expressed interest in participating in this research felt strongly about personal and corporate integrity and were actively involved in fostering integrity in their workplaces. However, this was aligned with the purpose of this research, which was to understand the meaning of integrity from the perspective of the senior executives and how they implement and foster their conceptualization and understanding of the concept in their organizations. Understandably, the senior executives had extremely busy schedules, but they took time out to talk about a subject they had passion for. Third, the information collected through the interviews is of self- reporting nature and may not be fully aligned with the perceptions of the informants' integrity of other members of the organizations (Hogan, Curphy, & Hogan, 1994).

Suggestions for Future Research

Despite these limitations, the findings of this study suggest several areas for future research on the topic. The results should be used as a basis for further research to substantiate or examine the findings in greater depth with larger samples in other industries. It will be useful to extend the study cross-culturally and investigate the extent to which cultural context changes the meaning of integrity. Future studies using multilevel methods to identify any gaps between business leaders' conceptualizations of integrity and followers' conceptualizations might be important future empirical developments.

In conclusion, this study has contributed to fill the gap existing in the current scholarly literature in management about the meaning of integrity from an upper echelons perspective. It has generated a rich narrative which has opened avenues for future research to consolidate a unified framework to highlight the variety of meanings of integrity.

Note

1. The United States ranked first, and the United Kingdom, Hong Kong, and Singapore ranked second, third, and fourth, respectively.

References

Audi, R. & Murphy, P. E. (2006). The many faces of integrity. *Business Ethics Quarterly, 16*(1), 3–21.

Australian Bureau of Statistics (2010). *Australian national accounts: National income, expenditure and product.* Catalogue number 52060. Canberra, Australia: Australian Bureau of Statistics.

Australian Trade Commission (2011). *Australia's banking industry.* Canberra, Australia: The Government of Australia.

Avolio, B. J. & Gardner, W. L. (2005). Authentic leadership development: Getting to the root of positive forms of leadership. *The Leadership Quarterly, 16*(3), 315–338.

Baccilli, P. A. (2001). *Organizationand manager obligations in a framework of psychological contract development and violation.* Unpublished dissertation, Claremont Graduate University, Claremont, CA.

Badaracco, J. L. & Ellsworth, R. R. (1992). Leadership intergrity and conflict. *Management Decision, 30*, 29–34.

Bandura, A. (1986). Social foundations of thought and action: A social cognitive theory. Englewood Cliffs. New Jersey: Prentice-Hall.

Barry, B. & Stephens, C. U. (1998). Objections to an objectivist approach to integrity. *Academy of Management Review, 23*(1), 162–169.

Batson, C. D., Thompson, E. R., Sueferling, G., Whitney, H. & Strongman, J. A. (1999). Moral hypocrisy: Appearing moral to oneself without being so. *Journal of Personality and Social Psychology, 77*, 525–537.

Bauman, D. C. (2013). Leadership and the three faces of integrity. *The Leadership Quarterly, 24*, 414–426.

Becker, T. E. (1998). Integrity in organizations: Beyond honesty and conscientiousness. *Academy of Management Review, 23*, 154–161.

Bews, N. F. & Rossouw, G. J. (2002). A role for business ethics in facilitating trsutworthiness. *Journal of Busienss Ethics, 39*, 377–389.

Braun, V. & Clarke, V. (2006). Using the thematic analysis in psychology. *Qualitative Research in Psychology, 3*, 77–101.

Brown, M. T. & Trevino, L. K. (2006). Ethical leadership: A review and future directions. *The Leadership Quarterly, 17,* 595–616.

Calhoun, C. (1995). Standing for something. *Journal of Philosophy, 92*(5), 235–260.

Carter, S. L. (1996). *Integrity.* Harper Perennial: New York.

Cox, D., LaCraze, M., & Levine, M. (2003). *Integrity and the fragile self.* Ashgate: Burlington, VT.

Craig, S. B. & Gustafson, S. B. (1998). Percieved leader integrity scale: An instrument for assessing employee perceptions of leader integrity. *Leadership Quarterly, 9,* 127–145.

Crittenden, W. F. (2005). A social leraning theory of cross-functional case education. *Journal of Business Research, 58*(7), 960–966.

De George, R. T. (1993). *Competing with integrity in international business.* New York: Oxford University Press.

Diddams, M. & Chang, G. C. (2012). Only human: Exploring the nature of weakness in authentic leadership. *The Leadership Quarterly, 23,* 593–603.

Duska, R. F. (2005). A look at integrity in financial services. *Journal of Financial Services Professionals, 59,* 26–28.

Eibach, R. P., Libby, L. K., & Ehrlinger, J. (2009). Priming family values: How being a parent affects moral evaluations of harmless but offensive acts. *Journal of Experimental Psychology, 45,* 1160–1163.

Fitzsimons, G. M. & Bargh, J. A. (2003). Thinking of you: Nonconscious pursuit of interpersonal goals associated with relationship partners. *Journal of Personality and Social Psychology, 84,* 148–164.

Gentry, W. A., Cullen, K. L., Sosik, J. J., Chun, J. U., Leupold, C. R., & Tonidandel, S. (2013). Integrity's place among the character strengths of middle-level managers and top-level executives. *The Leadership Quarterly, 24,* 395–404.

Gino, F. & Galinsky, A. D. (2012). Vicarious dishonesty: When psychological closeness creates distance from one's moral compass. *Organizational Behavior and Human Decision Processes, 119,* 15–26.

Gioia, D. A. & Chittipeddi, K. (1991). Sensemaking and sensegiving in strategic change initiation. *Strategic Management Journal, 12,* 433–448.

Gioia, D. A., Corley, K. G., & Hamilton, A. L. (2012). Seeking qualitative rigour in inductive research: Notes on Gioia methodology. *Organizational Research Methods, 16*(1), 15–31.

Graafland, J. J., & Ven, B. W. van de (2011). The credit crisis and the moral responsibility of professionals in finance. *Journal of Business Ethics, 103,* 605–619.

Greycourt White Paper (2008). The finacial crisis and the collapse of ethical behavior. *White Paper no. 44.* Greycourt and Co Inc.

Grojean, M. W., Resick, C. J., Dickson, M. W., & Smith, D. B. (2004). Leaders, values and organizational climate: Examining leadership strategies for establishing an organizational climate regarding ethics. *Journal of Business Ethics, 55,* 223–241.

Hogan, R., Curphy, G. J., & Hogan, J. (1994). What we know about leadership. Effectiveness and personality. *American Psychologist, 49,* 493–504.

House, R. J., Hanges, P. J., Javidan, M., Dorfman, P., & Gupta, V. (2004). *Culture, leadership and organizations: The GLOBE study of 62 societies.* Thousand Oaks, CA: Sage.

Howell, J. M. & Avolio, B. J. (1995). Charismatic leadership: Submission or liberation? *Business Ethics Quarterly, 60,* 62–71.

Jacobs, D. C. (2004). A pragmatic approach to integrity in business ethics. *Journal of Management Inquiry, 13*(3), 215–223.

Jensen, M. C. (2009, January 14). Integrity: Without it nothing works. *Rotman Magazine*, 16–20.

Kirkpatrick, S. A. & Locke, E. A. (1991). Leadership: Do traits matter? *The Executive*, 5, 48–60.

Koehn, D. (2005). Integrity as business asset. *Journal of Bsuiness Ethics*, 58, 125–136.

Kohlberg, L. (1969). State and sequence: The cognitive-development approach to socialization. In D. Goslin (Ed.), *Handbook of socialization theory and research* (pp. 347–480). Chicago: Rand-McNally.

Kottak, C. (2006). *Mirror for humanity*. New York: McGraw-Hill.

Locke, E. A. & Becker, T. E. (1998). Rebuttal to a subjectivist critique of an objectivist approach to integrity in organisations. *Academy of Management Review*, 23(1), 170–175.

Lowe, K. B., Cordery, J., & Morrison, D. (2004). A model for the attribution of leader intergrity: Peeking inside the black box of authentic leadership. *Paper presented at the 2004 Gallup Leadership Institute Conference*, Lincoln, NE.

McFall, L. (1987). Integrity. *Ethics*, 98, 5–20.

Maree, J. G. (2015). Career construction counseling: A thematic analysis of outcome. *Journal of Vocational Behavior*, 86, 1–9.

Martin, S. M., Keating, M. A., Resick, C. J., Szabo, E., Kwan, H. K., & Peng, C. (2013). The meaning of leader integrity: A comparative study across Anglo, Asian, and Germanic cultures. *The Leadership Quarterly*, 24, 445–461.

May, D. R., Chan, A. Y. L., Hodges, T. D., & Avolio, B. J. (2003). Developing the moral component of authentic leadership. *Organizational Dynamics*, 32(3), 247–260.

Minkes, A. L., Small, M. W., & Chatterjee, S. R. (1999). Leadership and business ethics: Does it matter? Implications for management. *Journal of Business Ethics*, 20, 327–335.

Monga, M. (2015, November 24–25). Integrity and its antecedent: A unified conceptual framework of integrity. *Proceedings of Asia Pacific Conference on Business and Social Sciences*, Kuala Lumpur, Malaysia, 171–180.

Monga, M. (2016). Meaning of integrity from upper echelons' perspective. *Journal of Developing Areas*, 50(6), 333–340.

Moore, C. (2009). Psychological perspectives on corruption. In D. De Cremer (Ed.), *Psychological perspectives on ethical behavior and decision making* (pp. 35–71). Charlotte, NC: Information Age Publishing.

Moore, C. & Gino, F. (2013). Ethically adrift: How others pull our moral compass from true North, and how we can fix it. *Research in Organizational Behavior*, 33, 53–77.

Moorman, R. H., Darnold, T. C., & Priesemuth, M. (2013). Perceived leader integrity: Supporting the construct validity and utility of a multi-dimensional measure in two samples. *The Learership Quarterly*, 24, 427–444.

Morrison, A. (2001). Integrity and global leadership. *Jounal of Business Ethics*, 31, 65–76.

Murray, D., Davis, K., Dunn, C., Hewson, C., & McNamee, B. (2014). *Murray Report on Financial System Inquiry*. Canberra, Australia: The Commonwealth of Australia.

Newman, B. (2003). Integrity and presidential approval, 1980–2000. *Public Opinion Quarterly*, 67, 335–367.

Noelliste, M. (2013). Integrity: An intrapersoanl perspective. *Human Resource Development Review*, 12(4), 474–499.

Orlitzky, M. & Jacobs, D. (1998). A candid and modest proposal: The brave new world of objectivism. *Academy of Management Review*, 23(4), 653–659.

Paine, L. S. (1997). Cases in leadership, ethics, and organization integrity: A strategic perspective. Chicago: Irwin Press.

Paine, L. S. (2005). Integrity. In P. H. Werhane & R. E. Freeman (Eds.), *The blackwell encyclopedia of management: Business ethics* (2nd ed., pp. 247–249). Malden, MA: Blackwell Publishing.

Palanski, M. E. & Yammarino, F. J. (2007). Intergrity and leadership: Clearing the conceptual confusion. *European Management Journal*, 25(3), 171–184.

Palanski, M. E. & Yammarino, F. J. (2009). Integrity and leadership: A multilevel conceptualization. *The Leadership Quarterly*, 20(3), 405–420.

Palanski, M. E. & Yammarino, F. J. (2011). Impact of behavioral integrity on follower job performance: A three-study examination. *The Leadership Quarterly*, 22, 756–786.

Parry, K. W. & Proctor-Thomson, S. B. (2002). Perceived integrity of transformational leaders in organisational settings. *Journal of Business Ethics*, 35, 75–96.

Peterson, C. & Seligman, M. E. P. (2004). *Character strengths and virtues*. New York: Oxford University Press.

Peterson, D. (2004). Perceived leader integrity and ethical intentions of subordinates. *Leadership & Organization Development Journal*, 25, 7–23.

Posner, B. Z. (2001). What does it mean to act with integrity? *Teaching Business Ethics*, 5, 461–473.

Rawls, J. (1971). *A theory of justice*. Cambridge: Harvard University Press.

Scandura, T. & Dorfman, P. (2004). Leadership reaserch in an international and cross-cultural context. *The Leadership Quarterly*, 15, 277–307.

Schlenker, B. R. (2008). Integrity and character: Implications of principled and expedient ideologies. *Journal of Social and Clinical Psychology*, 27(10), 1078–1125.

Simons, T. L. (1999). Behavioral integrity as a critical ingredient for transformational leadership. *Journal of Organizational Change Management*, 12, 89–104.

Simons, T. L. (2002). Behavioral integrity: The percieved alignment between managers' words and deeds as a research focus. *Organization Science*, 13, 18–35.

Simons, T.L. & McLean-Parks, J. (2000). *The sequential impact of integrity on trust, commitment, discretionary service behaviour, customer satisfaction, and profitability*. Paper presented at Academy of Management Conference, Toronto, ON.

Sims, R. R. (2000). Changing organization's culture under new leadership. *Journal of Business Ethics*, 25, 65–78.

Sims, R. R. & Brinkmann, J. (2002). Leaders as moral role models: The case of John Gutreund at Salmon Brothers. *Journal of Business Ethics*, 35, 327–339.

Solomon, R. C. (1992). Ethics and excellence: Cooperation and integrity in business. New York: Oxford University Press.

Solomon, R. C. (1999). A better way to think about business: How personal integrity leads to corporate success. New York: Oxford University Press.

Thyer, B. A. & Myers, L. L. (1998). Social learning theory. *Journal of Human Behavior in the Social Environment*, 1(1), 32–52.

Tracey, J. B. & Hinkin, T. R. (1994). Transformational leaders in hospitality industry. *Cornell Hotel and Restaurant Administration Quarterly*, 35, 18–24.

Trevino, L. K. (1986). Ethical decision making in organizations: A person-situation interactionist model. *Academy of Management Review*, 11, 601–617.

Trevino, L. K., Brown, M., & Hartman, L. P. (2003). A qualitative investigation of percieved executive ethical leadership: Perceptions from inside and outside the executive suite. *Human Relations, 56*(1), 5–37.

Trevino, L. K., Hartman, L. P., & Brown, M. (2000). Moral person and moral manager: How executives develop a reputation for ethical leadership. *California Management Review, 42*, 128–142.

Van Lange, P. A. M. (1991). Being better but not smarter than others: The Mohammad Ali effect at work in interpersonal situations. *Personality and Social Psychology Bulletin, 17*, 689–693.

Van Lange, P. A. M., & Sedikides, C. (1998). Being more honest but not necessarily more intelligent than others: Generality and explanations for the Muhammad Ali effect. *European Journal of Social Psychology, 28*, 675–680.

Vogelgesang, G. R., Leroy, H., & Avolio, B. J. (2013).The mediating effects of leader integrity with transparency in communication and work engagement/performance. *The Leadership Quarterly, 24*, 405–413.

Worden, S. (2003). The role of integrity as a mediator in strategic leadership: A recipe for reputational capital. *Journal of Business Ethics, 46*, 31–44.

Yukl, G. A. & VanFleet, D. D. (1992). Theory and research on leadership in organizations. 92nd Ed. In M. D. Dunette & L. M. Hugh (Eds.), *Handbook of industrial and organizational psychology (2nd ed.,*Vol 3, pp. 147–197). Palo Alto, CA: Consulting Psychologists Press.

Zenger, J. & Folkman, J. (2003). Leaders with integrity. *Executive Excellence, 20*(6), 20.

7 An Integrated Model of Managerial Integrity and Compliance

Duane Windsor

Introduction

This chapter proposes an integrated model of managerial integrity linked to a theory of compliance enforcement through relevant organizational governance and external mechanisms. By integrated, the author means systematically connecting managerial integrity and compliance enforcement in an operationally meaningful way within an organization. That linking requires both organizational governance mechanisms and external mechanisms for defining and enforcing standards of conduct. Step 1 concerns the prescriptive definition of managerial integrity. Step 2 concerns compliance enforcement. What is desirable is a fruitful cooperation among all participants to maximize the likelihood of managerial integrity and minimize the likelihood of employee misconduct.

The remainder of this chapter is structured as follows: The second section discusses the problem of defining integrity, compliance, and ethics in relationship to one another. The third section explicates the proposed integrated model of managerial integrity and compliance through discussion of Figure 7.1. The section considers two implications of the model: building integrity-based organizations and "giving voice to values" within integrity-based organizations. The fourth section illustrates the integrated model through mini-cases of two German companies and two Japanese companies that have engaged in documented misconduct. Siemens top management orchestrated a global corruption scheme operating across multiple countries. At Volkswagen (VW), top personnel management engaged in corruption of labor union leadership, and software engineers designed a way to evade diesel emissions testing standards. At Toshiba, top management cooked the books for a number of years. At Mitsubishi Motors, there was systematic cheating on mileage tests over decades. The fifth section explains the management implications of the proposed approach to an integrated model of managerial integrity and compliance. The explanation focuses on the General Electric (GE) approach to integrity (Heineman, 2007, 2008; Jones, 2008) as a contrast to the four mini-cases. A brief conclusion summarizes the key points of the chapter.

Integrity, Compliance, and Ethics

The three important concepts for an integrated model are integrity, compliance, and ethics. The meaning of ethics, for purposes of this chapter, is a normative conception of morally right and wrong actions. Paying bribes (at Siemens), corrupting union leaders and evading diesel emissions testing standards (at VW), cooking the books (at Toshiba), and cheating on mileage tests (at Mitsubishi) are all morally wrong acts. Generally, for purposes of this chapter, one can use the terms *ethical* and *moral* more or less interchangeably. There is, however, a more technical distinction in which morality is the behavior and beliefs of individuals, while ethics is the formal study of morality including by professional bodies of individuals that issue ethical codes of conduct for its members.

There is an important distinction, emphasized in the business ethics literature, between integrity (Cox, La Caze, & Levine, 2013) and compliance. Paine (1994) articulated a relationship in which compliance is the minimum and necessary requirement for the employees of an organization, and integrity goes well beyond that minimum. Paine (1994, pp. 106–107) defines integrity-based ethics as combining concern for the law with managerial responsibility for ethical behavior, in a way that "becomes the governing ethos of an organization." Compliance stresses strict adherence to law (and governmental regulations). Compliance helps promote integrity because "exemplary conduct may be the best way to prevent damaging misconduct" (Paine, 1994, p. 117). Organizational context and leadership are thus vitally important to the promotion of ethical behavior and discouragement of misconduct.

Compliance is relatively easy to define: individuals and organizations obey legal and moral rules. Compliance is rule-governed conduct. Individuals and organizations comply; if not, they deviate from compliance. To be ethical (or moral), compliance is insufficient. Ethical behavior is principle oriented rather than rule governed. A reason for this distinction is that, in order to be ethical (or moral), an individual may have to violate a rule. Ethics—as principled conduct—is thus superior to compliance—as rule-governed conduct (see Cheffers & Pakaluk, 2005). A difficulty in the distinction between rule and principle may be that the greater flexibility possibly implied in principle may tend to weaken moral compass (Gino, 2016).

Integrity is arguably more difficult to define and to place in relationship to compliance and ethics. Parry and Proctor-Thomson (2002, p. 76), drawing on earlier work, point out that "integrity is a concept commonly used within formal and informal discussions of leadership and organisational theory, but is not clearly defined and understood (Rieke & Guastello, 1995)." There may be a conflict between conceptions of personal integrity and moral integrity (McFall, 1987). Zarim and Zaki (2016) expand on this division of integrity into personal and moral spheres. The difficulty is that each sphere can have a different meaning with respect to how individuals understand what it means to be true to oneself. Integrity means willingness to take personal responsibility and to endure the consequences of personal convictions, however unpleasant (Zarim & Zaki, 2016). The relationship of integrity to ethics thus requires clarification and precision: The idea has been used so broadly as to cause diffuseness of interpretation and application (Audi & Murphy, 2006).

In general terms, integrity implies the ethical wholeness of an individual or an organization. A person of integrity holds herself or himself to consistent ethical principles and moral standards. There should be no inconsistency or discrepancy or fluctuation in beliefs and actions. Thus, a person of integrity is, by way of illustrations, honest, morally principled, truthful, conscientious, and faithful—a person of strong moral character.

A person of integrity has moral beliefs and values—and consistently carries through on those beliefs and values in her or his actions. Integrity especially has the implication of a person not yielding inappropriately on beliefs, values, or actions to external pressures. One may relate integrity to the notion of a moral compass pointing to a "true north" of ethics: A person of integrity has an internal moral compass and follows that compass consistently.

Integrity is not simply automated: Rather, integrity may require careful reflection and analysis. "In response to the ethical challenges of modern law practice, an expanded focus on ethics and problem-solving will help students learn the habits of reflection and analysis needed to develop and retain a professional 'moral compass'" (Rothenberg, 2009, p. 420).

An organization is a collection, or set, of individuals. The organization has full integrity when all individuals within the organization have integrity. Organizational integrity declines as more individuals misbehave. The moral role of leadership in an organization is to select employees who have integrity and to reinforce those individuals with an ethical climate. Leaders are moral exemplars for the inspiration of employees (see Bauman, 2013; Windsor, 2013a).

An Integrated Model of Managerial Integrity and Compliance

The author provides here a proposed integrated model of managerial integrity and compliance. Figure 7.1 depicts the model in general terms. The model treats managerial integrity—at the center of Figure 7.1—as the result of three internal sources of integrity (personal, professional, and positive) and a set of external positive reinforcement pressures. Internal sources of integrity are personal integrity, professional integrity, and positive integrity—defined in detail in the following. The interaction of the internal sources of integrity with a set of external positive reinforcement pressures increases managerial integrity and in consequence ethical behavior of individuals and the organization.

The integrated model functions as follows: Integrity, wholeness of an individual or organization (the set of employees), has an internal dimension and

Figure 7.1 An Integrated Model of Managerial Integrity and Compliance

an external dimension linked through a morally neutral theory of reputation. The internal dimension comprises three sources of integrity, of which positive integrity also functions as the link to external positive reinforcement pressures. Positive integrity is reputation with stakeholders. Ideally, the three sources should be mutually reinforcing within organizations comprised of managers, employees, and professionals concerned with positive reputation. This perspective on managerial integrity and compliance is formulated in a way that is consistent with the treatment of stakeholders, environmental integrity, human rights integrity, and other variations, which involve the specifications of content of integrity:

• The normative component of the internal dimension is *personal integrity*: an individual's ethics standards and voluntary compliance. While the understanding of personal integrity can be influenced by others in various ways, ultimately the understanding resides with the individual's sense of ethics (or morality). Here, the author treats personal and moral integrity as the same. That is, the core of personal integrity is moral integrity. Ideally, no violation of legal or ethical standards by an individual (or organization through noncompliance by any employee) should occur. One might characterize personal integrity in a number of ways: moral character (Paine, 1991), moral compass, compassion for others viewed as superior to self-interest narrowly defined (Seppälä, 2016), sense of corporate social responsibility, and resistance to corporate social irresponsibility (Windsor, 2013b, 2015b). The theory of personal and moral integrity is prescriptive. An executive or director should not engage in self-dealing (Ma, 2016) but exhibits in this sphere fiduciary loyalty under the corporate opportunity doctrine. Empirically, managers may develop their own behavioral codes for personal survival and advancement (Windsor, 2015c), which are not linked to conceptions of economic rationality (Windsor, 2016) or proper handling of peers and subordinates (Windsor, 2015a; forthcoming).

- The empirical component of the internal dimension is *professional integrity*, defined by canons of conduct for licensed professionals such as brokers, Certified Public Accountants, lawyers, medical doctors, and professional engineers; relevant legal standards; and relevant ethical standards. For licensed professionals, professional integrity and personal integrity should be mutually reinforcing. But professional integrity is absent for managers, such as Masters of Business Administration who are not licensed professionals—although arguments can be advanced that such managers should behave as if professionals on account of education and knowledge as well as responsibility (Donaldson, 2000). It is simply unlikely that such managers will do so. One aspect of professionalism (Tinker, Sy, & Saxe, 2016) is a healthy skepticism for the accuracy of information provided by others concerning a decision situation (Milgrom & Roberts, 1986). The theory of professionalism is prescriptive (Cheffers & Pakaluk, 2005). There is a definite possibility that professionalism, in various disciplines, is being eroded by increasing emphasis on the business success of professional service firms, such that they have become in reality businesses staffed by professionals rather than organizations of professionals engaged in services to businesses (Zeff, 2003a; 2003b). Such "professionals" do not serve any public interest (Huber, 2015) and may not be prepared to challenge or report management misconduct as effective gatekeepers (Avci & Seyhun, 2016).
- In addition to personal integrity (which has a moral core) and professional integrity (which is an agreed canon of conduct), there is Erhard, Jensen, and Zaffron's (2009) proposed conception of *positive integrity*: To preserve reputation for integrity, a person or organization should keep promises or pay adequate compensation in instances of noncompliance. This conception is morally neutral: the objective is reputation maintenance for individual or organizational advantage (see Erhard & Jensen, 2015). Essentially, Erhard et al. argue that honoring one's word (or providing compensation) is an unambiguous standard for conduct. The standard should provide superior performance and competitive advantage for individuals and organizations. The authors argue further that honoring one's word will "empower" virtues of ethics and legality (see Jensen, 2014).

The precise relationship among the three internal sources is arguable, at least in certain circumstances. For instance, while integrity is typically considered to be an important military virtue, one inquiry raises questions concerning whether individuals in the military can act according to personal values and principles (Olsthoorn, 2009). That author suggests, because integrity has "many, often contradicting, meanings" (Olsthoorn, 2009, p. 90), other virtues might serve better to the same purpose. In a military context, ethics and legality may be in collision (Reid, 2011): Legality may override personal ethics.

Figure 7.1 adds an external dimension of desirably positive reinforcement actors—especially regulators and stakeholders. Karnani (2010), in reemphasizing a case against corporate social responsibility, stresses that a market economy for proper functioning does require regulations and vigilant stakeholders. This external dimension should function as positive reinforcement of personal integrity, professional integrity, and positive integrity—by providing positive and negative incentives for individuals and organizations. Ideally, lack of compliance does not arise as a practical problem. Realistically, professionals should serve as a check on managerial misconduct. A professional canon supersedes profit-seeking behavior. Governance mechanisms, including the board of directors, should similarly serve as a check on managerial misconduct. Legal compliance and ethical standards supersede profit-seeking behavior (Kang & Wood, 1995). Ethical standards must be enforced by governance mechanisms and stakeholder pressures. External regulation is the final check on misconduct. There was a systematic failure of professional checks, governance mechanisms, and external regulators in both Enron (United States) and Satyam (India). Professionals and regulators appear to have failed systematically in the Enron and Satyam corporate frauds.

Building Integrity-Based Organizations

An important consideration in integrity theory is how to move an organization from compliance to integrity (Kayes, Stirling, & Nielsen, 2007). Paine (1994) provides case instances of how organizations have moved toward integrity from compliance. However, there is as yet relatively little literature on the process—which must include the role of leadership (Manz, Anand, Joshi, & Manz, 2008) in conditions in which an organization is in a condition of noncompliance, much less of integrity, beyond compliance. Verhezen (2010) conceptualizes movement from a compliance-oriented organizational culture to an integrity-based culture. The movement begins with formal and informal corporate governance mechanisms that steer an organization toward creativity, moral excellence, and organizational value. Verhezen thinks that formal mechanisms (such as codes and regulations emphasizing compliance) are necessary but not sufficient, while informal mechanisms based on relationship building will more likely achieve moral excellence. The movement is a transformation strategy to encourage giving voice to values in place of moral silence concerning violations of personal or corporate values. This strategy can be reinforced by dialogue and training to help foster moral awareness, trust in compliance, and ethical innovation.

Zwilling (2012) proposes five standards (or ways) for exhibiting business integrity in the context of entrepreneurship (see Yusoff, Kazi, Arisar, Jamil, & Hishan, 2016): (1) meet commitments (illustrated by being on time and meeting product quality commitments), (2) honesty to a fault as seen by others (illustrated by including in an apology the real reason for nondelivery of a service), (3) consistently meeting the moral code expectation of the customer or investor, (4) always treating others with respect, and (5) building and maintaining trust with others through personalizing the company through actions of the owner.

Giving Voice to Values in Integrity-Based Organizations

Gentile (2010, 2013) launched a "giving voice to values" movement for business ethics education. The motive for this movement was an expressed concern that conventional business ethics education tended to reinforce learning how to rationalize misconduct rather than to foster moral character development. Gentile proceeded from an assumption that business individuals know the difference between right and wrong, and, thus, the vital issue was to help morally oriented individuals to learn how to express value issues in business decision contexts. She suggested that there are seven pillars for effective voice and action concerning values discussions in business. These seven pillars can be expressed succinctly as follows: (1) appeal to widely shared values within the organization, (2) realize that individuals do have choices, (3) make voicing values and dealing with conflict normal action, (4) define personal and professional values, (5) define how to narrate values, (6) practice articulation, and (7) anticipate typical rationalizations and counterarguments to one's values appeal.

Gonzalez-Padron, Ferrell, Ferrell, and Smith (2012) provide a critique of the giving voice to values approach. They point out that the assumption is that while most individuals would prefer to provide input to ethical conflicts based on their own values, many individuals may lack sufficient courage to act. In part, this lack of courage may be grounded in a lack of confidence in effective options for acting. While viewing giving voice to values as an effective tool, the authors argue that the approach is not a comprehensive or holistic approach for either ethics education or corporate ethics programs.

The present author adds a consideration in evaluating giving voice to values. The approach may operate quite differently in non-integrity-based organizations than in integrity-based organizations. The difference is that the former discourage giving voice to values and encourage moral muteness—and intentionally or purposively so—while the latter foster giving voice to values and moral courage as normal aspects of business. If so, the organizational context for giving voice to values is vitally important to effectiveness.

Four Mini-Cases in Germany and Japan

Practical illustrations are developed through mini-cases of two German companies and two Japanese companies: Siemens corruption strategy; VW emissions falsification, following corruption of labor union leaders; Toshiba accounting fraud; and Mitsubishi Motors mileage falsification. The cases are selected in order to (1) highlight failures of integrity in major corporations outside the United States (where there are plenty of instances), (2) examine some different industries, and (3) examine afford some limited comparison of conditions in Germany and Japan (which with the United States and the United Kingdom are the largest economies other than China).

Friedman and Gerstein (2016) provide a partial list of major corporate scandals in recent years. The list includes instances from a number of industries: accounting, automobile, financial, and retailing. The authors conclude that any moral compass at many businesses remains broken by greed. They argue that executives and boards of directors at such businesses pay "lip service" to integrity and ethics while behaving otherwise. Similar pressure may occur at companies to undermine safety (Tomlinson, 2016).

A recent instance of failure of corporate integrity occurred at Wells Fargo & Co. bank. Basically, the bank dismissed some 5,300 employees over 5 years, under management pressure for performance results, creating some 2 million fake accounts—in some instances causing financial harm to bank customers (Merle, 2016; Ridlehuber, 2016). Ridlehuber attributes the pressure to quarterly earnings results, resulting in cross-selling of services to customers. The CEO, who is also chairman of the board of directors, was called to testify before the U.S. Senate Banking Committee; at the hearing, Senator Elizabeth Warren (D-Mass) called on the CEO to resign. The CEO forfeited some $45 million in unvested stock awards and will not receive a bonus for the year; another executive heading the involved division forfeited some $19 million in unvested stock awards. Wells Fargo agreed to pay $185 million to federal regulators and the Los Angeles City Attorney's Office. The CEO will forgo pay during an inquiry by an external law firm hired by the independent directors (Koren, 2016). A group of employees dismissed or demoted for not meeting performance requirements are joining two lawsuits, seeking class-action status (Cowley, 2016). The CEO frequently stated a goal that each customer should have at least eight accounts with the bank (Cowley, 2016, p. B1). The Wells Fargo situation may be referred to other federal agencies for investigation of potential criminal charges (Cowley, 2016, p. B6).

Siemens (Germany): Global Corruption From Top Management

U.S. and German investigations revealed that Siemens had operated a global strategy of bribery across perhaps 20 or more countries and orchestrated in part through a system of more than 2,700 business consultant agreements (Abdella, Di Tella, & Schlefer, 2008; Baron, 2008; Klinkhammer, 2013; Löscher, 2012; Schembera & Scherer, 2014; Schubert & Miller, 2008; Sidhu, 2009). The corruption approach was centered in telecommunications, especially for mobile phone system contracts, but was not restricted to that area; reports also concerned medical and hospital equipment, high-voltage lines for power transmission, and metro transport lines and related signaling equipment. Countries included in U.S. and German reports included Bangladesh, China, Malaysia, and Vietnam (Miller, 2009; Montero, 2009; ProPublica, n.d.). There were also countries in Eastern Europe and other regions of the world.

In December 2008, Siemens was fined heavily by U.S. and German authorities. The estimated fines amounted to $800 million in the U.S. to the Security and Exchange Commission (SEC) and the Department of Justice, and €395 million in Munich concerning failure of supervisory duties of the Siemens board, following a fine a year previously of €201 million for bribery by the telecommunications division. To that point Siemens had also paid some €850 million in legal and accounting fees. The total costs amounted to some €2.5 billion in December 2008 (Gow, 2008).

The convicted German employee, who orchestrated the bribery scheme for top management, was quoted as follows: "People will only say about Siemens that they were unlucky and that they broke the 11th Commandment." . . . "The 11th Commandment is: 'Don't get caught.'" (Schubert & Miller, 2008). An effort by Canada to bar Siemens (and some other countries such as Hewlett-Packard and BAE Systems) for doing business with the Canadian government for some time was met by a report for the Canadian Council of Chief Executives that there could be a World Trade Organization challenge and North American Free Trade Agreement investor lawsuits concerning such a policy (McKenna, 2014).

Volkswagen (Germany): Emissions Cheating— and Union Corruption

In September 2015, U.S. regulators announced the discovery of software in certain 2-liter VW diesel vehicles that turned on during emissions testing and turned off during normal driving, resulting in discharge of considerably more than legally allowed nitrogen oxide (Masunaga, 2016). VW admitted to the scheme (Klier & Linn, 2016), which has been labeled "Dieselgate" (Bovens, 2016). Two software engineers are believed to have developed this method of evading emissions testing when the diesel technology at VW would not meet the standards. Some evidence suggests that at least 30 VW executives may have collaborated in this fraud (Zhang, 2015). Some 11 million vehicles were involved, of which nearly 500,000 were in the United States (Zhang, 2015). The Environmental Protection Agency (EPA) estimate was 482,000 (Reitze, 2016). Boston (2015) traces the problem at VW back to conflicts within the company over diesel strategy. In June 2016, VW agreed to a settlement amount of up to $14.7 billion including buying back or terminating leases of nearly 500,000 vehicles in the United States (Masunaga, 2016). One study attributes the deception to middle management, which arguably collaborated in this scheme over years (Nelson, 2016). The ethics of this scheme is the subject of increased research interest (Bovens, 2016; Cavico & Mujtaba, 2016; Rhodes, 2016).

The EPA did not uncover the scheme through its regulatory procedures. Rather, there was an inquiry by the European environmental group the International Council on Clean Transportation (ICCT), which was interested in how VW was meeting more stringent U.S. standards, in order to promote an increase in European Union standards (Reitze, 2016). ICCT hired a research team at West Virginia University to test certain VW and BMW vehicles (Raby, 2015). The research team reported its findings to the EPA and the California Air Resources Board in May 2014.

In 1993, an earlier top management cultivated union leaders (Abdella, Di Tella, & Schlefer, 2008). Germany has a codetermination law, which includes a provision that firms pay worker representatives. VW wanted to undertake serious restructuring, which required union cooperation. The head of personnel created a position for a personnel liaison official to work closely with worker representatives. Reports indicate that the liaison official's job was to keep those representatives "satisfied"—effectively by any means necessary. There were organized annual retreats to tourist locations. In January 1996, a trip to Brazil apparently included nightlife and prostitutes in Rio de Janeiro, through a detour. The liaison official allegedly submitted real and false receipts so that VW covered the entire cost of the detour to Rio. Over 9 years, there were approximately €2 million in expenses. Essentially, trips to various countries were little more than country tours with prostitutes. Eventually, VW fired the liaison official (and another manager) over alleged embezzlement. At that point, information about the trips came out. The head of personnel resigned, and then was indicted and convicted on criminal charges of authorizing the payments. The liaison official was also convicted. The chief worker representative involved was later convicted and sentenced to 2 years 9 months in prison. That representative had reportedly spent €400,000 on a lover in Brazil. The two management officials involved received suspended sentences. The head of personnel was also fined €576,000.

Toshiba (Japan): Persistent Accounting Fraud in an Economic Downturn

In July 2015, the CEO, the vice chairman of the board of directors, and an adviser of Toshiba resigned following results of an independent investigation by external attorneys and accountants revealing that the company's profits had been seriously inflated for several years (Edwards, 2015). The chairman of the board took over as interim president. The investigation concluded that operating profit had been overstated by about $1.22 billion over several years. Another estimate is about 1.9 billion (Friedman & Gerstein, 2016). This conclusion was about three times the initial estimate reported by the company. The investigators also concluded that the CEO and the CEO's immediate predecessor had been aware of the overstatement. The investigators reportedly spoke to some 200 Toshiba personnel. The investigation was headed by a former senior prosecutor (Verschoor, 2015).

The investigation report attributed the situation to "institutional" accounting malpractices and a "corporate culture" preventing employees from complaining about demands for "increasingly unachievable profits" (Edwards, 2015). The report stated, "There existed a corporate culture at Toshiba where it was impossible to go against the boss' will" (Edwards, 2015). The report concluded that top management's involvement in profit inflation was systematic and deliberate (Edwards, 2015).

The Toshiba scandal began in February 2015 (Verschoor, 2015) with an investigation by the Securities and Exchange Surveillance Commission of Japan into profit recognition on certain large long-term projects in various business lines of the company (including air-traffic control, nuclear, hydro-electric, and wind-powered equipment). Essentially, for accounting purposes, management was required to estimate "percentage of completion" of long-term projects in order to recognize for each accounting period the proportionate share of estimated total profit (or loss) of each project. Estimation of project progress over time is under control of management, and essentially is a subjective matter (Friedman & Gerstein, 2016). Evidently, during and following the fiscal crisis of 2008, operating results were so bad that employees were unwilling to report them accurately (Verschoor, 2015). Thus, improper accounting practices occurred under the then CEO and the next two CEOs. Reportedly, the CEO in 2008 had told personnel to "get it done like your life depends on it" (Verschoor, 2015). The next two CEOs were in the same situation (Verschoor, 2015). The investigation report concluded that improper accounting became "a de facto policy of the management" (Fukase, 2015).

Some evidence of inflation was also uncovered in the United States, where Westinghouse Electric Co. is a unit of Toshiba (Friedman & Gerstein, 2016). There is some evidence reported that the CEO and CFO of Toshiba acted to influence Westinghouse managers during late 2013 and early 2014 not to report too high a quarterly loss (Schoenberg & Robinson, 2016).

Mitsubishi Motors (Japan): Mileage Falsification—for Decades

In April 2016 (Soble, 2016), Mitsubishi Motors reported that company engineers had deliberately falsified fuel-economy test results, in violation of Japanese testing standards, for an ultrasmall car (or microcar) called the eK and produced in Japan for sale in that country. The then president of Mitsubishi Motors reported at a news conference that about 620,000 cars sold in Japan from 2013 were affected. However, he also stated that the same testing method had been used on other models in Japan and that a broader investigation was being launched. It was reported that company executives had aggressively pressured employees for fuel efficiency (Bomey, 2016). In May 2016, the president resigned, without admitting any personal wrongdoing (Bomey, 2016). The resignation followed an acquisition of 34% of Mitsubishi Motors by Nissan Motor (Bomey, 2016). The eK model had also been sold under a Nissan label (Kageyama, 2016b). Apparently, Nissan testing had discovered the mileage problem (Kageyama, 2016a). As a result of the revelation, the Japanese government ordered all automakers to check mileage tests (Kageyama, 2016b). An internal investigation at Mitsubishi Motors found evidence of mileage falsification back to 1991 (Kageyama, 2016a).

In June 2016 (Kageyama, 2016b), the company offered each Japanese owner a compensation payment of $960. The company planned to take a $913 million charge for the expenses. A compensation payment of $290 was made for some other Mitsubishi models. The company denied there was any falsified mileage information for models sold outside Japan. Subsequently, the Japanese government ordered sales of more models—beyond the eK models—halted and reported that the cruise range on an electric car had been overstated (Kageyama, 2016c). A company spokesman stated that the firm had used best mileage results rather than average mileage results—there being a range of data on results (Kageyama, 2016c).

In August 2000, Mitsubishi Motors had admitted to hiding some tens of thousands of reported vehicle defects since 1977 (Tanikawa, 2000). It appeared that this concealment of customer complaints was systematic. The company recalled over 600,000 vehicles during July and August 2000, largely in Japan—including perhaps 50,000 vehicles exported to the United States. (The U.S. unit reduced the estimate of affected vehicles to perhaps 10,000.) At that time, company sales dropped nearly in half, and Mitsubishi Motors was close to bankruptcy as a result (Soble, 2016), recovering subsequently. Although there was at the time no evidence of fatal or serious accidents linked to the concealed defects, Mitsubishi Motors was legally obligated to report the defects to both U.S. and Japanese government authorities (Tanikawa, 2000). The reported reason for concealment of defects was that the company both avoided costly recalls and the public humiliation in Japan of such recalls (Tanikawa, 2000).

The General Electric (GE) Approach
to Integrity-Based Business

The German and Japanese instances can be contrasted to a General Electric (GE) model of integrity about which there is public information provided by the former chief legal officer Heineman (Heineman, 2007, 2008; Jones, 2008). The information concerns the building and operation of the GE model under CEOs Welch and Immelt. Heineman was a senior member of the top management team under both CEOs for some 20 years.

It is important here to point out that one should not interpret the decision to contrast a U.S. company with German and Japanese companies as any comment concerning national business cultures or regulatory regimes. It is simply the case that GE has a well-reported integrity-based approach, whereas the German and Japanese companies illustrate specific and reasonably common forms of noncompliance and absence of integrity (especially corruption and falsification of different kinds of reports). Wells Fargo bank would serve as an illustration of noncompliance and absence of integrity, but the incident is brand new and thus not as well reported or documented at this point. Jennings (2015) comments on the Toshiba scandal that one can be too judgmental of the specific situation at a particular company (Toshiba) and in a particular country (Japan). The problem of building and operating integrity-based organizations is much more universal.

The behavioral problem (Bazerman & Gino, 2012; Elsass, Park, Adkins, & April, 2016) concerns why (as well as how) managers engage in misconduct (and how frequently). The empirical problem concerns how various compliance enforcement mechanisms fail (and how frequently). There are some key defects in prescribing managerial behavior. First, the manager has to be virtuous; an honorable manager is the core assumption of integrity-based business. MBAs are not licensed, but they are well educated and knowledgeable with respect to proper conduct (Donaldson, 2000). Second, there must be reasonably clear rules, standards, and principles. In particular, legal or institutional corruption, defined as gaps and loopholes in standards, generate considerable grayness within which opportunistic personnel can operate (Kaufmann & Vicente, 2011; Patibandla, 2016). Gray standards combined with managerial discretion and absence of personal or professional integrity present a recipe for misconduct. Third, agency theory reinforces the managerial imperative to meet profit targets without much respect for rules, principles, or standards—much less integrity as defined in this chapter. Agency theory implies different behavior than do stewardship or trustee theories of responsibility for organizations and toward stakeholders. Undermining of moral integrity of individuals may be increased by interpersonal relationships. Gino and Galinsky (2012) tested for vicarious dishonesty and generosity in four studies using multiple manipulations of psychological closeness among individuals. Closeness to individuals who are selfish or dishonest or scoundrels can result in less moral behavior and greater moral disengagement. In effect, individuals may be more lenient with people to whom they are close. Closeness to generous individuals can increase one's own generosity. Psychological closeness can increase the distance from one's moral compass. Morality arguably has an important social nature in which socio-psychological processes are important influences (Moore & Gino, 2013).

This description is adapted from Heineman (2007) and Jones (2008). Heineman (2008) is the lengthier book version. Heineman's exposition of the GE approach begins with the "dark side" of market capitalism: the intense pressure on and in publicly traded firms for short-term earnings. This pressure appears highlighted in the Wells Fargo situation by news reports. As Heineman points out, when there is discovery, the costs to managers, employees, investors and other financial stakeholders can be quite high. (Here the chapter does not make an estimate concerning the likelihood of discovery.) Goldman Sachs settled for a $550 million fine on the ABACUS portfolio transaction, in which the firm made a $15 million fee (Baron, 2011). In the quarter of the settlement, Goldman Sachs likely cleared $3 billion profit. The CEO of Goldman Sachs was quoted in a 2010 interview as saying (Baron, 2011, p. 1): "We did a good job of managing risks [to Goldman Sachs,] but we did a less good job of managing our reputation." (Baron cites the *Economic Times* of India, 2010). Here the present author refers the reader back to the concept of positive reputation in business (Eccles, Newquist, & Schatz, 2007).

Heineman presents the case that the CEO must (the argument is stronger than should) develop an integrity-based culture that goes beyond compliance with rules through penalties. The essential features of this integrity-based culture are leadership, transparency, positive incentives, and appropriate processes. A key assumption is that business performance (including financial performance) is enhanced, rather than impeded, by integrity principles and practices. "Ultimately, it is a company's culture that sustains high performance with high integrity" (Heineman, 2007, p. 101). This culture requires continuous reinforcement from the CEO. Heineman (2007, p. 101) cites instances in which some senior managers were terminated for "knowingly or recklessly" violating company rules—whether for business or personal reasons. One manager failed to conduct required due diligence on third-party distributors with reputations for making improper payments in another. Dismissal decisions were independent of the business consequences for GE. Managers might also be dismissed for failure to create an integrity-based culture, demonstrated through concealment of improper acts intended to satisfy customers in other countries through procurement contract fraud or falsification of supplier documents for regulatory filings. (Similarly, a CEO should praise upright conduct that results in loss of business.) Heineman provides a set of seven principles and practices: (1) consistent and committed leadership; (2) transcending formal rules to a higher standard of global integrity; (3) anticipate systematically "financial, legal, and ethical developments" around the globe (Heineman, 2007, p. 104); (4) driving standards into business processes; (5) making key staff functions (finance, legal, and human resources) both partner and guardian; (6) providing voice to employees through an ombuds system, bottom-up annual review of compliance performance of each business unit, internal corporate audit, and the key staff functions of each business unit—financial, legal, and human resources; and (7) use of integrity metrics to hold executives and managers accountable. This culture—and the embedded principles and practices—was plainly absent at Siemens, VW, Toshiba, and Mitsubishi Motors. Siemens has been engaged in trying to build a new culture (Löscher, 2012). In July 2013, the reform CEO Peter Löscher was dismissed—partly for disappointing earnings performance and other difficulties—in favor of the CFO Joe Kaeser. The decision by the supervisory board of Siemens does illustrate the continuing difficult balancing problem at the company. VW, Toshiba, and Mitsubishi had not moved far enough along from their recent problems to gauge reform effectiveness presently.

Conclusion

This chapter explicates a proposed integrated model of managerial integrity and compliance. Figure 7.1 depicts this integrated model. Integrity is a term in increased use in business and professional situations to suggest strict ethical behavior in accord with personal and professional moral values. The idea is essentially that demands for business performance through improper actions (basically any means necessary) should be resisted by executives, directors, managers, and employees. Defining integrity does involve some problems, as discussed in the chapter. However, the basic approach is that integrity-based organizations build on, but transcend a foundation of compliance with regulations and similar standards for conduct. Compliance is rule oriented. Integrity is principled, in contrast. Compliance will tend to fail in an organization that is not integrity based; compliance should flourish in an organization that is integrity based.

The chapter discusses four mini-cases of companies in Germany and Japan that have had fairly recent scandals: global corruption as a business strategy at Siemens (Germany); union leadership corruption and diesel emissions-test falsification through software at Volkswagen (Germany); cooking the books at Toshiba (Japan); and mileage test falsification at Mitsubishi Motors (Japan). The absence of compliance and integrity at these companies is contrasted to the description of an integrity-based, and thus compliance-oriented, approach at General Electric (GE). The chapter also includes some discussion of building integrity-based organizations and of "giving voice to values" in such organizations.

References

Abdella, R., Di Tella, R., & Schlefer, J. (2008, July 30). *Corruption in Germany.* Harvard Business School case 9–709–006. Cambridge, MA: Harvard Business School.

Audi, R., & Murphy, P. E. (2006). The many faces of integrity. *Business Ethics Quarterly, 16*, 3–21.

Avci, S. B. & Seyhun, H. N. (2016, July 3). Why don't general counsels stop corporate crime? *Ross School of Business Paper No. 1326.* Retrieved from http://ssrn.com/abstract=2804352 or http://dx.doi.org/10.2139/ssrn.2804352.

Baron, D. P. (2008). *Siemens anatomy of bribery.* Stanford Graduate School of Business, Case No. P68. Stanford, CA: Stanford Graduate School of Business.

Baron, D. P. (2011). *Goldman Sachs and its reputation.* Stanford Graduate School of Business, Case No. P77. Stanford, CA: Stanford Graduate School of Business.

Bauman, D. C. (2013). Leadership and the three faces of integrity. *The Leadership Quarterly, 24*, 414–426.

Bazerman, M. H. & Gino, F. (2012). Behavioral ethics: Toward a deeper understanding of moral judgment and dishonesty. *Annual Review of Law and Social Science, 8*, 85–104.

Bomey, N. (2016, May 18). Mitsubishi motors president to resign over mileage scandal. *USA Today.* Retrieved from www.usatoday.com/story/money/cars/2016/05/18/mitsubishi-motors-president-resign-over-mileage-scandal/84530388/.

Boston, W. (2015, October 5). Volkswagen emissions investigation zeroes in on two engineers: Company investigation focuses on two men elevated after Winterkorn was made CEO. *Wall Street Journal*. Retrieved from www.wsj.com/articles/vw-emissions-probe-zeroes-in-on-two-engineers-1444011602.

Bovens, L. (2016). The ethics of Dieselgate. *Midwest Studies in Philosophy*, *40*(1), 262–283.

Cavico, F. J. & Mujtaba, B. G. (2016). Volkswagen emissions scandal: A global case study of legal, ethical, and practical consequences and recommendations for sustainable management. *Global Journal of Research in Business & Management*, *4*(2), 303–311.

Cheffers, M. & Pakaluk, M. (2005). *A new approach to understanding accounting ethics: Principles, professionalism, pride* (Chapter 2, From Rules to Principles, pp. 28–59). Manchaug, MA: Allen David Press.

Cowley, S. (2016, September 27). Wells Fargo: Fired for doing the right thing? *Houston Chronicle*, *115*(350), Tuesday, B1, B6 (Business).

Cox, D., La Caze, M., & Levine, M. (2013, January 25). Integrity. *Stanford Encyclopedia of Philosophy* (online). Retrieved from http://plato.stanford.edu/entries/integrity/.

Donaldson, T. (2000). Are business managers "professionals?" *Business Ethics Quarterly*, *10*(1), 83–93.

Eccles, R. G., Newquist, S. C., & Schatz, R. (2007, March–April). Reputation and its risks. *Harvard Business Review*, *85*(2), 104–114. Reprint R0702F.

Economic Times (ET) Bureau (2010, May 21). India is a very good investment: Lloyd Blankfein, CEO, Goldman Sachs. *Economic Times* (India). Retrieved from http://economictimes.indiatimes.com/opinion/interviews/india-is-a-very-good-investment-lloyd-blankfein-ceo-goldman-sachs/articleshow/5955955.cms.

Edwards, J. (2015, July 21). Toshiba CEO resigns over massive accounting scandal. Retrieved from www.businessinsider.com/r-toshiba-ceo-resigns-over-massive-accounting-scandal-2015-7.

Elsass, P., Park, J., Adkins, C., & April, K. (2016). Behavioral ethics exploring the global landscape in ethics education. *Journal of Management Education*, *40*(2), 220–222.

Erhard, W. & Jensen, M. C. (2015). *Putting integrity into finance: A purely positive approach*. Retrieved from http://ssrn.com/abstract=1985594.

Erhard, W., Jensen, M. C., & Zaffron, S. (2009, March 23). *Integrity: A positive model that incorporates the normative phenomena of morality, ethics and legality*. Retrieved from http://ssrn.com/abstract=920625 or http://dx.doi.org/10.2139/ssrn.920625.

Friedman, H. H. & Gerstein, M. (2016, September 14). Are we wasting our time teaching business ethics? Ethical lapses since Enron and the Great Recession. Retrieved from http://ssrn.com/abstract=2839069.

Fukase, A. (2015, December 7). Toshiba accounting scandal draws record fine from regulators. *Wall Street Journal*. Retrieved from www.wsj.com/articles/toshiba-accountingscandal-draws-record-fine-from-regulators-1449472485.

Gentile, M. C. (2010). Giving voice to values: How to speak your mind when you know what's right. New Haven, CT: Yale University Press.

Gentile, M. (2013). Giving voice to values: The "how" of values-driven leadership. *Oskin Thought Leader Series*, *1*(2), 1–5. Chester, PA: Widener University, Oskin Leadership Institute. Retrieved from www.widener.edu/about/widener_values/leadership/oskin_leadership/_docs/VoiceToValues.pdf.

Gino, F. (2016). How moral flexibility constrains our moral compass. In J.-W. van Prooijen & P. A. M. van Lange (Eds.), *Cheating, corruption, and concealment: The roots of dishonesty* (pp. 75–98). Cambridge, UK: Cambridge University Press.

Gino, F. & Galinsky, A. D. (2012). Vicarious dishonesty: When psychological closeness creates distance from one's moral compass. *Organizational Behavior and Human Decision Processes, 119*(1), 15–26.

Gonzalez-Padron, T. L., Ferrell, O. C., Ferrell, L., & Smith, I. A. (2012). A critique of giving voice to values approach to business ethics education. *Journal of Academic Ethics, 10,* 251–269.

Gow, D. (2008, December 15). Record US fine ends Siemens bribery scandal. *The Guardian* (Manchester). Retrieved from www.theguardian.com/business/2008/dec/16/regulation-siemens-scandal-bribery.

Heineman, B. W. (2007). Avoiding integrity land mines. *Harvard Business Review, 85*(4), April, 100–108. Reprint R0704G.

Heineman, B. W. (2008). *High performance with high integrity.* Boston, MA: Harvard Business Press.

Huber, W. M. (2015). Public accounting and the myth of the public interest. *Journal of Accounting, Ethics & Public Policy, 16*(2), 251–272.

Jennings, M. M. (2015). Toshiba lessons: On not being so judgmental of the company or Japan. *Corporate Finance Review, 20*(2), 36–39.

Jensen, M. C. (2014, April 6). Integrity: Without it nothing works (interview with K. Christensen). *Rotman Magazine: The Magazine of the Rotman School of Management,* Fall 2009, pp. 16–20. Retrieved from http://ssrn.com/abstract=1511274.

Jones, A. (2008, July 11). *On integrity and performance: A chat with former GE GC Ben Heineman.* Retrieved from http://blogs.wsj.com/law/2008/07/11/on-integrity-and-performance-a-chat-with-former-ge-gc-ben-heineman/.

Kageyama, Y. (2016a, April 27). Mitsubishi fuel-economy fibs date back a quarter-century. *Houston Chronicle, 115*(197), Wednesday, B5 (Business).

Kageyama, Y. (2016b, June 20). Drivers offered cash over rigged mileage. *Houston Chronicle, 115*(225), Monday, B6 (Business).

Kageyama, Y. (2016c, September 1). Mileage scandal grows in Japan. *Houston Chronicle, 115*(324), Thursday, B3 (Business).

Kang, Y.-C. & Wood, D. J. (1995). Before-profit social responsibility: Turning the economic paradigm upside-down. In D. Nigh & D. Collins (Eds.), *Proceedings of the 6th Annual Meeting of the International Association for Business and Society (IABS)* (pp. 408–418). Vienna, Austria: International Association for Business and Society (IABS).

Karnani, A. (2010, August 23). The case against corporate social responsibility. *Wall Street Journal, 9986,* p. R1.

Kaufmann, D. & Vicente, P. C. (2011). Legal corruption. *Economics and Politics, 23*(2), 195–219.

Kayes, D. C., Stirling, D., & Nielsen, T. M. (2007). Building organizational integrity. *Business Horizons, 50,* 61–70.

Klier, T. H. & Linn, J. (2016). The VW scandal and evolving emissions regulations. *Chicago Fed Letter.* Retrieved from www.chicagofed.org/~/media/publications/chicago-fed-letter/2016/cfl357-pdf.pdf?la=en.

Klinkhammer, J. (2013). On the dark side of the code: Organizational challenges to an effective anti-corruption strategy. *Crime, Law and Social Change, 60*(2), 191–208.

Koren, J. R. (2016, September 28). Wells Fargo: Bank's CEO will forfeit millions. *Houston Chronicle, 115*(351), Wednesday, B1, B9 (Business).

Löscher, P. (2012, November). The CEO of Siemens on using a scandal to drive change. *Harvard Business Review, 90*(11), 39–42.

Ma, F. (2016). Business integrity v. business efficiency: The corporate opportunity doctrine in China. *Journal of Financial Crime, 23*(1), 201–215.

McFall, L. (1987). Integrity. *Ethics, 98*(1), 5–20.

McKenna, B. (2014, November 14). Ottawa could face lawsuits for strict corruption rules: Report. *The Globe and Mail.* Toronto, Canada. Retrieved from www.theglobeandmail.com/report-on-business/international-business/ottawa-could-face-lawsuits-for-strict-trade-corruption-rules-report/article21739211/.

Manz, C. C., Anand, V., Joshi, M., & Manz, K. P. (2008). Emerging paradoxes in executive leadership: A theoretical interpretation of the tensions between corruption and virtuous values. *The Leadership Quarterly, 19*(3), 385–392.

Masunaga, S. (2016, September 9). Engineer in U.S. pleads guilty in VW emissions scandal. *Houston Chronicle, 115*(333), Friday, B6 (Business).

Merle, R. (2016, September 8). *Wells Fargo books 5,300 employees for creating accounts its customers didn't ask for.* Retrieved from www.washingtonpost.com/news/business/wp/2016/09/08/wells-fargo-fined-185-million-for-creating-accounts-its-customers-didnt-ask-for/.

Milgrom, P. & Roberts, J. (1986). Relying on the information of interested parties. *Rand Journal of Economics, 17*, 18–32.

Miller, T. C. (2009, December 22). Help us name names in Siemens *Corruption Scandal.* Retrieved from www.propublica.org/article/help-us-name-names-in-siemens-corruption-scandal-1222.

Montero, D. (2009, April 1). *Bangladesh: Following the Siemens bribery trail: Sons of former prime minister charged in large corruption sweep.* Retrieved from www.pbs.org/frontlineworld/stories/bribe/2009/04/bangladesh-following-the-siemens-bribery-trail.html.

Moore, C. & Gino, F. (2013). Ethically adrift: How others pull our moral compass from true North, and how we can fix it. *Research in Organizational Behavior, 33*, 53–77.

Nelson, J. S. (2016, April 19). *The criminal bug: Volkswagen's middle management.* Retrieved from http://ssrn.com/abstract=2767255.

Olsthoorn, P. (2009). A critique of integrity: Has a commander a moral obligation to uphold his own principles? *Journal of Military Ethics, 8*(2), 90–104.

Paine, L. S. (1991). Ethics as character development: Reflections on the objective of ethics education. In R. E. Freeman (Ed.), *Business ethics: The state of the art* (pp. 67–88). New York: Oxford University Press.

Paine, L. S. (1994, March–April). Managing for organizational integrity. *Harvard Business Review, 72*(2), 106–117. Reprint 94207.

Parry, K. W. & Proctor-Thomson, S. B. (2002). Perceived integrity of transformational leaders in organizational settings. *Journal of Business Ethics, 35*(2), 75–96.

Patibandla, M. (2016, May). Institutional Corruption: Few Issues. Indian Institute of Management Bangalore, Working Paper No. 516. Retrieved from www.iimb.ernet.in/research/sites/default/files/WP%20No.%20516.pdf.

ProPublica (n.d.). *The world wide web of Siemens's corruption.* Retrieved from www.propublica.org/special/the-world-wide-web-of-siemenss-corruption.

Raby, J. (2015, September 28). W. Virginia unit a pioneer in testing fuel emissions. *Houston Chronicle, 114*(350), Monday, B8 (Business).

Reid, M. (2011). Where ethics and legality collide. *Canadian Military Journal, 11*(3), 5–13. Retrieved from www.journal.forces.gc.ca/vol11/no3/doc/03-reid-eng.pdf.

Reitze, A. W. (2016). The Volkswagen air pollution emissions litigation. *Environmental Law Reporter, 46*(7), July, 10564–10571. Retrieved from http://ssrn.com/abstract=2805186.

Rhodes, C. (2016, April 7). Democratic business ethics: Volkswagen's emissions scandal and the disruption of corporate sovereignty. *Organization Studies* (Online First ahead of print), doi:10.1177/0170840616641984.

Ridlehuber, R. (2016, September 25). Guest Columnist: Here's what went wrong at Wells Fargo. *Houston Chronicle, 115*(348), Sunday, B5 (Business).

Rieke, M. L. & Guastello, S. J. (1995). Unresolved issues in honesty and integrity testing. *American Psychologist, 50*, 458–459.

Rothenberg, K. H. (2009). Recalibrating the moral compass: Expanding "thinking like a lawyer" into "thinking like a leader." *University of Toledo Law Review, 40*, 411–420.

Schembera, S. & Scherer, A. G. (2014, February 25). *Organizing Corruption Controls after a Scandal: Regaining Legitimacy in Complex and Changing Institutional Environments.* University of Zurich, Institute of Business Administration, UZH Business Working Paper, No. 343. Retrieved from http://ssrn.com/abstract=2400936 or http://dx.doi.org/10.2139/ssrn.2400936.

Schoenberg, T. & Robinson, M. (2016, March 17). *Toshiba shares plunge as U.S. unit faces accounting probe.* Retrieved from www.bloomberg.com/news/articles/2016-03-17/toshiba-said-to-face-u-s-probeover-westinghouse-accounting.

Schubert, S. & Miller, T. C. (2008, December 20). *At Siemens, bribery was just a line item.* Retrieved from www.nytimes.com/2008/12/21/business/worldbusiness/21siemens.html?_r=0.

Seppälä, E. (2016, January 25). Why compassion serves you better than self-interest. *Knowledge@Wharton.* Retrieved from http://knowledge.wharton.upenn.edu/article/compassion-serves-better-self-interest/.

Sidhu, K. (2009). Anti-corruption compliance standards in the aftermath of the Siemens scandal. *German Law Journal, 10*(8), 1343–1354. Retrieved from www.germanlawjournal.com/volume-10-no-08.

Soble, J. (2016, April 20). Mitsubishi admits cheating on fuel-economy tests. *New York Times.* Retrieved from www.nytimes.com/2016/04/21/business/mitsubishi-fuel-economy-tests.html?_r=0.

Tanikawa, M. (2000, August 23). *New York Times.* Retrieved from www.nytimes.com/2000/08/23/business/mitsubishi-admits-to-broad-cover-up-of-auto-defects.html.

Tinker, T., Sy, A., & Saxe, E. (2016). Professionalism and professionalisation ethics in business and industry. *International Journal of Critical Accounting, 8*(1), 19–29.

Tomlinson, C. (2016, September 25). Safety expert says danger in broken corporate cultures. *Houston Chronicle, 115*(348), Sunday, B5 (Business).

Verschoor, C. C. (2015). Toshiba's toxic culture: In Japan, where it's disrespectful to disobey orders, a poor tone at the top can be detrimental to a company. *Strategic Finance, 97*(5), 18–20.

Verhezen, P. (2010). Giving voice in a culture of silence: From a culture of compliance to a culture of integrity. *Journal of Business Ethics, 96*(2), 187–206.

Windsor, D. (2013a). A typology of moral exemplars in business. In M. Schwartz & H. Harris (Eds.), *Moral saints and moral exemplars: Research in ethical issues in organizations* (Vol. 10, pp. 63–95). Bingley, UK: Emerald Group Publishing.

Windsor, D. (2013b). Corporate social responsibility and irresponsibility: A positive theory approach. *Journal of Business Research, 66*(10), 1937–1944.

Windsor, D. (2015a). Ethics in managing corporate power and politics. In K. Ogunyemi (Ed.), *Teaching ethics across the management curriculum* (pp. 277–302). New York: Business Expert Press.

Windsor, D. (2015b). Identifying reasons why some firms maximize corporate social irresponsibility and some firms minimize corporate social responsibility. In A. Stachowicz-Stanusch (Ed.), *Corporate social performance* (pp. 67–89). Charlotte, NC: IAP—Information Age Publishing.

Windsor, D. (2015c). Philosophy for managers and philosophy of managers: Turf, reputation, coalition. *Philosophy of Management, 14*(1), 17–28.

Windsor, D. (2016). Economic rationality and a moral science of business ethics. *Philosophy of Management, 15*(1), 135–149.

Windsor, D. (forthcoming). The ethical sphere: Organizational politics, fairness and justice. In E. Vigoda-Gadot & A. Drory (Eds.), *Handbook of politics* (2nd ed.). Cheltenham, UK & Northampton, MA: Edward Elgar Publishing.

Yusoff, R. B. M., Kazi, A. G., Arisar, M. M. K., Jamil, F., & Hishan, S. S. (2016). Role of integrity in the success of freelancing and entrepreneurship: A conceptual review. *International Review of Management and Marketing, 6*(4S), 250–254. Retrieved from www.econjournals.com/index.php/irmm/article/view/2495/pdf.

Zarim, Z. A. & Zaki, H. O. (2016). Ethics and integrity in building employee's perceptions. *Management, 4*(3), 131–137. Retrieved from www.davidpublishing.org/Public/uploads/Contribute/566e5bd282e35.pdf.

Zeff, S. A. (2003a). How the U.S. accounting profession got where it is today: Part I. *Accounting Horizons, 17*(3), 189–205.

Zeff, S. A. (2003b). How the U.S. accounting profession got where it is today: Part II. *Accounting Horizons, 17*(4), 267–286.

Zhang, B. (2015, October 7). *This is the real cause of the Volkswagen cheating scandal.* Retrieved from http://finance.yahoo.com/news/real-cause-vw-cheating-scandal-191153186.html;_ylt=AwrT6Vthd.pXYtQAXn8PxQt.;_ylu=X3oDMT Byb3B2a242BHNlYwNzcgRwb3MDMwRjb2xvA2dxMQR2dGlkAw.

Zwilling, M. (2012, March 30). *5 ways to see if your business integrity is showing.* Retrieved from www.forbes.com/sites/martinzwilling/2012/03/30/5-ways-to-see-if-your-business-integrity-is-showing/#2e22f7fc53bd.

8 Pragmatism and Integrity
A Second Look

David C. Jacobs

Introduction

As the contributors to this volume affirm, integrity is a central concept in business ethics and ethics in general. While it is often defined simply as honesty or trustworthiness, in its multiple uses it shows a plasticity of meaning, adapting to context and the concerns of actors. Managers and corporate leaders have attempted to harness it to benefit their organizations. Social scientists have operationalized it as a variable. Becker (1998) and others have noted that integrity has been employed in empirical research as a predictor of job performance, as a central trait of effective leaders, as a determinant of trust in organizations, as an influence on organizational citizenship behaviors, as an element of transformational leadership, as a determinant of employee attitudes, and so on (Tomlinson, Lewicki, & Ash, 2014; Parry & Proctor-Thomson, 2002). Stakeholder groups have targeted deficits in integrity in managers and regulators. Public figures have responded to criticism with bold claims of integrity.

What is it about integrity that elevates its apparent priority in practical ethical discussions? Integrity symbolizes a hope that sustains members of organizations and reassures members and leaders that rules will be properly observed, and gives hope to outsiders and members of disparate constituencies that they will find means to satisfy their claims. It is an antidote to anomie and alternative to desperation. If integrity is nowhere to be found, how can we engage with the organizations that surround us? Integrity is also an invitation to negotiations as alternate conceptions meet.

On the other hand, sometimes integrity is a shield, a means for those in embattled organizations to represent their practices as sound even when there is good reason to doubt them. It helps to disguise moments at which rules and rigid dogma prove damaging to some and inspire resistance. The assertion of integrity may suggest the opposite. Think of moments when the defenders of controversial public figures claim "the utmost integrity" for their friends.

The concept of integrity reflects several dimensions of human consciousness. It may embody a natural urge that coincides with the evolution of ethical awareness. At the most basic level, it manifests the urge to protect self and family as one whole. It also refers to the development of rules through which organizations preserve some combination of authority and fairness. It emerges from reflexivity, routine, and rule making.

In this chapter, I extend and modify my previous arguments for a pragmatist integrity (Jacobs, 2004), guided by the social consequences of one's decisions, with the potential to motivate individuals and groups in their negotiations with the world of organizations, blending John Dewey with Reinhold Niebuhr. A pragmatist approach subjects organizations and organizational routines to question. Organizations are understood as merely provisional instruments of human collaboration.

As prelude, I introduce a typology of conceptions of integrity. Second, I describe several ideas that contribute to the development of a pragmatist model: integrity as wholeness, virtue as memory, and the problem of power. I introduce the moderate pessimism of Reinhold Niebuhr as a corrective to excessive optimism about any model of social change. Third, I turn to John Dewey for an elaboration of philosophical pragmatism. Finally, I propose social bargains as a form of problem solving deriving from pragmatist integrity.

Typologies of Integrity

Multiple conceptualizations of integrity are presented in this volume. Palanski and Yammarino (2007) identify five different interpretations of integrity among the many: integrity as wholeness, consistency between words and deeds, stalwart and principled behavior under conditions of adversity, personal authenticity, and morally sound behavior. Peck (1987) links integrity with the whole person. Some, including Solomon (1992), describe integrity primarily as an attribute of individuals. Integrity thus incorporates a set of virtues. Objectivists (Becker, 1998) stress honesty in rational contracting in order to fashion a conception of integrity that upholds their vision of individualism and laissez-faire capitalism. Consistency is important insofar as it serves market transactions. Others focus on organizations or corporations as potential embodiments of integrity and therefore apply consistency, authenticity, and other values to the degree that they have organizational analogues. Maak (2008) is among those formulating integrity for the corporation, in his case evaluation commitment, conduct, content, context, consistency, coherence, and continuity. Petrick and Quinn (2000) and Monga (2016) also seek to develop models of corporate integrity, blending concerns of organizational maintenance and social responsibility.

Underlying the cacophony of competing notions, one notes that several thinkers assume the legitimacy and priority of some institution as critical to integrity, whether it be business, capitalism as a whole, the church, or democratic governance. In comparing conceptions of freedom, Bergmann (1977) writes of "areas of self-identification," within which one might regard oneself as free. Similarly, many cannot speak of integrity without embedding it within the contexts with which their identities are bound.

I would propose an alternate threefold typology of conceptions of integrity: (a) plain consistency; (b) consistency in the pursuit of a moral standard, possibly consideration for self and others, prior to the demands of existing organizations; and (c) consistency as a means to organization or system maintenance. This last classification, arguably, includes Objectivists and corporate integrity thinkers. Sometimes the rigorous rule-enforcement definition of integrity is fundamentally about authority or hierarchy.

Some have hoped to arrive at an integration of these conceptions, but there are significant differences between them. I would not argue that there are unbridgeable gaps between "moral tribes" (Greene, 2013). The various conceptions emerge from and are modified by social interaction, cooperation, and conflict.

Elements of Pragmatist Integrity

Wholeness

I would now like to explore several ideas that will ultimately align with a pragmatist perspective: wholeness, virtue as memory, and resistance to concentrated power.

The Stanford Encyclopedia of Philosophy (2013) describes the physical interpretation of integrity as follows:

> One may speak of the integrity of a wilderness region or an ecosystem, a computerized database, a defense system, a work of art, and so on. When it is applied to objects, integrity refers to the wholeness, intactness or purity of a thing—meanings that are sometimes carried over when it is applied to people.

The *Oxford English Dictionary* notes that the origin of the word integrity is the Latin *integritas*, meaning wholeness or completeness. First among the definitions is

> the condition of having no part or element taken away or wanting; undivided or unbroken state; material wholeness, completeness, entirety.

Many writers emphasize this theme of physical wholeness in the ethical context. They suggest that an individual with integrity respects no partitions or fissures in his or her thinking and action. They submit that integrity requires that an individual confront opportunities and dilemmas with full humanity, without compartmentalizations, blending reason and emotion, self-regard, and social consciousness. In the whole person, both reason and emotion are recognized as sources of knowledge. In fact, considering the complexities of cognition, even theory and practice, the intellectual and manual, may not be as distinct as is commonly supposed (Stanley & Krakauer, 2013).

This wholeness-centered interpretation of integrity may reflect the natural origins of ethical awareness. Daniel Dennett (1995), among others, has stressed the evolutionary origins of ethical awareness. The natural urge to protect oneself and family, bodily and family integrity, may be extended and elaborated in human evolution, manifesting a broadening social consciousness.

Peck (1987) worried that

> we human beings [often] take matters that are properly related to each other and put them in separate, airtight mental compartments where they don't rub up against each other and cause us any pain . . . [but we must] . . . fully experience the tension of conflicting needs, demands, and interests . . . even be emotionally torn apart by them.
>
> (p. 235)

Peck notes an interesting contradiction: The whole self experiences tension and conflict, given competing demands. Wholeness does not guarantee harmony with others. The whole person may find peril in the modern power- and profit-seeking organization. (David Weil (2014) has written of the "fissured workplace," the corporation that relies on a proliferating array of subcontractors pressed to preserve brand standards often at the expense of labor standards.)

Virtue

Integrity defined as personal virtue is prior to and independent from organization. Solomon (1992) submitted that integrity is a "supervirtue," binding a complex of virtues and directing the interactions of individuals and groups, qualifying organizational loyalty with the constraints of autonomy and humility and incorporating "a pervasive sense of social context and a sense of moral courage that means standing up for others as well as oneself" (Solomon, 1992, p. 174). Carson (1995, p. 16) also connected integrity cast as virtue. He argued that "an unwavering commitment to acting for the benefit of others, standing up for those who are under attack, loyalty to people to whom we have committed ourselves, acting honorably, and so on" (p. 6) would earn the designation of integrity. Needless to say, these definitions of integrity do not prioritize the organization.

Aristotle defined virtue as a disposition to behave morally and in moderation. Virtue emerges from practice; it is informed by the memory of choices and consequences. The understanding of virtue sets some constraints on experimentation and opportunism. One's choices should be guided by past experience, by a receptivity to the evidence of social consequences as they unfold, from which memories the virtues are inferred. (The reader will see that a pluralist pragmatism accepts heuristics and codes as provisional tools, all to be further tested in experience.)

Resistance to Concentrated Power

As writers have applied conceptions of integrity in the context of business practice, they have sought to embed integrity in the structure of organizations. This seems to represent a qualitative shift in the character of the idea, or at least a shift in its locus. As will soon be evident, the pragmatist perspective must contend with organizations but is not anchored by them.

Petrick (2007) and Monga (2016), among others, have sought to develop an approach to integrity that reflects corporate organization, but is also responsive to external concerns. Petrick, for example, has written that

> integrity is both a personal and a social capacity to coherently process moral awareness, deliberation, character, and conduct, to regularly render balanced and inclusive judgments regarding moral results, rules, character, and context, to routinely demonstrate mature moral reasoning and relationship development, and to design and/or sustain morally supportive intraorganizational and extraorganizational systems. The four dimensions of integrity are process, judgment, development, and system capacities; they both enable and reflect moral coherence, moral wholeness, moral maturity, and moral environment.
>
> (2007, p. 1141)

Petrick mixes personal and organizational processes in a manner that defies easy understanding. One might wonder if his approach is so entangled with existing organizations that it cannot distinguish many problematic situations. Would it extend to the distant reaches of global supply chains? The modern "fissured" and "leveraged" organization has power centers that fall outside the boundaries of "integrity management" and "integrity capacity" (see Appelbaum & Batt, 2014; Weil, 2014).

Maak (2008) finds "corporate social responsibility" wanting and proposes "corporate integrity" in its place. Maak's corporate integrity depends upon the "7 Cs": commitment, conduct, content, context, consistency, coherence, and continuity. It would appear that Maak assumes a unitary character to the organization that corresponds poorly to the modern enterprise pressed by investors, including private equity funds, to emphasize return over organizational integrity or survival.

Monga (2016) adds to Maak's framework two dimensions: intrinsic and extrinsic, which helpfully illuminate the seven elements of the framework. In Monga's analysis, commitment and coherence are intrinsic to the person and enterprise; the other factors are extrinsic. Like Maak, Monga seeks to superimpose coherence on a differentiated and protean institutional configuration which depends on one's accepting the organization as defined by an impermanent management faction rather than by a collection of occupational communities.

Many corporations have established ethical compliance systems that cite integrity as a fundamental principle. Consulting firm KPMG (now KPMG Forensics), among others, has had a division focusing on "integrity management," whose stated purpose was

> to help clients achieve the highest levels of business integrity in an efficient and effective way. Our focus is always to assist our clients in their efforts to 'do the right thing in the right way.' We can also support organizations in 'measuring' integrity, enabling the implementation of an effective 'integrity policy'. For this purpose, we developed a number of practical, tried-and-tested tools, based on specialist knowledge of integrity risks and dilemmas, as well as specific industry knowledge.

Win Swenson, a former principal with KPMG Integrity Management, stated that he had been distressed by the weakness of KPMG's ethical compliance program (CCR, 2006). Swenson had actually been the director of the U.S. Corporate Sentencing Guidelines Commission, which stipulated lesser sentences in cases of corporate law-breaking if the corporation had enacted legal compliance systems. In 2005, KPMG admitted to fraud amounting to at least $2.5 billion in tax evasion and was granted a deferred prosecution agreement.

Converting integrity to a technique of management and purchasing it from a consultant in an industry recently bedeviled by conflicts of interest seems to compound the deficits of a conception of integrity anchored by a corporate organization. There are perils in the managerial frame of reference that underlie many of these views of integrity, particularly the corporate form last mentioned. Some larger questions are easily obscured. The autonomous choices of managers, however modulated, ordinarily presuppose that the enterprise is a higher end to which managerial choices are means.

Absent from the consciousness of those who argue for corporate integrity is a concern for the corruptions of power. In his *The Children of Light and the Children of Darkness* (Niebuhr, 1944), Reinhold Niebuhr (a Protestant theologian with an Augustinean view of sin) wrote,

> The left and the right have both been guilty of an illusion that people in power can be trusted to do good [. . .]. Inordinate power tempts its holders to abuse it, which means to use it for their own ends.
>
> (1944, p. 53)

Niebuhr specifically had in mind both corporate executives and political leaders. He would not have been convinced that managerially derived conceptions of integrity would be sufficient to check the abuse of power. Although corporate or organizational integrity systems may impose significant constraints on the behavior of corporate officers and employees, it still takes the enterprise as a given, and the corporation is now highly unstable terrain, as private equity funds press for restructuring. Corporate integrity possibly compartmentalizes a divided and increasingly fractured corporate self limited in moral reach. There are likely to be practices that escape sufficient scrutiny from within such a system.

Despite the bizarre conception of the corporation as a legal person with unlimited life, it is not a human actor, and its identity and boundaries are fluid. When managers formulate an integrity program and instruct subordinates to comply, they may actually preempt necessary deliberations among employees and other managers in the pursuit of integrity. Integrity applies more forcefully, I think, to individuals and groups, self-conscious human actors who do not need to fixate on the impermanent boundaries of organizations.

In their integrative social contracts theory (ISCT), Donaldson and Dunfee (1999) undertake a challenging project: to fashion a locally and globally relevant business ethics model utilizing social contract theory. They explained that globally apparent hypernorms should guide the negotiation of microsocial contracts within which business enterprise is formed. In *Ties That Bind* (Donaldson & Dunfee, 1999), they listed integrity along with fairness and respect for others as timeless principles that should shape and limit social contracting. They specifically refused to consider the details of enterprise creation to verify their conception of social contracting. Donaldson and Dunfee (1999) and later Gosling and Huang (2009) embrace an integrity focused on managers, not the whole of the community. All appeal to hypernorms as a constraint on micronorms, but hypernorms should motivate all organizational and community members in the shaping of institutions, not managers alone.

In ISCT, who are the parties to the microsocial contract? Private equity intervention can dissolve any such contracts. Peak institutions can discipline corporate actors. This exacerbates the fiction of the social contract. But Gosling and Huang's analysis stipulates hypernorms that provide standards for microsocial contracts and require that integrity be more than consistency.

The Children of Light and the Children of Darkness once again provides some corrective insights. Donaldson and Dunfee do not appear to consider the possibility that leaders of organizations are routinely corrupted by their power and may consult insufficiently with employees or neighbors to give meaning to the putative social contracts to which the authors refer. However, the value of integrative social contracts theory is that it can be severed from its assumptions about existing markets and retooled to provide the basic of a critical reconstruction (just as the rational contracting illusions of Objectivism can inspire a search for meaningful alternatives) as the reader will see (Donaldson & Dunfee, 1999, p. viii). In my view, ISCT fails, in part, because of a false picture of freedom of contract or social contract. As Gilbert Preiss (2014) explains so well, choice among a narrow set of options may constitute rational choice, but it is not free choice. The choices that appear to the individual lacking collective power are of lesser value than choices assuming collective power.

Private Equity at Work by Appelbaum and Batt (2014) and *The Fissured Workplace* by Weil (2014) do pose difficult challenges for organization-based models of integrity.

Appelbaum and Batt (2014) describe the transformation of enterprises and degradation of work that seem to accompany private equity interventions. Weil explores the rampant labor law violations occurring in complex organizations depending upon corporate headquarters and networks of contractors. In what unit of disintermediated enterprise can inclusive integrity regimes emerge?

(Note that neoclassical economists who view all economic activity as rational contracting can justify new forms of enterprise in the "fissured workplace" as rational responses to market forces, but they fail to consider the actual consequences for workers.)

Pragmatism and Business Ethics

Several scholars have suggested that philosophical pragmatism would be an appropriate framework for business ethics. Frederick (2000), Buchholz and Rosenthal (1997), Wicks and Freeman (1998), and others have emphasized the nuanced understanding of individuals and organizations as well as the rejection of dichotomies between facts and values, reason and emotion, mind and body that characterizes pragmatism.

Dewey denied any notion of a transcendent reality or absolute truth visible only to pure reason. Similarly, he disputed the value of abstract theory asserted over concrete situations. He would not, for example, affirm the market logic of factory production over the apparent reality of low wages, speedups, and supervisory abuse. Nor would he treat the "working class" as an abstraction, either in Marxist or neoclassical economics. Dewey would not embrace an ideal of "free markets," "class struggle," or technological progress stripped from material reality. Rather, he would insist upon the evaluation of experience and experimentation in individual action and collective choices. From Dewey's perspective, individuals and groups deliberate about their options and discover provisional truths to guide them (Dewey, 1958, p. 74).

Deweyan pragmatism finds "scientific" experimentation to be within the capacity of every individual. Although professional scientists practice experimentation with rigor, ordinary individuals learn from experiments and broader experience as well. Children cannot learn to speak or walk without trying sounds and exploring movements. Members of organizations learn from experience as well, and their experience does not respect temporary organizational boundaries. Individuals can enhance their contributions to their organizations and society if they regard themselves as participants in craft and professional communities and continue to practice and experiment. (Needless to say, Dewey did not assign a special function to managers. Dewey would deny that ethics applies in different ways to managers and workers.)

Dewey's approach to ethics combined careful and deliberate case-by-case analysis as well as reflection on experience. Dewey (1920) provided a sketch of a *moral situation*:

> A moral situation is one in which judgment and choice are required antecedently to overt action. The practical meaning of the situation— that is to say the action needed to satisfy it—is not self-evident. It has to be searched for. There are conflicting desires and alternate apparent goods. What is needed is to find the right course of action, the right good. Hence, inquiry is exacted: observation of the detailed makeup of the situation; analysis into its diverse factors; clarification of what is obscure; discounting of the more insistent and vivid traits; tracing the consequences of the various modes of action that suggest themselves; regarding the decision reached as hypothetical and tentative until the anticipated or supposed consequences that led to its adoption have been squared with actual consequences. This inquiry is intelligence.
>
> (pp. 163–164)

There are economies of effort; that is, the individual can learn from analogous situations and consider the insights reflected in conceptions of virtue. Moral decision making is an iterative process, incorporating feedback and course correction.

Pragmatism does not require the use of a fixed algorithm for the assessment of experience and consequences. Rather, it calls for judgment. Moreover, the social consequences to be predicted or assessed extend to social and institutional details and local circumstances. Dewey inquired as to the specific conditions of people's lives, hesitating to generalize about a generic public. In fact, Dewey used the word *public* to mean a specific social group that came into existence to challenge some existing practice and to offer remedies based on particular experiences. He argued that the understandings of such publics were indispensable to social problem solving.

Dewey's publics perhaps resemble the "mediating structures" that Peter Berger and Richard Neuhaus (1977) regarded as critical to democracy, but they are more fluid and improvisational and inhabit traditional intermediate organizations. One might also compare Dewey's publics to "stakeholders" in business ethics scholarship. However, Dewey's approach is not associated with a style of managing or question of technique in management. Rather, it is a guide for democratic social change.

Dewey's concept of publics is evident in the text of the *Port Huron Statement*, a radical manifesto of the 1960s. Note the following definition of *participatory democracy*:

In a participatory democracy, the political life would be based in several root principles:

> that decision-making of basic social consequence be carried on by public groupings; that politics be seen positively, as the art of collectively creating an acceptable pattern of social relations; that politics has the function of bringing people out of isolation and into community, thus being a necessary, though not sufficient, means of finding meaning in personal life; that the political order should serve to clarify problems in a way instrumental to their solution; it should provide outlets for the expression of personal grievance and aspiration; opposing views should be organized so as to illuminate choices and facilities the attainment of goals; channels should be commonly available to related men to knowledge and to power so that private problems—from bad recreation facilities to personal alienation—are formulated as general issues.
>
> (Hayden & the Students for a Democratic Society, 1963)

Dewey's focus on emergent experience (and social consequences) requires attention to the conditions of others and invites their perspectives even if they are "low" in station and lacking in credentials. Dewey (1939, p. 401) wrote, "The individuals of the submerged mass may not be very wise. But there is one thing they are wiser about than anybody else can be, and that is where the shoe pinches, the troubles they suffer from." Judgments based on the prediction of consequence can, of course, fail when the prediction is faulty. There may be unintended consequences, for which reason a feedback loop is essential.

Thus, Dewey's pragmatism (and pragmatist integrity) requires a larger view of the social reality including the condition of the least well-off and attention to their voices. What particularly distinguishes the pragmatism is the critical approach to office and organization as means not ends in themselves. The pragmatist avoids ethical compartmentalization as he or she works within and without the organization, seeking to improve the social reality and to avoid unintended negative social consequences.

It must be noted that the individual and the collective are often blurred in the consideration of business. The corporation is a collective instrument and yet is treated in the law as a person and is sometimes accorded the personality of an individual. Pragmatism is particularly helpful in its illumination of the false view of business as an extension of the individual. It should be noted that pragmatism is equally hostile to an individualism that denies social context and a statist philosophy that denies all claims of the individual.

Dewey emphasized personal change and development in his version of pragmatism, and thus, a pragmatist integrity will admit the constancy of change. Dewey believed that engagement with the world of experience and moral decision necessarily alters the individual: "In short, the thing actually at stake in any serious deliberation is not difference of quantity, but what kind of person one is to become, what sort of self is in the making, what kind of a world is making" (Dewey, 1983, p. 150).

To summarize, a pragmatist approach to integrity requires that individuals consider the objective social consequences (immediate and emergent) of their actions and stress personal growth and an integrated personality. However, this approach has some flaws which can be addressed with a dose of Niebuhrian pessimism. In order to correct for Dewey's excessive optimism about the potential of "intelligence" to revolutionize social institutions, one must add some vigilance to correct for the perils of authoritarianism, whether emerging from popular prejudice or elite condescension.

Limits to Intelligence

Peter Levine (2016) writes,

> When everything is left open to experimentation and learning, people may spend hundreds of years "learning" that they can own other people or that Jews are blood-sucking parasites. We should rather treat as sacred and unamendable such passages as Article One of the German Constitution: (1) Human dignity shall be inviolable [. . .]

Levine worries that a freewheeling pragmatism might reproduce and amplify popular misconceptions. Niebuhr (1960) located the danger in the conceits of groups:

> In every human group there is less reason to guide and to check impulse, less capacity for self-transcendence, less ability to comprehend the needs of others and therefore more unrestrained egoism than the individuals, who compose the group, reveal in their personal relationships. . . . The thesis to be elaborated in these pages is that a sharp distinction must be drawn between the moral and social behavior of individuals and of social groups, national, racial and economic; and that thus distinction justifies and necessitates political policies which a purely individualistic ethic must always find embarrassing.
>
> (p. xxix)

As I indicated previously, Niebuhr (1944) also worried about the illusions of organizational and political leaders in *The Children of Light and The Children of Darkness*.

A Few Practical Applications

What would pragmatist integrity (with a dose of Niebuhrian pessimism) mean for business practice? Members of organizations, whether managers or in different roles, would seek a heightened (but not unsustainable) consciousness of the consequences of their decisions. They would not merely assert the appropriateness of some "rational" business decision or impose an abstract theory. They would seek solutions for immediate problems that offer desirable bargains for associated parties. They would exercise restraint, consult across hierarchies, distribute decision making, and consider alternatives.

A pragmatist regards an organization as a means to human ends, and flexible in form, not as a possession to be defended. He or she would consider coordinated strategies with government and other groups to generate responsive networks and maximize problem-solving capacity. Practitioners would be aware of the interdependence of means and ends. They would not justify low wages, poor working conditions, and cheap production by their organization's need to be competitive and profitable. The so-called sweatshop (with wages low relative to basic needs and hours of work an obstacle to family obligations) or so-called zero-hours contract (with no regularity of employment) would not be tolerated as legitimate means to the end of organizational success. Firm competitiveness would be an intermediate end, and approaches to it would be compared with regard to social consequences.

The recent nail salon controversy in New York City provides an opportunity to delineate a pragmatist approach to integrity. Journalist Sarah Maslin Nair (2015) described an exploitive system of apprenticeship in which new immigrants received subminimum wages or no compensation at all and endured abuse in order to permit nail salons to offer inexpensive manicures. Nail salon owners and neoclassical economists seemed to largely agree that immigrant recruits to the salons must have adequate wages and benefits because they "freely" accepted their terms. The interests of nail shop owners and neoclassical observers seem to coincide in the denial of the empirical evidence of harm to workers. Pragmatist integrity would not allow theory to trump the reality of exploitation.

Joshua Preiss (2014) has sharply illuminated the problem of labor exploitation. He notes that rational choice among poor and constrained options is not equivalent to free and voluntary choice, even if the choice is the "non-worse" option (Powell & Zwolinski, 2012). By distinguishing between voluntary choice and rational choice, Preiss finds a potential defect in the employment of neoclassical theory. Reformers with "pragmatist integrity" might legitimately seek to win improvements in working conditions and refuse to support employers who fail to honor the autonomy and dignity of their workers.

Employment at will is a common law legal doctrine that emerges from an abstract understanding of freedom of contract. Despite the claims of the 19th-century legal scholar Horace C. Woods, employment at will does not represent the free choice of the parties. In both England and America, the annual hiring rule was common. Given a dialogue of equals, employees and managers would choose a mutually advantageous regime. The pragmatist perspective would support due process practices and the recognition of emerging interests in organizations (Feinman, 1976).

A pragmatist would be inclined to favor due process in employment decisions, sociological inquiry to guide wage determination and maximum opportunity for just social bargains. Pragmatism would require that employment bargains be examined with respect to the objective conditions of the workers. An employer who contracts with suppliers who deny their employees' reasonable expectations of wages exceeding subsistence levels and a healthy and safe working environment fails to demonstrate integrity. Wages and the cost of living in a community can be compared to establish whether wages are adequate. Although this is not an entirely mechanical exercise, and it requires judgments, it is far cry from considering integrity as a matter of process in contracting.

Pragmatist integrity would alter management responses to union organizing or worker demands for voice. There is considerable evidence of employee interest in voice mechanisms. Freeman and Rogers (1999) found that most unorganized workers would like some form of representation with independence from management, including both traditional unionism and representative fora. Freeman and Medoff (1984) observed a productivity advantage in unionized enterprises, and other scholars have noted that employee commitment is enhanced in responsive organizations. Managers practicing pragmatist integrity would not seek to suppress unionism or ignore the "publics" arising within the workplace. They would seek methods to reconcile profitability with mutually advantageous bargains.

Pragmatist integrity is a solvent that, when successful, dissolves or contains encrusted privilege and opportunism that otherwise obstruct the flow of information and resources to those who must use them. It is to be expected that cabals and restrictive networks will continue to form and seek to preserve the organizational structure for their benefit. Not every existing hierarchy will and must be undone, but all require questioning and resistance. Dewey and pragmatism offer considerable hope that activists and craftsmen can apply intelligence to the redesign of organizations along more ethical lines. Niebuhr provides a warning that hierarchies and publics will err in their interventions.

Pragmatist integrity is a demanding but not impossible standard. The experiences of Robert Owen and Edward Filene, among other experimenting managers, provide some guidance as to the struggle required to bring pragmatist integrity to business. Although they attained prosperity as individuals, their critical stance toward business as usual brought them into conflict with many of their colleagues. Their achievements are evident in a pattern of experimentation that transcends the individual enterprise. In the 19th century, Owen created an exemplary workplace and community in New Lanark, Scotland, as well as contributing to the development of the British labor movement. In the 20th century, Edward Filene introduced a robust worker representation plan at his department store, pioneered cross-class community centers, and founded the important think tank, the Twentieth Century Fund (Quarter, 2000).

Pragmatism and Integrity 169

More recently, Saru Jayaraman (Gelles, 2016) and Ai-Jen Poo (Alonso, 2012) have practiced a pragmatic experimentalism. Jayaraman was one of the founders of the Restaurant Opportunities Center, an employee association that originated in a campaign to serve the laid-off employees of the rooftop restaurant of the World Trades Center after the 9/11 attacks. She helped create a "public" composed of restaurant workers suffering from low wages and lack of sick leave and has led them in initiatives to enhance professionalism in the industry. Ai-Jen Poo has helped organize domestic workers in a legal environment that affords them few rights. To bring domestic workers out of anarchy and empower them is to heal the whole community.

Integrity and Social Bargains

The pragmatist model of integrity stimulates a reconceptualization of markets. Given the illusion of choice in many market contexts, the conflation of the "least worse" among unsatisfactory options with robust choice, pragmatist integrity demands honesty about the underlying reality and corrective action. It motivates questions about the quality of choices available in contexts that match large corporate organizations with unorganized individuals. One alternative might be "codetermination," broadly conceived. This term, of course, derives from the example of the German system of works councils and worker representation in management. However, I have in mind any local instance of inclusive determination of organizational conditions by workers, managers, and consumers and resistance to unilateral authority. This can be a small enterprise constituted by the deliberation of its partners or a large corporation characterized by multiple forms of stakeholder representation and bargaining. In either case, there is an opportunity for organizational experimentation guided by the consideration of consequences by the multiple actors themselves. Deliberations among organized equals involve the whole of the organization and its publics and move beyond the consideration of price toward the appreciation of value.

Pragmatist integrity requires an approach to the workplace that deemphasizes organizational boundaries, does not treat management or labor as factors of production or black boxes but considers a complex of workplace communities. As I have suggested, pragmatist integrity expands the conception of fraud in contracting that motivates Objectivists and construes it as false choices that confirm the relative weakness of the many compared to the dominant corporate form. To make choices based on the consideration of consequences, one must have the reality of choices. Pragmatist integrity demands constructivism, a plurality of actors and organizational forms.

However, Niebuhr's worries about the tendencies of organizations must be heeded. Oligarchies will reassert themselves, publics will err, and experiments will disappoint us. Then again, publics will reorganize and renew the experiments. It is a story that never ends.

References

Alonso, N. (2012). The home front. *Columbia College Today*. Retrieved from www. college.columbia.edu/cct/archive/fall12/features3. Accessed November 14, 2016.

Appelbaum, E. & Batt, R. L. (2014). *Private equity at work: When wall street manages main street*. Cambridge, MA: Harvard University Press.

Becker, T. E. (1998). Integrity in organizations: Beyond honesty and conscientiousness. *Academy of Management Review*, 23(1), 154–161.

Berger, P. L. & Neuhaus, R. J. (1977). *To empower people: The role of mediating structures in public policy*. Washington, DC: American Enterprise Institute for Public Policy Research.

Bergmann, F. (1977). *On being free*. South Bend, IN: University of Notre Dame Press.

Buchholz, R. A. & Rosenthal, S. B. (1997). Business and society: What's in a name. *International Journal of Organizational Analysis*, 5(2), 180–201.

Carson, A. S. (1995). The nature of a moral business person. *Review of Business*, 17(2), 16–22.

Corporate Crime Reporter (2006, January 4). Swenson: KPMG compliance program didn't meet Thompson Memo criteria. *Corporate Crime Reporter*, 2(1). Retrieved from www.corporatecrimereporter.com/swenson010406.htm. Accessed November 14, 2016.

Cox, D., La Caze, M., & Levine, M. (2013). Integrity. In E. N. Zalta (Ed.), *Stanford Encyclopedia of Philosophy*, (Winter 2016 ed.). Retrieved from http://plato. stanford.edu/archives/win2016/entries/integrity/. Accessed November 4, 2016.

Dennett, D. C. (1995). *Darwin's dangerous idea*. New York: Simon & Schuster.

Dewey, J. (1920). *Reconstruction in philosophy*. New York: Henry Holt.

Dewey, J. (1939). The democratic form. In J. Ratner & E. A. Post (Eds.), *Intelligence in the modern world: John Dewey's philosophy* (pp. 400–404). New York: Random House.

Dewey, J. (1958). *Experience and nature*. New York: Dover.

Dewey, J. (1983). Human nature and conduct. In J. A. Boydston (Ed.), *The middle works: 1899–1924* (Vol. 14, pp. 146–153). Carbondale, IL: University of Southern Illinois Press.

Donaldson, T. & Dunfee, T. (1999). *Ties that bind: A social contracts approach to business ethics*. Boston: Harvard Business School Press.

Feinman, J. (1976). The development of the employment at will rule. *American Journal of Legal History*, 20(2), 118–135.

Frederick, W. (2000). Pragmatism, nature, and norms. *Business and Society Review*, 105(4), 467–479.

Freeman, R. B. & Medoff, J. L. (1984). *What do unions do?* New York: Basic Books.

Freeman, R. B. & Rogers, J. (1999). *What workers want* (updated ed.). Ithaca, NY: ILR Press.

Gelles, D. (2016, February 10). An outspoken force to give food workers a seat at the table. *New York Times*. Retrieved from www.nytimes.com/2016/02/21/business/an-outspoken-force-to-give-food-workers-a-seat-at-the-table.html. Accessed November 14, 2016.

Greene, J. D. (2013). Moral tribes: Emotion, reason, and the gap between us and them. New York: Penguin.

Gosling, M. & Huang, H. J. (2009). The fit between integrity and integrative social contracts theory. *Journal of Bus Ethics*, 90(supplement 3), 407–417.

Hayden, T. & the Students for a Democratic Society (1963). *Port Huron Statement*. Retrieved from http://coursesa.matrix.msu.edu/~hst306/documents/huron.html. Accessed on November 7, 2016.

Jacobs, D. C. (2004). A pragmatist approach to integrity in business ethics. *Journal of Management Integrity, 13*(3), 215–223.

Levine, P. (2016). Pragmatism and the power of evil. *A Blog for Civic Renewal*. Retrieved from http://peterlevine.ws/?p=17091. Accessed November 14, 2016.

Maak, T. (2008). Undivided corporate responsibility: Towards a theory of corporate integrity. *Journal of Business Ethics, 82*(2), 353–368.

Monga, M. (2016). Integrity and its antecedents: A unified conceptual framework of integrity. *The Journal of Developing Areas, 50*(5), 415–421.

Nair, S. M. (2015, May 7). The price of nice nails. *New York Times*. Retrieved from www.nytimes.com/2015/05/10/nyregion/at-nail-salons-in-nyc-manicurists-are-underpaid-and-unprotected.html. Accessed November 14, 2016.

Niebuhr, R. (1944). The children of light and the children of darkness: A vindication of democracy and a critique of its traditional defense. New York: C. Scribner's Sons.

Niebuhr, R. (1960). Moral man and immoral society: A study in ethics and politics. New York: Scribner.

Palanski, M. E. & Yammarino, F. J. (2007). Integrity and leadership: Clearing the conceptual confusion. *European Management Journal, 25*(3), 171–184.

Parry, K. W. & Proctor-Thomson, S. B. (2002). Perceived integrity of transformational leaders in organisational settings. *Journal of Business Ethics, 35*(2), 75–96.

Peck, M. S. (1987). *The different drum: Community making and peace*. New York: Simon & Schuster.

Petrick, J. A. (2007). Integrity. In R. W. Kolb (Ed.), *Sage encyclopedia of business ethics and society* (pp. 1141–1144). Thousand Oaks, CA: Sage.

Petrick, J. A. & Quinn, J. F. (2000). The integrity capacity construct and moral progress in business. *Journal of Business Ethics, 23*(1), 3–18.

Powell, B. & Zwolinski, M. (2012). The ethical and economic case against sweatshop labor: A critical assessment. *Journal of Business Ethics, 107*(4), 449–472.

Preiss, J. (2014). Global labor justice and the limits of economic analysis. *Business Ethics Quarterly, 24*(1), 55–83.

Quarter, J. (2000). Beyond the bottom line: Socially innovative business owners. Westport, CT: Quorum Books.

Solomon, R. C. (1992). Ethics and excellence: Cooperation and integrity in business. New York: Oxford University Press.

Stanley, J. & Krakauer, J. (2013). Motor skill depends on knowledge of fact. *Frontiers in Human Neuroscience, 7*, 503. Retrieved from http://journal.frontiersin.org/article/10.3389/fnhum.2013.00503. Accessed on November 7, 2016.

Tomlinson, E. C., Lewicki, R. J., & Ash, S. R. (2014). Disentangling the moral integrity construct: Values congruence as a moderator of the behavioral integrity citizenship relationship. *Group and Organization Management, 39*(6), 720–743.

Weil, D. (2014). *The fissured workplace: Why work became bad for so many and what can be done to improve it*. Cambridge, MA: Harvard University Press.

Wicks, A. C., & Freeman, R. E. (1998). Organization studies and the new pragmatism: Positivism, anti-positivism, and the search for ethics. *Organization Science, 9*(2), 123–140.

9 Virtue Signaling

Oversocialized "Integrity" in a Politically Correct World

Marc Orlitzky

Integrity. If you can fake that, you've got it made.

—Joke cited in Solomon (1999, p. 40)

Most people pretend that morality, ethics, justice, and indeed integrity still carry substantive meaning today. However, in a post-Enlightenment world that has lost its virtue, all that remains of an earlier morality are linguistic husks (MacIntyre, 2007) in which shallow external value markers of goodness have replaced genuine internal commitments to a true North. To be sure, in a world of pastiche, faint pastels, and appearances (Boje, 1995; Kilduff & Mehra, 1997), we—scholars and business executives alike—never cease to invoke values underpinning our judgments and actions, but it is no coincidence that the meaning of these values is almost exclusively and most firmly grounded in social reality—*outside* of the individual. Because of these trends, integrity may be an ethical concept whose substantive meaning has irretrievably been lost on, and for, the vast majority of people.

In this chapter, I present a partly sociological, partly psychoanalytic account of integrity in its historical context. First, I explain the etymological roots of the Latin *integer* and *integritas* in order to illustrate how our modern concept of integrity has dropped almost all reference to the word's meaning in ancient Rome. Second, I describe how ubiquitous virtue signaling has replaced genuine integrity-based decision making. Third, I offer several examples that illustrate the recovery of the true meaning of integrity—rather than merely the appearance of integrity—and a few potential, promising directions for future research.

Back to Basics

Researching the Latin roots, one finds that, etymologically, integrity can be traced back to *integer*, with the original meaning of this adjective best translated as *pure, unspoiled*, and *wholesome* (see also Jacobs, 2017; Orlitzky & Monga, 2017). For example, Horatius contrasted foul-smelling food (*vitiatum commodius*) with fresh food (*vitiatum integrum*) (Petschenig,

1936, p. 422). That is, the etymological foundation of integrity seems more reminiscent of an ethic of sanctity that emphasizes purity, chastity, and the absence of (moral or any other) stain (see also Haidt, 2012; Shweder, Much, Mahapatra, & Park, 1997). In this type of moral system, impurity produces emotional reactions of disgust—and avoiding impurity is the highest virtue (Haidt, 2012).

Such an ethic, focused on purity and sanctity and, therefore, also called an ethic of divinity (Shweder et al., 1997), sharply contrasts with the currently common Western focus on rational explanations of ethical behavior—a secular morality that is centered on the aim of avoiding harm and injustice (Haidt, 2012). This zeitgeist (of moral guidelines as assistance in shunning harm and injustice) is important because the social and institutional context in which all actors, including researchers, are embedded affects at least in part the way they conceive of the world and what they regard as the taken-for-granted appropriate standards—not only in their theories (Orlitzky, 2011a) but also in their methods (Orlitzky, 2011b, 2012). University researchers and Western elites have largely been socialized in a WEIRD environment—where the acronym WEIRD stands for Western, educated, industrialized, rich, and democratic (Henrich, Heine, & Norenzayan, 2010). So, the temptation is high for researchers to prefer conceptualizations of moral concepts that are consistent with the contemporary WEIRD theorizing about harms and injustice.

As almost all chapters in this volume illustrate, contemporary researchers of integrity in management largely eschew the etymological roots of the concept because going back to these etymological basics would also necessitate a rejection of the typical secular rationalism in moral theorizing (Haidt, 2008). Instead, contemporary practitioners and researchers ascribe, to integrity, moral content of a particular, currently acceptable mold. For one, among psychologists and other social scientists, the moral content is close to the narrower virtue called honesty (see also Becker, 1998; Jacobs, 2017; Orlitzky & Monga, 2017). Furthermore, whenever integrity is imbued with moral-normative content (which frequently occurs), integrity researchers draw on a smorgasbord of different values and virtues (see also Palanski & Yammarino, 2007), which are invariably embedded in the contemporary WEIRD morality. Among most contemporary management researchers, such a morality is mainly focused on producing benefits for stakeholders and creating a "socially just" society in which the equality of outcomes (also known as egalitarianism) is generally desirable. In general, these current conceptualizations of morality are based on the idea that social relationships and institutions can be socially engineered and that society can ultimately be perfected by deliberate human design (Hayek, 1976, 1988, 2001, 2011). Such social design is currently suffused with the values of political correctness (Fairclough, 2003), which through the regulation of speech is a device to shape the thinking of managers and other members of a politically correct society. The reference points of such social design are external to the social actor (probably most clearly articulated by Jacobs, 2017—the chapter on pragmatism). Yet, because such an external perspective does not capture the full spectrum of moral reference points (Haidt, 2012), one can plausibly charge such viewpoints as rather narrow reflections of ethics.

Values Bias

Any scientifically persuasive exploration of integrity must minimize the impact of values bias, that is, the assertion that the content of values affects the factual statements the researcher employs in the research process (Cohen, 1989). However, such values bias is difficult to minimize when it is presumed that the fact–value dichotomy is merely a cognitive mirage (Frederick, 1994). In a (politically correct) world where the difference between facts and values is assumed to be artificial, values bias is viewed not so much as a problem as it assumes a "taken for granted" characteristic of any scientific endeavor. According to the most radical postmodern theoreticians of science, this fundamental epistemological assumption affects not only social science, but all science (see Nola, 2003). However, in the final analysis, the premise of the supposed obsolescence of the fact–value dichotomy gives rise to a peculiar kind of antirationalism in the acquisition of human knowledge (Cohen, 1989; Nola, 2003).

Because social scientists, but especially those embracing the philosophy of pragmatism (see also Jacobs, 2017), do not problematize such values bias in scientific inquiry anymore, all types of norms and values, including researchers' political ideologies, can intrude in scientific research, as has already been demonstrated in detail elsewhere (Duarte et al., 2015).[1] For example, researchers of corporate social responsibility generally assume that implementing "social responsibility," a concept steeped in leftwing ideology (Orlitzky, 2015), benefits organizations, markets, and societies (Orlitzky, 2013). All contrasting views that point to the inherent dangers of corporate social responsibility, regardless of whether they are analyzed from a left-wing or right-wing perspective (e.g., Friedman, 1970; Levitt, 1958; Reich, 2008), have inherently been delegitimized by this ideologically biased literature—and increasingly so since the late 1950s (Orlitzky, 2015).

This problem would be serious enough if only cognitive omissions were allowed to persist. Such omissions could take a variety of forms. For example, accounts of ethical decision making in management have omitted any in-depth investigation of moral emotions, intuitions, and more generally subconscious processes (Haidt, 2001, 2008, 2013). Another omission is the clear preference for altruism over egoism in almost all of the business ethics literature (Locke, 2006).

With respect to integrity, however, this bias becomes acute because the moral anchor points are vague definitions of "moral behavior" (Audi & Murphy, 2006; Bauman, 2013; Palanski & Yammarino, 2007) and, as already mentioned, the meanings of integrity are circumscribed by social reality exclusively. Thus, from such an (overly) social perspective, the business ethicist's gaze turns toward the actor's social environment as the primary determinant of the value of any given individual action (see also Jacobs, 2017). However, when individual wholeness and authenticity become mere afterthoughts in ethical decision making, scholars abandon and subvert this incisive definition of integrity by Ayn Rand:

> Integrity is that quality in man which gives him the courage to hold his own convictions against all influences, against the opinions and desires of other men; the courage to remain whole, unbroken, untouched, to remain true to himself.
>
> (Rand in Harriman, 1997, p. 260)

Here, it should be noted that Rand's emphasis on the importance of individual independence is also consistent with empirical evidence demonstrating the myriad moral temptations presented by others when the ethical decision-maker has a socially *inter*dependent mind-set (Gino & Galinsky, 2012).

Integrity Properly Conceived

Integrity, properly concerned with an individual's whole and wholesome sense of self (see facets 4 and 5 in Orlitzky & Monga, 2017) in order to regain one's own true North (see also Moore & Gino, 2013), must acknowledge the specific psychodynamic preconditions of wholeness in character. Searching for one's moral compass in conformity with the demands, interests, or wishes of others would only lead to the identification of one's false, or compliant, self (Winnicott, 1965). By contrast, developing an autonomous self (which is inevitably interrelated with others) is one of the most important tasks in every individual's human development (Kohut, 2009, 2013; Winnicott, 1965). In other words, any critique of the Randian conceptualization of integrity ought to be tempered by realistic psychological considerations of individual human development. Jacobs (2004, p. 217) has argued that

> Objectivism fails as a philosophical basis for integrity because of its fundamentally flawed conception of human nature. Objectivists err in their unfounded concept of the individual as prior to and fully distinguishable from the social and in their understanding of reason as an enterprise wholly of the self.

Yet, Jacobs's own pragmatist conceptualization seems to fall short of the psychological prerequisites for a coherent and, indeed, authentic self. Because self-denial and self-sacrifice (see also Avolio & Locke, 2002) are not viable paths to integrity, individuals must learn to establish and maintain a healthy and mature sense of self. The affirmation of one's human individuality and autonomy requires deep self-awareness and sensitivity to one's *own* moral emotions (Moore & Gino, 2013). However, these intrapersonal requirements of integrity have become extremely difficult to develop and nourish in a world without (any real) virtue left (MacIntyre, 2007), as the next section shows.

Virtue Signaling

In a post-Enlightenment world where moral traditions have largely been replaced by social and emotive appeals, such as compassion (MacIntyre, 2007), appeals to so-called ethical action or integrity primarily serve as signals of high repute, trustworthiness, and so on. What matters now is not so much whether one's decisions authentically reflect one's genuine principles and one's own coherent value system, but the (social) value these decisions confer on the decision maker, who is trying to live up to *others'* notions of the Good and/or the Right rather than to his or her own. In a politically correct, but morally vacuous, world, ethics is most closely associated with those values and concepts whose (normative and substantive) meaning is most flexible. For example, the malleable concept of "sustainability" can now be defined not only in ecological but also in social terms (Beckerman, 1994; Dunphy & Griffiths, 1998) and has been included as a reasonable aim of integrity-based managerial behavior (see, e.g., Monga, 2017; Crossman & Perera, 2017; Seaman & Bent, 2017).

The virtue signaler desires to be socially recognized for his or her moral respectability. Filled with the discomforting suspicion that the real meaning of virtues has been lost after the introduction of Kantian, utilitarian, feminist, and various other ethical systems (MacIntyre, 2007), "ethical" decision makers are now most concerned with how they are perceived by others in terms of moral worth, strictly defined as a social perception conferring moral worth. In the same way as the narcissist is driven by the need to fill personal emptiness and a gnawing lack of self-worth (Chessick & Kohut, 1985; Freud, 1991; Glickauf-Hughes & Wells, 1997; Kohut, 2013; Maccoby, 2004), the virtue signaler is driven by the need to be admired for their moral worth. Accomplishing this goal typically requires moral grandstanding (Tosi & Warmke, 2016) in a public arena. Naturally, the implicit goals of virtue signaling are easier to achieve when the socially constructed "virtues" and values of the virtue signaler conform with the moral zeitgeist and are difficult to measure or verify. What matters more than the objective consequences of ethical action are the inferences of others about the virtue-signaler's motives. For example, the same virtue-signaling politicians that have earned a worldwide reputation as leading proponents of "sustainability" also tend to be those that have allowed Islamofascism into their countries and, thus, objectively undermined the sustainability of social harmony in the nations they govern so ineffectively. Oblivious to these inherent contradictions, but earning great admiration from the politically correct media (for such alleged motives as their "compassion," "opposition to racism," etc.), the pro-sustainability leaders portray, at least publicly, their unsustainable decisions as grand acts of integrity and compassion. In such a politically correct environment, every ethical decision is reduced to a social signal. In a post-Enlightenment world, this cannot be otherwise because the internal, substantive criteria by which actions were once ethically judged have lost their meaning (MacIntyre, 1988, 2007). In such a social environment, the signal *is* the message.

Signals: True and False

To be sure, signaling, which refers to social actors' use of visible attributes that convey information to, or change the beliefs of, other social actors (Connelly, Certo, Ireland, & Reutzel, 2011; Spence, 1974), is not inherently problematic in all cases, regardless of its context. By itself, a signal does not imply that the underlying characteristic—be they job skills, productivity, integrity, or some other virtue—is absent (Spence, 2002). Signals are typically seen as mutually beneficial for sender and receiver alike (Dawkins, 1989), although in exceptional cases, such as the peacock's tail or male paradise birds, signals may actually handicap the sender (Grafen, 1990; Johnstone & Grafen, 1993). Undeniably, signals can convey true or false information (Akerlof, 1970; Dawkins, 1989, pp. 64–65). Contrary to the arguments of some recent defenders of virtue signaling (Bowman, 2016), signals need not be honest to be properly considered "signals." For example, harmless animals (e.g., butterfly *Papilio polytes*) may deceptively mimic the external appearance of other, toxic species (e.g., *Pachliopta aristolochiae*). Or cuckoos exploit the mothering instincts of other bird species by using deception. These animal signals are not only deceptive (Dawkins, 1989) but also credible; they can only be effective signals because they are credible. Regardless of the ontological quarrel about the underlying honesty of the signaler, the main feature of signals, in any context, is that they are intended to manipulate the receiver (Dawkins & Krebs, 1978; Krebs & Dawkins, 1984). This is as true in biology as in economics where a signal, such as a higher education degree, is intended to change or influence the beliefs, perceptions, attitudes, or behaviors of the receiver (Spence, 1974, 2002).

In the context of human morality, the manipulative characteristic of signals raises serious concerns about the inherent morality of signaling when the signal is deliberate (rather than instinctual) and substantively vacuous. This moral vacuity can largely be explained by the particular historical moment in which we find ourselves: an era with no moral anchor points of genuine, shared virtues (MacIntyre, 2007). In such times, the self is not anchored in traditions or a coherent philosophical worldview, such as Objectivism (Locke, 2006) or an Aristotelean virtue ethic. Instead, individuals attempt to define themselves always in reference to others' (equally amoral) judgments. In turn, when the influence of others' judgments—as in stakeholder theory—becomes the primary goal of (supposedly) moral behavior, then the signal is no longer the authentic expression of an underlying moral, psychological, emotive, or other reality. Instead, it devolves into a merely manipulative social device.

The Psychopathology of Virtue Signaling

Furthermore, virtue signaling is pathological insofar as it misses the two fundamental goals of traditional ethics that have largely been lost in a post-Enlightenment world. First, ethics assumes meaning only in relation to the strengthening of social ties rather than rendering (often uncomfortable) judgments of approval or disapproval, which tends to run counter to these social goals (Luhmann, 1990; Tosi & Warmke, 2016). Second, because the virtue signaler enacts a social role, in essence virtue signaling involves the role-playing of emotions or some other inner reality. Thus, each of these play acts further disconnects (or, one may also conclude, alienates) the decision maker from his or her true emotional self.

In the long run, the consequences of virtue signaling and moral grandstanding are likely to be dire for the individual and society. Because of the two aforementioned pathologies involved in virtue signaling, circumspect observers will quickly lose confidence in the substantive meaningfulness of the various signals of virtue. Therefore, in the long run, virtue signaling has an extremely corrosive effect on many social institutions, trust, and ultimately even social harmony. This harm can be considered oversocialized insofar as it is expressed as a constant obsession with others' affirmations of one's own moral worth. Because virtue signaling to a large extent consists of play-acting, it is not concerned with authentically expressing authentic, innate moral emotions (Orlitzky, 2016; Wolf, 1993).

What living in an oversocialized, virtue-signaling world means in practice is nicely illustrated by the diverging farewell addresses of Presidents Ronald Reagan and Barack Obama. President Reagan was sitting at his Oval Office desk—by himself—and downplaying the accomplishments of his administration ("Not bad . . . not bad at all"). In contrast, President Obama performed a long farewell address in front of a large auditorium of thousands of supporters cheering all his claims of the good he brought to America. The virtue signaler's self-styled accomplishments are only validated by the mirrored presence of an audience—either large or small.

Acts of Integrity

Complex institution-wide problems, such as the demise of any meaningful morality, resist easy solutions (see, e.g., Orlitzky, 2012). Nonetheless, a preliminary list of examples of integrity may be helpful to illustrate possible first steps in recovering the true meaning of integrity in a virtueless society. As implied in my theorizing so far, one major conceptual precondition is that integrity, when properly conceived, is the reverse of conformity with prevalent, ideologically biased, and merely social norms of goodness (e.g., in support of the collectivist and ambiguous value of "sustainability" or "social responsibility") or vague admonitions to be morally "appropriate" or "ethical." Thus, integrity can only manifest in opposition to prevailing notions of social propriety. In addition, genuine acts of (true rather than merely espoused) integrity are often quiet acts rather than public acts (of grandstanding). Unfortunately, these features make acts of true integrity difficult to discern. So, a few examples may be instructive.

Examples of Personal Integrity

When business executives duck trends and take actions that run contrary to the political zeitgeist (e.g., support for conservative-nationalist rather than secular-progressive or neoliberal causes) they act with integrity (Orlitzky, 2015). If such actions are pursued publicly, despite the threat of severe sanctions and retributions (e.g., violence), such acts of integrity especially deserve admiration for the actor's moral courage.

When social scientists have the courage to speak out against the groupthink, bias, and anticonservative discrimination that pervade the social sciences (e.g., Duarte et al., 2015; Tetlock, 1994) they demonstrate great integrity. By contrast, value conformity with the crowd can hardly be considered an act of integrity. For example, when other researchers provide clear evidence that this problem of prejudice in psychology is observable in many other Western countries but downplay the universality of their empirical data (Bilewicz, Cichocka, Gorska, & Szabo, 2015) or become defensive, an unwillingness to acknowledge the sacred cow of the interconnection between social science research and the researcher's own personal politics is an example of diminished integrity.

We should also admire the integrity of any political candidate who is willing to call out the most serious social, economic, and other problems starkly, unequivocally, and without regard for political correctness. When the values these unconventional politicians promote are opposite to those of the mainstream media and political or business elites and, therefore, cause severe backlash from those in positions of entrenched power (the "establishment"), such a high-risk demonstration of integrity is even more praiseworthy—because the act of integrity occurred in the face of great adversity.

Suggestions about the Definition and Context of True Integrity

What these illustrative examples of integrity have in common is that they are manifestations of individual actors being true to themselves, their own most deeply held beliefs, regardless of the personal consequences. Integrity represents wholeness of character (Solomon, 1999), which reflects a clear consistency between words and actions (Palanski & Yammarino, 2007, 2009). First, it is important to note that no one can justifiably claim to have acted with integrity without having faced great adversity because of those decisions. (Analogously, a pilot's capabilities and skills are not put to the test when the plane is on autopilot at cruising altitude.) Second, the concept should avoid any reference to any objective ethics because, by now, it should be obvious that this universalizing project of moral philosophy has failed (MacIntyre, 1990; Nietzsche, 1994). Because of the lack of evidence for any "transcendentalist" (Wilson, 1998, p. 266), objective truth to moral concepts (Orlitzky, 2016), the moral content will be difficult to specify (more on this in the section Promising Directions for Future Research). Thus, the best one can probably do from a definitional perspective is to declare integrity an adjunctive virtue, like moral courage, inquisitiveness, or conscientiousness, which are qualities supportive of achieving moral uprightness (Audi & Murphy, 2006). Unlike substantive moral virtues, adjunctive virtues are not good in themselves. The desire of ethicists and laypeople to infuse integrity with moral content is psychologically understandable; however, it requires further foundational normative research before we can proceed with only one definition of integrity. So long as the normative grounding remains debatable because of the lack of a universalistic normative foundation, moral integrity remains a rather nebulous and, thus, conceptually problematic concept.

The conceptual distinction between personal integrity and moral integrity is vital and, therefore, must be preserved. Personal integrity is a deep commitment to personal values, demonstrating wholeness in character by being true to oneself (Blustein, 1991; McFall, 1987; Taylor, 1985). Without consistency in words and actions, personal integrity does not exist and, therefore, can also be called behavioral integrity (Bauman, 2013). At the same time, it can only exist if the individual exhibiting integrity is devoted to values that others do not find morally palatable (see, e.g., Haidt & Graham, 2007). In contrast, moral integrity requires a commitment to morally justified principles (Becker, 1998; Graham, 2001; Schlenker, Miller, & Johnson, 2009)—it is "acting consistently from moral values" (Bauman, 2013, p. 419).

Promising Directions for Future Research

Consistent with the previous section, future research should continue on at least two separate tracks: a descriptive track on personal integrity and a normative track on moral integrity. The descriptive track ought to clarify and delineate the conceptual dimensions of personal integrity and investigate its drivers. Because integrity may be an identity-conferring commitment (Bauman, 2013), its relationship to human nature and functioning warrants closer empirical scrutiny. Human nature consists of those hereditary regularities (i.e., epigenetic rules) of mental development that connect genes to culture (Barkow, Cosmides, & Tooby, 1992; Wilson, 1975, 1998). From this biological definition of human nature it is clear that future studies would benefit from more in-depth grounding not only in cognitive science but also evolutionary psychology. Integrity is a particularly interesting phenomenon because evolutionary psychology has shown that moral emotions are not only about social cooperation, empathy, or (reciprocal) altruism; rather, moral emotions and judgments cover a very broad range of adaptive problems in human evolution (Haidt, 2008, 2012). In general, the current evidence suggests that moral beliefs and judgments are mainly cognitive mechanisms to choose sides in conflicts and thus regulate coordination rather than social cooperation (DeScioli & Kurzban, 2013). For this reason, integrity, when interpreted from an evolutionary perspective, offers great promise in taking moral theory beyond cooperation, harm avoidance, and altruism. As my preferred definition of integrity highlighted before, integrity is a concept that focuses on mental development of the self. So, future study of personal integrity would probably be most enriched by the empirical investigation of its evolutionary-cognitive foundations and the integration of the distinct parts of the self-system—the development of authentic selfhood in relation to others and perceived moral obligations of identity-conferring commitments (Bauman, 2013; Hinde, 2002).

In the study of common pathologies of integrity—either the complete and transparent absence thereof or the hypocritical virtue signaling so common today and highlighted before—psychodynamic theories, such as object relations (Glickauf-Hughes & Wells, 1997; Summers, 1994), Jungian analytic psychology, or Freudian psychoanalysis, may offer interesting perspectives, which are compatible with evolutionary psychology (Nesse & Lloyd, 1992). Social relationships often reward individuals for acting out social roles that are departures from the True Self, as understood by Winnicott (1965). For example, self-deception may be an important cognitive mechanism for the effective persuasion of others, manipulated by virtue-signaling individuals, that the professed integrity is a credible reflection of one's true self. The self-deception may go so far that the other side, opposed to one's own subjective-ideological definition of "virtue," is denigrated as evil against which acts of violence are justified. In other words, without a certain degree of self-deception, virtue signaling would be easier to detect as a manipulative, fundamentally selfish device (Alexander, 1975; Trivers, 1985). Furthermore, a psychodynamic focus on self-actualization (rather than these pathologies) may be even more constructive. In general, psychodynamic theories may be able to elucidate the components of human mental development that are key to personal integrity: individual wholeness, wholesomeness (or purity), and authenticity.

In addition to these descriptive studies of personal integrity, further in-depth research on the normative foundations of moral integrity is necessary. The contemporary rather vague ideas about moral appropriateness must give way to more critical thinking, with a focus on the normative foundations of moral judgments and behaviors. The Enlightenment's reply to these theoretical challenges is most commonly represented by encyclopedic moral philosophy—a type of moral inquiry that now, in general, is considered highly problematic (MacIntyre, 1990, 2007). Encyclopedic moral inquiry understands truth as "the relationship of *our* knowledge to *the* world, through the application of those methods whose rules are the rules of rationality as such" (MacIntyre, 1990, loc 811 of Kindle eBook). In encyclopedic normative foundations, objective, neutral knowledge about morality and progress toward ever greater moral truth are possible (Orlitzky, 2016). The encyclopedic project has failed for several reasons, one of which is encyclopedists' rejection of a teleological view of human nature (MacIntyre, 2007). Then, there is the failure to provide a persuasive psychological foundation for moral impartiality (MacIntyre, 1990). Arguably, Objectivism may be the most valid attempt to circumnavigate these failures (see also Becker, 1998) by resurrecting Aristotelean teleology and introducing an egoist psychology, which is certainly more persuasive than Kant's psychology (MacIntyre, 1990). At this point, though, several problems persist with the ontology and epistemology of Objectivism (Orlitzky & Jacobs, 1998). Certainly, the Objectivist's confidence in Reason is reflective of all encyclopedists' key failures.

To what extent Thomist or other traditionalist moral theorizing may take the place of encyclopedic foundations of moral integrity remains an open question worthy of future inquiry. Perhaps MacIntyre's (1990) optimism is appropriate. Yet, his optimism strikes me as unjustified, at least in the increasingly secular West. Similarly, Nietzsche's and other genealogists' work, which subverts the nonperspectival encyclopedic foundations of ethics (e.g., utilitarianism, deontology) by emphasizing individual subjectivity, seems problematic as a normative foundation of the principles inherent in moral integrity because, in genealogy, the only truth is "truth-from-a-point-of-view" (MacIntyre, 1990, loc 811). Grounding in genealogical inquiry may never be successful in theory because it reduces moral values to personal, subjective values (see also Orlitzky, 2016). In general, attaching either intersubjective (as in traditionalist moral inquiry) or subjective (genealogical) moral content to what is supposed to be a scientific concept is problematic (Cohen, 1989).

In addition, to what extent a collective (such as a corporation) rather than an individual can authentically reflect their own (collective) value systems in their actions is another topic that warrants future, careful investigation (see also Maak, 2008). For example, one may reasonably wonder whether a coherent collective value system, characterized by high integrity, would expect each individual member to demonstrate such an extreme commitment to the collective's values that such a system could plausibly be considered antithetical to individual liberty (Boaz, 1997; Carey, 1998; Hayek, 2011; Rothbard, 1998). In other words, such a collective could plausibly be considered totalitarian. So, at this point, social scientists studying integrity may, in fact, be better off adhering, for now, to methodological individualism (Homans, 1967; Nozick, 1977) in the study of personal *and* moral integrity. At the collective level, the term may merely, yet legitimately, be a useful metaphor.

Conclusion

This chapter argued that often talk of "integrity" could merely be considered an act of virtue signaling in societies that have lost any sense of a (relatively homogeneous) community held together by virtues. This is first and foremost a psychological and sociological problem because wholeness of character and authenticity of expression have lost their meaning in a politically correct world. Faced with the demands of political correctness, individuals cannot help but become political and, thus, act out their social roles, hypocritically. Honoring one's promises (Erhard, Jensen, & Zaffron, 2017) is certainly a good start when aiming to recover the true meaning of integrity—wholeness and authenticity. However, this chapter also argued that research informed by psychodynamic theories and evolutionary psychology may offer invaluable insights in the re(dis)covery of integrity.

Note

1. What can happen when the fact–value dichotomy is abandoned is perfectly illustrated by the fate of the journalistic profession in the United States and most other Western countries between 2015 and 2017. The U.S. public now holds the media in contempt at record low levels (Gallup, 2016). Social scientists better pay attention to these societal developments because another once-powerful institution, journalism, lost a large portion of its influence in society because of the evaporation of the public's trust in their objectivity and impartiality.

References

Akerlof, G. A. (1970). The market for lemons: Quality uncertainty and the market mechanism. *Quarterly Journal of Economics, 84*, 488–500.

Alexander, R. D. (1975). The search for a general theory of behavior. *Systems Research and Behavioral Science, 20*(2), 77–100.

Audi, R. & Murphy, P. E. (2006). The many faces of integrity. *Business Ethics Quarterly, 16*(1), 3–21.

Avolio, B. J. & Locke, E. E. (2002). Contrasting different philosophies of leader motivation: Altruism versus egoism. *The Leadership Quarterly, 13*(2), 169–191.

Barkow, J. H., Cosmides, L., & Tooby, J. (Eds.). (1992). *The adapted mind: Evolutionary psychology and the generation of culture.* New York: Oxford University Press.

Bauman, D. C. (2013). Leadership and the three faces of integrity. *The Leadership Quarterly, 24*(3), 414–426.

Becker, T. E. (1998). Integrity in organizations: Beyond honesty and conscientiousness. *Academy of Management Review, 23*(1), 154–161.

Beckerman, W. (1994). Sustainable development: Is it a useful concept? *Environmental Values, 3*, 191–209.

Bilewicz, M., Cichocka, A., Gorska, P., & Szabo, Z. P. (2015). Is liberal bias universal? An international perspective on social psychologists. *Behavioral & Brain Sciences, 38*, 17–18.

Blustein, J. (1991). *Care and commitment: Taking the personal point of view.* New York: Oxford University Press.

Boaz, D. (Ed.). (1997). *The libertarian reader: Classic and contemporary readings from Lao-tzu to Milton Friedman.* New York: Free Press.

Boje, D. M. (1995). Stories of the storytelling organization: A postmodern analysis of Disney as "Tamara-Land." *Academy of Management Journal, 38*, 997–1035.

Bowman, S. (2016). *Stop saying 'virtue signalling'.* Retrieved from www.adamsmith.org/blog/stop-saying-virtue-signalling.

Carey, G. W. (1998). *Freedom and virtue: The conservative/libertarian debate* (Rev. and updated ed.). Wilmington, DE: Intercollegiate Studies Institute.

Chessick, R. D. & Kohut, H. (1985). *Psychology of the self and the treatment of narcissism.* Northvale, NJ: Aronson.

Cohen, B. P. (1989). *Developing sociological knowledge: Theory and method* (2nd ed.). Chicago, IL: Nelson-Hall.

Connelly, B. L., Certo, S. T., Ireland, R. D., & Reutzel, C. R. (2011). Signaling theory: A review and assessment. *Journal of Management, 37*(1), 39–67.

Crossman, J., & Perera, S. (2017). Time theft: An integrity-based approach to its management. In M. Orlitzky & M. Monga (Eds.), *Integrity in business and management* (pp. 40–65). New York: Routledge/Taylor & Francis.

Dawkins, R. (1989). *The selfish gene.* New York: Oxford University Press.

Dawkins, R. & Krebs, J. R. (1978). Animal signals: Information or manipulation? *Behavioural Ecology: An Evolutionary Approach, 2,* 282–309.

DeScioli, P. & Kurzban, R. (2013). A solution to the mysteries of morality. *Psychological Bulletin, 139*(2), 477–496.

Duarte, J. L., Crawford, J. T., Stern, C., Haidt, J., Jussim, L., & Tetlock, P. E. (2015). Political diversity will improve social psychological science. *Behavioral and Brain Sciences, 38,* 1–13.

Dunphy, D. & Griffiths, A. (1998). *The sustainable corporation: Organisational renewal in Australia.* St. Leonards, Australia: Allen & Unwin.

Erhard, W. H., Jensen, M. C., & Zaffron, S. (2017). Integrity: A positive model that incorporates the normative phenomena of morality, ethics, and legality. In M. Orlitzky & M. Monga (Eds.), *Integrity in business and management* (pp. 11–39). New York: Routledge/Taylor & Francis.

Fairclough, N. (2003). 'Political correctness': The politics of culture and language. *Discourse & Society, 14*(1), 17–28.

Frederick, W. C. (1994). The virtual reality of fact versus value: A symposium commentary. *Business Ethics Quarterly, 4*(2), 171–174.

Freud, S. (1991). *On narcissism: An introduction.* New Haven, RI: Yale University Press.

Friedman, M. (1970, September 13). The social responsibility of business is to increase its profits. *New York Times Magazine, 74,* 33.

Gallup (2016). *Americans' trust in mass media sinks to new low [Press release].* Retrieved from www.gallup.com/poll/195542/americans-trust-mass-media-sinks-new-low.aspx.

Gino, F. & Galinsky, A. D. (2012). Vicarious dishonesty: When psychological closeness creates distance from one's moral compass. *Organizational Behavior and Human Decision Processes, 119*(1), 15–26.

Glickauf-Hughes, C. & Wells, M. (1997). Object relations psychotherapy: An individualized and interactive approach to diagnosis and treatment. Northvale, NJ: Aronson.

Grafen, A. (1990). Biological signals as handicaps. *Journal of Theoretical Biology, 144*(4), 517–546.

Graham, J. L. (2001). Does integrity require moral goodness? *Ratio, 14*(3), 234–251.

Haidt, J. (2001). The emotional dog and its rational tail: A social intuitionist approach to moral judgment. *Psychological Review, 108*(4), 814–834.

Haidt, J. (2008). Morality. *Perspectives on Psychological Science, 3*(1), 65–72.

Haidt, J. (2012). The righteous mind: Why good people are divided by politics and religion. New York: Pantheon.

Haidt, J. (2013). Moral psychology for the twenty-first century. *Journal of Moral Education*, 42(3), 281–297.

Haidt, J. & Graham, J. (2007). When morality opposes justice: Conservatives have moral intuitions that liberals may not recognize. *Social Justice Research*, 20(1), 98–116.

Harriman, D. (Ed.). (1997). *The journals of Ayn Rand*. New York: Penguin Putnam.

Hayek, F. A. (1976). *The mirage of social justice*. Chicago: University of Chicago Press.

Hayek, F. A. (1988). *The fatal conceit: The errors of socialism*. Chicago: University of Chicago Press.

Hayek, F. A. (2001). *The road to serfdom*. London: Routledge.

Hayek, F. A. (2011). *The constitution of liberty* (R. Hamowy Ed. Definitive ed.). Chicago, IL: University of Chicago Press.

Henrich, J., Heine, S., & Norenzayan, A. (2010). The weirdest people in the world? *Behavioral and Brain Sciences*, 33, 61–83.

Hinde, R. A. (2002). *Why good is good: The sources of morality*. London, UK: Routledge.

Homans, G. C. (1967). *The nature of social science*. San Diego: Harcourt Brace Jovanovich.

Jacobs, D. C. (2004). A pragmatic approach to integrity in business ethics. *Journal of Management Inquiry*, 13(3), 215–223.

Jacobs, D. C. (2017). Pragmatism and integrity: A second look. In M. Orlitzky & M. Monga (Eds.), *Integrity in business and management* (pp. 156–171). New York: Routledge/Taylor & Francis.

Johnstone, R. A. & Grafen, A. (1993). Dishonesty and the handicap principle. *Animal Behaviour*, 46(4), 759–764.

Kilduff, M. & Mehra, A. (1997). Postmodernism and organizational research. *Academy of Management Review*, 22(2), 453–481.

Kohut, H. (2009). *The restoration of the self*. Chicago: University of Chicago Press.

Kohut, H. (2013). The analysis of the self: A systematic approach to the psychoanalytic treatment of narcissistic personality disorders. Chicago: University of Chicago Press.

Krebs, J. R. & Dawkins, R. (1984). Animal signals: Mind-reading and manipulation. *Behavioural Ecology: An Evolutionary Approach*, 2, 380–402.

Levitt, T. (1958). The dangers of social responsibility. *Harvard Business Review*, 36(5), 38–44.

Locke, E. A. (2006). Business ethics: A way out of the morass. *Academy of Management Learning & Education*, 5(3), 324–332.

Luhmann, N. (1990). Paradigm lost: Über die ethische Reflexion der Moral. Frankfurt a.M.: Suhrkamp.

Maak, T. (2008). Undivided corporate responsibility: Towards a theory of corporate integrity. *Journal of Business Ethics*, 82(2), 353–368.

Maccoby, M. (2004). Narcissistic leaders: The incredible pros, the inevitable cons. *Harvard Business Review*, 82(1), 92–102.

McFall, L. (1987). Integrity. *Ethics*, 98, 5–20.

MacIntyre, A. (1988). *Whose justice? Which rationality?* London: Duckworth.

MacIntyre, A. (1990). Three rival versions of moral enquiry: Encyclopaedia, genealogy, and tradition. Notre Dame, IN: University of Notre Dame Press.

MacIntyre, A. (2007). *After virtue: A study in moral theory* (3rd ed.). Notre Dame, IN: University of Notre Dame Press.

Monga, M. (2017). 'Doing the right thing' in the banking sector: Integrity from an upper ecehelons perspective. In M. Orlitzky & M. Monga (Eds.), *Integrity in business and management* (pp. 105–135). New York: Routledge/Taylor & Francis.

Moore, C. & Gino, F. (2013). Ethically adrift: How others pull our moral compass from true North, and how we can fix it. *Research in Organizational Behavior, 33,* 53–77.

Nesse, R. M. & Lloyd, A. T. (1992). The evolution of psychodynamic mechanisms. In J. H. Barkow, L. Cosmides, & J. Tooby (Eds.), *The adapted mind: Evolutionary psychology and the generation of culture* (pp. 601–624). New York: Oxford University Press.

Nietzsche, F. (1994). *On the genealogy of morality* (C. Diethe, Trans.). New York: Cambridge University Press.

Nola, R. (2003). Rescuing reason: A critique of anti-rationalist views of science and knowledge. Boston, MA: Kluwer Academic.

Nozick, R. (1977). On Austrian methodology. *Synthese, 36*(3), 353–392.

Orlitzky, M. (2011a). Institutional logics in the study of organizations: The social construction of the relationship between corporate social and financial performance. *Business Ethics Quarterly, 21*(3), 409–444.

Orlitzky, M. (2011b). Institutionalized dualism: Statistical significance testing as myth and ceremony. *Journal of Management Control, 22*(1), 47–77.

Orlitzky, M. (2012). How can significance tests be deinstitutionalized? *Organizational Research Methods, 15*(2), 199–228.

Orlitzky, M. (2013). Corporate social responsibility, noise, and stock market volatility. *Academy of Management Perspectives, 27*(3), 238–254.

Orlitzky, M. (2015). The politics of corporate social responsibility or: Why Milton Friedman was right all along. *Annals in Social Responsibility, 1*(1), 5–29.

Orlitzky, M. (2016). How cognitive neuroscience informs a subjectivist-evolutionary explanation of business ethics [Advance online publication]. *Journal of Business Ethics.* doi: 10.1007/s10551-016-3132-8.

Orlitzky, M. & Jacobs, D. (1998). A candid and modest proposal: The brave new world of objectivism. *Academy of Management Review, 23,* 656–658.

Orlitzky, M., & Monga, M. (2017). The multiple facets of integrity in business and management. In M. Orlitzky & M. Monga (Eds.), *Integrity in business and management* (pp. 1–10). New York: Routledge/Taylor & Francis.

Palanski, M. E. & Yammarino, F. J. (2007). Integrity and leadership: Clearing the conceptual confusion. *European Management Journal, 25*(3), 171–184.

Palanski, M. E. & Yammarino, F. J. (2009). Integrity and leadership: A multi-level conceptual framework. *The Leadership Quarterly, 20*(3), 405–420.

Petschenig, M. (1936). Stowassers lateinisch-deutsches Schul-und Handwoerterbuch. Wien: Hoelder-Pichler-Tempsky.

Reich, R. (2008). The case against corporate social responsibility (Publication no. GSPP08–003). Retrieved Sept. 23, 2009, from Goldman School of Public Policy Working Paper No. GSPP08–003. Available at http://ssrn.com/abstract=1213129.

Rothbard, M. N. (1998). *The ethics of liberty.* New York: New York University Press.

Schlenker, B. R., Miller, M. L., & Johnson, R. M. (2009). Moral identity, integrity, and personal responsibility. In D. Narvaez & D. K. Lapsley (Eds.), *Personality, identity, and character: Explorations in moral psychology* (pp. 316–340). New York: Cambridge University Press.

Seaman, C. & Bent, R. (2017). The role of family values in the integrity of family business. In M. Orlitzky & M. Monga (Eds.), *Integrity in business and management* (pp. 91–104). New York: Routledge/Taylor & Francis.

Shweder, R. A., Much, N. C., Mahapatra, M., & Park, L. (1997). The 'big three' of morlaity (autonomy, commubnity, and divinity), and the 'big three' explanations of suffering. In A. Brandt & P. Rozin (Eds.), *Morality and health* (pp. 119–169). New York: Routledge.

Solomon, R. C. (1999). A better way to think about business: How personal integrity leads to corporate success. New York: Oxford University Press.

Spence, M. (1974). Market signaling: Informational transfer in hiring and screening processes. Cambridge, MA: Harvard University Press.

Spence, M. (2002). Signaling in retrospect and the informational structure of markets. *American Economic Review*, 92(3), 434–459.

Summers, F. (1994). Object relations theories and psychopathology: A comprehensive text. Hillsdale, NJ: Analytic Press.

Taylor, G. (1985). *Pride, shame, and guilt: Emotions of self-assessment*. Oxford, UK: Oxford University Press.

Tetlock, P. E. (1994). Political psychology or politicized psychology: Is the road to scientific hell paved with good moral intentions? *Political Psychology, 15*(3), 509–529.

Tosi, J. & Warmke, B. (2016). Moral grandstanding. *Philosophy & Public Affairs, 44*(3), 197–217.

Trivers, R. L. (1985). *Social evolution*. Menlo Park, CA: Benjamin/Cummings.

Wilson, E. O. (1975). *Sociobiology: The new synthesis*. Cambridge, MA: Belknap.

Wilson, E. O. (1998). *Consilience: The unity of knowledge*. London: Abacus.

Winnicott, D. W. (1965). Ego distortion in terms of true and false self. In D. W. Winnicott (Ed.), *The maturational processes and the facilitating environment* (pp. 140–152). New York: International Universities Press.

Wolf, A. P. (1993). Westermarck redivivus. *Annual Review of Anthropology, 22*, 157–175.

Index

Note: Page numbers in *italics* indicate figures.